Theatre for Children in Hospital

Theatre for Children in Hospital
The Gift of Compassion

Persephone Sextou

intellect Bristol, UK / Chicago, USA

First published in the UK in 2016 by
Intellect, The Mill, Parnall Road, Fishponds, Bristol, BS16 3JG, UK

First published in the USA in 2016 by
Intellect, The University of Chicago Press, 1427 E. 60th Street,
Chicago, IL 60637, USA

A catalogue record for this book is available from the
British Library.

Copy-editor: Emma Rhys
Cover designer: Holly Rose
Production manager: Amy Rollason
Typesetting: Contentra Technologies

Print ISBN: 978-1-78320-645-2
ePDF ISBN: 978-1-78320-646-9
ePub ISBN: 978-1-78320-647-6

Printed and bound by 4edge

Contents

Foreword

Theatre for Children in Hospital: The Gift of Compassion explores the practice of theatre in clinical settings as an important strategy of normalizing children's experience of illness while spending time in hospital for treatment. This book breaks new ground in applied theatre practices and processes for young people. It provides insights into the world of the hospitalized child through the under-researched area of the dramatic and examines ways that participatory and intimate performance can alleviate passivity, boredom and clinical anxiety associated with hospital life. It witnesses ways of preparing children for painful procedures, relaxing them before and after surgery, and enhancing emotional and social wellbeing. It brings theatre into hospital wards and reconnects the artist to the realities of children's everyday burdens. Through engagement with disciplines such as health and wellbeing, creativity, philosophy of illness and psychology, the book provides a basis for understanding the use of theatre for a better experience of life during illness.

The book researches and analyses a unique type of bedside theatre performance to argue for an approach that is sensitive, compassionate and attentive to the needs of children. *Theatre for Children in Hospital: The Gift of Compassion* includes original research of practice that is acutely sensitive to the problems and possibilities of this work. It focuses on a five-year research study conducted with children, their families and artists in NHS (National Health Service) hospitals in the United Kingdom (paediatrics, general pathology and cardiac and oncology wards). It offers explicit examples of one-to-one and moment-by-moment interventions for children (4–10 years old) incorporating storytelling, live music, soft toys and relaxation practice. Transcriptions of exciting dialogues, breathtaking incidents and observations of children participating in bedside performance illustrate what really happens when theatre *goes* to hospitals. Special moments between the child and the artist in performance; happy and enthusiastic reactions to characters; incidents of empathetic communication; challenging moments of ambiguity and clinical emergencies; 'magical' moments of escape from the clinical through the fictional; and true stories of children and artists being present together *in* theatre and *in* illness become material to interrogate the claim that theatre in hospital can only be theatre for entertainment.

The book is a critical handbook for the artist. It is a 'what is', 'who for', 'why do it' and 'how to' guide on bedside performance-making for those with an interest in theatre, children and healthcare. It seeks to inform readers about a special type of participatory drama aimed at making a challenging time (being ill in hospital) easier. It also aims at educating the reader on this applied theatre intervention from the perspective of the child-patient, the family and the nursing staff who share the hospital experience with the child, as well as the artist who participates in the theatre event. The book provides a concise summary for professionals and trainees in drama, theatre studies and performing arts and healthcare; primarily actors, facilitators and community artists, and secondarily play specialists, nurses, teachers in educational centres in hospitals, and therapists who work with children in clinical environments. It reveals the importance of applied theatre as a way of adding a playful dimension to illness with sensitivity, respect, empathy and compassion for the audience. The book will appeal to both experienced practitioners and newcomers with an interest in using theatre to entertain, relax and help children and their families maintain their optimism about life in hospital and during recovery. Readers will identify with many aspects of the theatrical experience as artists and drama students, or as parent/carers of children and nurses in children's hospital wards, and perhaps make new meanings of theatre through performing in contexts of illness. This book uses research evidence and personal reflections to articulate that Theatre for Children in Hospital (TCH) is a powerful, narrow slice of applied theatre practice with major potential.

Prologue

In medical dictionaries a heart is defined as a hollow muscular organ in a person's chest that pumps blood through veins and arteries (Merriam-Webster 2014). In biblical dictionaries, a heart (*kardía*) is defined as the affective centre of our being, of all physical and spiritual life, and the capacity of moral preference (Thayer 1995; Hughes 2006).

What if a heart is transformed from a pump into a place where emotions are felt, an organ that can flow affection and compassion into human relationships and can bring humans into communion with each other? If we, the artists, are to contribute to the wellbeing of children who experience illness through theatre, we need a heart that behaves like a *kardía*. We need the gift of compassion. The gift of compassion is perhaps the most important of the many gifts that a warm and caring heart can offer to humanity. Seeing through the heart is not a cliché. To see through the heart means that the artists do not use their talents to show children as less able to do things because they are ill. Theatre for Children in Hospital (TCH) is interested in using the art form to encourage children to believe in themselves and participate in the performance, hoping that they will use this confidence to do things outside the performance too. This is an ambitious investment because, usually, the child is associated with illness and disability. TCH aims to disassociate children from their illness. By this, I mean that TCH avoids any possible stigmatization of children as disadvantaged compared to children who are able to go to the theatre and might feel more advantaged. Children in hospital are limited to the things they can do but TCH offers them opportunities to revise this condition. It offers them experiences of aesthetic involvement. Children are invited to make decisions about the aesthetics of the performance, to do things and participate cognitively, verbally and physically, as far as the condition of the child allows. A compassionate heart acknowledges the child as important to the theatrical process and as a vital part of the aesthetics of TCH.

We often feel alone in our efforts to care for others, as others do not necessarily have the same desire that we do. We feel that the conditions of contemporary life are such that compassionate life is almost impossible. Life is often a chain of struggles, injustices, misunderstandings, misjudgements, disapprovals, betrayals and, therefore, almost justified actions of error, intimidation, pain, rage and revenge. But if we are to visit hospitals to perform to children, we should first consent to work with compassion. Compassion allows us to enter into a relationship with our audiences and develop an empathetic understanding of children who experience illness as other equal members of our community. I remember a colleague who asked me at a conference what I mean by 'community' in a hospital context. I replied, 'I mean sharing'. He asked 'Do you mean the sharing of hospital as a location, or the sharing of common health experience?' This was such a great question! I said to him that I want to share the experience of illness with the children who get entertainment in hospital. I want each bedside theatre performance to become a means towards sharing and monitoring their hospital experience and diverting their minds away from the anxiety of not living a life at home. Undoubtedly, there can be a lot of pain in a child's life when illness knocks at their door but there are also many little things to celebrate such as birthdays, the smell of chocolate, the warmth of the sun coming through the window, painting, creativity, family, friendships, happy memories, dreams for the future and so on. Theatre is, in my view, such a unique way of celebrating life and all the little things that it consists of because it is a lived experience. Lived experience by definition is a celebratory condition! We participate in theatre in the *now*, which is always inspiring because it reminds us of our ability to be alive, creative, appreciative and imaginative even through difficult times. It is my view that if we use theatre to participate in the reality of a child's experience in hospital, with respect and attention to the needs of the child, we find as much, and even more, reward and meaning in our art as can be found in the main theatre. For this reason, we bring theatre into hospitals with artistic quality and sensitivity, as well as openness to learning through exposure to images of pain. In that effort, there is hope for the artist's personal and professional growth too. Performing for children in hospital is a meaningful participation in the lives of those who suffer. TCH may pave the way for a more compassionate healthcare system and caring world.

I may sound very optimistic and overconfident in my belief that Theatre for Children in Hospital can make a better world, but I believe that this is already happening with a number of community artists in healthcare and that we can generalize it. All we need to do is to never get used to what we think we know about theatre, audiences and life, so that our minds and our hearts remain free for transformation.

Introduction

Motivations and beliefs

This book is addressed to the intellectually curious and passionate practitioners of theatre who want to get actively involved in Theatre for Children in Hospital (TCH) and work towards a compassionate healthcare for children and communities through the aesthetic of performance. The intention of the book is to lay out the features of theatre, combining participatory dramas in clinical settings as a basis for exploring and understanding the distinctive practical aspects of TCH, and the demands of the clinical context on the art form in healthcare settings. My aim is that, using experience from ten years' practice and evaluation of applied theatre processes in hospitals, this book will make an argument for the benefits of theatre provision for children, their families and the artists who participate in TCH. My aim is also that it will provide an insight into the methodology, the energy and the passion that is required for this job and the values that have inspired me. This methodology can then inspire other professionally experienced theatre practitioners, but also young actors, artists and volunteers who can see a personal meaning in developing theatre in child healthcare and beyond.

The opportunity to write this book came to me through my work as the research director of the Newman University Community & Applied Drama Laboratory (CADLab). CADLab researches bedside theatre in partnership with the Birmingham Children's Hospital (general pathology, cancer and cardiac wards) and Heartlands Hospital (paediatrics), both belonging to the NHS Trust in the United Kingdom. I have been privileged to receive an Entrepreneurship Award followed by funding from HEfCE and Unlimited in 2010, and play a leading part in the foundation and development of CADLab research, alongside volunteer drama students, colleagues from the area of social work with children and families, and professionals from the hospitals' arts departments and play centres. As an academic lecturer engaged in applied theatre since 1995, the scope for research on the impact of theatre on children's wellbeing in clinical settings caught my professional interest. CADLab gathered together the expertise and interest that has formed during that time, and the first stage of the bedside theatre study was the judges' highly commended theatre project for the 2013 West Midlands Award in Arts & Health. In 2015, CADLab secured a grand from BBC Children in Need to develop a three-year (2016–2019) participatory arts project for children in West Midlands hospitals and schools, including bedside theatre, after-show art activities and art exhibitions.

My Greek origins also led me to dedicate my research to this field. TCH reminds me that the arts, health and wellbeing are entwined. Theatre has been an integral part of entertainment and care for complete physical, mental, social and spiritual wellbeing in medical and healing centres since antiquity. Dedicated to Asclepius, the god of medicine in ancient Greek mythology, the Asclepieion Sanctuaries (fifth and fourth centuries BCE) were healing centres that adopted a holistic approach to treatment; recognizing the importance of physiological, psychological and social factors in the healing procedure. Patients were introduced to the 'Dream Healing Pilgrimage', where healing, science, the arts and belief in the supernatural were married together. There is an apparent connection between theatrical activities and the healing temple (Christopoulou-Aletra, Togia and Varlami 2010). Theatre, poetry and music were offered to patients as part of their cure in many of these sanctuaries, such as the one in the town of Epidaurus (fourth century BCE), which had its own theatre. The patients and pilgrims participated in the festivities in the god's honour and watched comedies, tragedies and satirical plays. As anticipated by Aristotle, the Greek philosopher and polymath (384–322 BCE), the tragedies had a purifying effect on their audiences through the cathartic emotion of 'pity and terror': the purgation of the pity and fear that arose in an audience. Attendance at theatrical plays in the sanctuary demonstrates that the inseparable connection between wellbeing and theatre has been recognized for millennia, although the notion of 'hospital theatre' has rested over the years. The works of Aristotle and Heraclitus's theory of life as an evolving phenomenon are mentioned in this book to contextualize wellbeing (*eudaimonia*) and the acceptance of illness as an overpowering life change. The possibility of joining the threads of my academic work in the United Kingdom and my ancestors' understandings of health and wellbeing was compelling. Essentially, illness, happiness, acceptance, empathy and compassion are emphasized in this book because of the nature of TCH and because the opposite – avoidance of meeting illness with acceptance, empathy and compassion – can be so problematic for the artist who performs with children in hospital.

The personal pull was equally strong. I recall myself as a parent in a children's hospital in 2006, in the midst of children lying on beds, most of them in pain and bored, alongside other overwhelmed parents. My compassion rose out from within me, possibly rooted in my 'circumstantial knowledge of the other' – the parents (Prádier 2011). Being a parent myself led me to gain some understanding of the parents' emotions about their children, but at the same time it gave me an external perspective on how I felt about my child and the circumstances of that time. In the middle of difficult times, I was thinking about emotions, the suffering of negative feelings in hospital both as a child and as a parent. I was also thinking about the possibility of using theatre in an environment like this to generate children's positive feelings through the experience of arts in hospital. Reflections of joyful moments with my children in theatre shone back at me from the clinical floors of the ward. That image actually caused me to reflect back on many joyful moments with children in the main theatre. The belief that theatre can draw smiles on children's faces and give comfort to parents and families through watching their children being happy motivated me to put a proposal forward to the National

Theatre of Northern Greece (NTNG). The proposal turned out to be successful and gained funding from the Hellenic Lottery scheme and the General Secretariat of Your People of the Ministry of Education. Through the invaluable experience that I gained with NTNG in witnessing the audience's response to the performances in paediatric, orthopaedic, cardiac and oncology departments in five hospitals in Thessaloniki – a historic city in the north of Greece – my engagement with TCH became a passion and a mission.

My enthusiasm during that time and my continuing research in the United Kingdom is informed by the aspiration that the arts can gradually make a difference to people's lives in healthcare. It may be a small difference in their thinking at the beginning, but it could lead to the opening of new channels with which to value the importance of the arts in health and wellbeing. There is an assumption and a hope in this belief. In making arts in healthcare, the artist is continually on the search for specific audiences with common health experiences and medical conditions; either to address their work toward or to engage in creative, interactive processes. This book is underpinned by an objective to examine the role of theatre as a potential methodology that could contribute to healthcare through portable theatre representations, dramatizations and adaptations of children's narratives and bedside storytelling. It is my intention with this book to approach the field of aesthetics of the theatre and assist our understanding of audience participation in hospital: to bring joy to children and families in the hospital. As I consider TCH's complexity, I foresee that it will be a difficult subject matter to examine. And yet, writing this book connects me with others: actors, children, parents, artists and health professionals. My aspiration to help children re-win a lost sense of joy, confidence and hope through theatre gives a purpose to my efforts. I am deeply connected to this purpose in my heart.

Arts and health

It is an exciting time to be engaged in this work. There is a growing sense of the potential of the arts and health field in the United Kingdom and internationally, and promising evidence about the purpose and value of arts-based activities in healthcare. TCH is situated in the growing field of arts and health and focuses on a particular aspect of the current interest in arts-based participatory approaches to child healthcare. More specifically, the book is about intimate bedside theatre performance, offered one-to-one for children with health problems during their stay in hospital. TCH is largely overlooked and untheorized. It is not mentioned in arts and health reviews and reports, and there is not much written work on theatre in hospitals in research journals. Therefore, the book aims to make an important contribution to the literature. Whilst recognizing the place of TCH in arts and health, we should define the developments in the field by the achievement of passionate artists, health professionals and researchers worldwide.

Since the beginning of the new millennium, the current evidence base for the impact of arts-focused initiatives on patients' physical health and emotional and social wellbeing shows a wealth of enthusiastic approaches to similar cultural initiatives by higher education institutions, research networks and cultural organizations around the world, which currently support Applied Theatre, Health Humanities, Medical Humanities and Arts in Education and Psychology. Evidence about the progression of the arts in healthcare in the United Kingdom in particular is reflected by the growth of the National Alliance for Arts, Health and Wellbeing, a leading UK organization with nine regional representatives supported by the Arts Council of England, such as the London Arts in Health Forum (LAHF), the West Midlands Arts and Health & Wellbeing (WMAH&W) the Arts and Health South West (AHSW), the North West Arts and Health Network, and others. From 2009 onwards, LAHF has been working with associations from across the United Kingdom to develop the National Alliance for Arts, Health and Wellbeing and developed a Charter for Arts and Health. The Charter proposes liaising with the government to embed arts in health practice and raise the profile of arts in healthcare:

> We are holistic in approach and believe the arts and humanities have a crucial role to play in medical training, clinician wellbeing and awareness. We believe the arts help us to see and value the patient as a whole person, not just an illness or symptom. We believe the arts will contribute to a culture within health services that is more supportive, empowering, enlightened, personal and humane.
>
> (LAHF 2012a)

The Alliance defines arts in health in the following terms:

> By supplementing medicine and care, the arts can improve the health of people who experience mental or physical health problems. Engaging in the arts can promote prevention of disease and build wellbeing. The arts can improve healthcare environments and benefit staff retention and professional development.
>
> (LAHF 2012c)

The definition of arts and health was followed by the taxonomy of arts-based activities in four main areas of practice: (1) arts in the health environment aiming to improve the experience of patients and staff; (2) participatory arts programmes providing opportunities for patients to get involved in the arts; (3) medical training and medical humanities using the arts to aid in understanding wellbeing and the accompanying ethics; and (4) arts therapy practised by qualified therapists working with patients in psychotherapy. In similar ways to the Alliance, Hemingway and Crossen-White's (2014) review of arts in health literature mainly organizes arts in health initiatives into two categories; community-based and hospital-based initiatives. They also consider arts therapies, drama in schools, music in playgrounds and arts sessions for young people in community venues. In the review they develop a clear interest in examining the impact on local people of particular types of projects in community and hospital settings, as well as contributing to the improvement of patients' quality of life.

The taxonomy of activities is useful as far as its limitations are accepted. Taxonomy helps with creating the evidence base for quality improvement that the arts can have on public health practice. It can also help to codify the best examples of practice. However, the cataloguing of projects in one area of work or another could be problematic for the artist whose work does not fit into only one category. TCH is an example of practice that crosses over the areas of work that have been created by the Alliance. TCH combines (1) the arts as a means to improve children's experience in a healthcare environment, (2) the child's participation in performance and (3) training a new generation of community actors and healthcare professionals. Considering the Hemingway and Crossen-White (2014) review, in its broadest form TCH could be defined as both a community-based and a hospital-based activity. It is difficult to separate the community from the role of hospitals because hospitals aim at quality health provision and care for the community and are vital components of community life. TCH is community-driven (inspired by community values and priorities) and hospital-based (located in hospital wards). At the same time, it can be hospital-commissioned (funded by the health sector) and community-based (created by members of the art community for a hospital community of patients). TCH is simply too inclusive and wide-ranging to classify, and as far as I am concerned that is the beauty of it, although the anxious practitioner may be concerned that their work will not be easily identified by others in the field. Therefore, it would be useful to revisit the area of arts and health practice.

Arts and health is an evolving field and needs to stay open to the development of new, creative arts-based approaches to health and wellbeing: new combinations of aims, practices and techniques; new mixed methodologies and audiences; and a variety of social settings and priorities: artistic and clinical. The artist needs to be liberated from labels (my work is 'this' or 'that') and encouraged to produce creative cross-disciplinary work in arts and health. If actors aimed for their work to suit only one set of aims and audiences, there would be very little theatre to see. The challenge for those involved in the documentation of arts-focused initiatives in health is to present the existent work whilst promoting innovative (outside the box) practice across the areas of health and wellbeing.

At the moment, activity in all areas of arts and health is reflected in the 'Creativity and Wellbeing' week, a lively major event that is organized by the LAHF. According to the organizers,

> Over 20,000 people attended events in 2014 and over 25,000 in 2015. They took part in a huge range of activity celebrating the impact of the arts on wellbeing. In the last five years, the week has grown to be a focal point for arts and health and this is in huge part down to the individuals and organisations across London who ran events.
>
> (LAHF 2014, 2015)

LAHF activity widens the participation of arts in healthcare by involving more actors, local governors, charities and trusts, individuals and organizations in shared projects. It creates more regional and national opportunities for partnerships between theatre practitioners and health professionals, and better prospects for arts-based research, professional development and employment in the community. LAHF events are not the only ones of their kind in the country, but they are based in the capital city and, therefore, attract large audiences of intellectually curious practitioners and audiences.

A series of government reports provide a review of the evidence for the benefits of the arts to health and the policy context of commissioning arts in health projects within professional and educational contexts, such as within therapy and medical training. For example, reports on the role of the arts in health and the national strategy for arts and health and wellbeing were produced by the Arts Council England (2004, 2006, 2007, 2014). Reviews of the literature expressing the range of arts-based activities from music to design and architecture were also commissioned by organizations such as the Global Alliance for the Arts in Health and the Health Development Agency; the Sidney De Haan Research Centre for Arts and Health; and the Royal Society for Public Health Working Group on Arts, Health and Wellbeing. A systematic review of the impact of the performing arts on adolescent health and behaviour (Daykin, Orme, Evans et al. 2008) reported on music, performance, drama and dance in community settings and mainstream education. Although the study was conducted with populations outside of clinical settings, it defined implications for key public health issues affecting young people, such as obesity, sexual health and mental health. In 2014, an international research database of evidence-based art projects in healthcare was looking at the long-term benefits of the arts on patients' physical and emotional health. The project was funded by the United Kingdom's Arts and Humanities Research Council (AHRC) as part of the Cultural Value Project (2014) examining the evaluation of art practices.

These reviews are significant because they provide an overview of the state of the arts and health field in England through the examination of practice and research, including projects, publications, conferences and symposia. Reviews help both artists and communities to understand the impact that the arts are making at all levels and improve the quality and effectiveness of the projects. They share evidence from the evaluation of activities to inform the development of policy and provision, and they make recommendations to improve how the government makes funding and delivery decisions about the arts in health. Sometimes, there is disappointment when the policy recommendations in these documents are not acted upon (Clift, Camic, Chapman et al. 2009), but these reports at least contribute to the development of renewed efforts to encourage debates about the need for changes in the leadership and implementation of the arts in healthcare.

TCH practice in the United Kingdom does not exist in isolation from the achievements of international organizations that support paths of collaboration between artists and researchers worldwide. Some of these are Arts and Health Australia, the Institute for Creative Health (formerly Arts and Health Foundation) and Regional Arts NSW in Australia; Arts for Health: VicHealth, the Global Alliance for Arts & Health, the Creative Centre (New

York) and the Arts in Medicine Children's Centre (Texas) in the United States; the Arts and Health Network Canada; and many others in Europe, which provide evidence for a strong and committed community of arts and health practitioners in these continents. Such achievements show that artists are not alone in their efforts to sustain their passion and commitment to the arts in healthcare. Their efforts are supported by encouraging and reassuring research about the positive impact of the performing arts on health and wellbeing experiences. Indicative examples of international practice in the United States, Australia, Canada, Norway and Sweden are included in the Royal Society for Public Health (RSPH) (2013) report on Arts, Health and Wellbeing, which offers supportive evidence about the raised status of the arts in healthcare outside the United Kingdom. Research evidence strengthens the development of the arts in health and illustrates the benefits of arts-based community projects.

Some key areas of research development in the field are the impact of the arts on wellbeing, mental illness and public care. Christine Putland (2012) identifies the contexts and types of research linking the arts to health and wellbeing, and offers evidence on the known effects of arts and health interventions on prevention and care, the management of chronic conditions and the cost-effectiveness of arts programmes for health and wellbeing, especially in relation to mental illness. Angus (2002), Philipp (2010) and Brodzinski (2010) offer indicative evidence that artistic methods can change the way artists and audiences interact with each other, forging a different relationship from the traditional artist–audience hierarchy in the theatre and affecting their wellbeing in clinical contexts. A growing interest in the role of the arts in child healthcare was also evidenced. 'Theme-based magic' is a particularly interesting example of practice with children. In this study, an interdisciplinary group of researchers from the United Kingdom and Israel (Green, Schertz, Gordon et al. 2013) paid attention to the dynamic interconnections between improving physical skills and supporting wellbeing by achieving long-held physical goals. The study investigated the effects of a theme-based ('magic') variation of the hand–arm bimanual intensive therapy programme for improving physical performance in children with hemiplegia. It explored the role of 'performing' in its broadest sense. By training children to become skilful magicians, the study looked into the correlation between physical activity (during magic sessions for children) and the improvement of their kinaesthetic performance. These observations are interesting because they implicate the use of performing activities in enhancing child wellbeing through the development of skills and the improvement of confidence and self-esteem.

Other research projects combine artwork, creative writing, digital photography and musical performances for children with cancer and blood disorders and their siblings. Cowell, Herron and Hockenberry's (2011) thirteen-year research study suggests that artistic activities (puppeteers, storytellers, musicians, dance troupes, photographers and playwrights, etc.) have a positive impact on children with cancer, creating a 'healing' environment and treatment experience. An earlier study by Athanassiadou, Tsiantis, Christogiorgos and Kolaitis (2009) also argues that puppet play improves children's pre- and post-operative distress management in hospitals. Such emerging work in this field stimulates new thinking and conversations about what directions artists might consider in the future and how they might evaluate the social, educational and economic value of the arts in healthcare. Although further research is necessary to test the effectiveness of these studies on larger groups of patients, they contribute important findings to the TCH practitioner about new methods to prepare children emotionally for surgery and support patient wellbeing in recovery.

Following the growth of arts in health, international publishers and audiences have developed a curiosity about research findings, ideas and debates within the field. Research journals such as *Arts & Health: An International Journal of Research, Policy and Practice* and the *Journal of Applied Arts & Health* investigate the efficacy of the interdisciplinary use of the arts in healthcare internationally. Evidence is presented through initiatives that include artists, healthcare professionals, community workers and researchers in the public, private and voluntary sectors. Journals about applied theatre practices and processes in education and the wider community, such as *Research in Drama Education: The Journal of Applied Theatre*, *National Drama* and *Applied Theatre Research* also give voice to new ideas and research that takes place with non-traditional audiences, amongst whom are children and young people. Conferences and journals provide researchers with space to express their views about the importance of evaluating their practical work and raise awareness about emerging theories, methodologies and practices in the fields of drama, theatre, education and communities. Not all the published works suggest specific models of arts-based practices in society, but the majority provide remarkable evidence of using the arts to bring meaning and make a difference to people's lives. The extended effort, creativity, passion and determination that have been invested in the arts in health and wellbeing by practitioners and researchers give academic communities hope for systematic investigation and improved healthcare experience through theatre.

Although only a little TCH evidence is presented here, this book is invested in is hope, passion and determination to inspire further investigations and practical experimentation with the art form in hospitals. The book brings TCH practice to life and proposes a unique mixed research methodology as a potential way of addressing and evaluating the effectiveness of bedside interventions. It examines TCH from multiple viewpoints: artist, child-patient, parents, clinical staff and principal researcher. In doing so, it highlights the complex relationship between the artistic and clinical, and at the same time offers a holistic analysis of the potential of TCH. It aims to offer in-depth insight into TCH's different elements (artistic, ethical, social) through a combination of anecdotal stories and transcribed interviews in an example of small-scale, bedside theatre practice. The risk of presenting TCH practice through one approach is that it might be perceived as the only way of learning how to make theatrical interventions for children in clinical environments, which is not the case. Van de Water (2012) for example acknowledges that TCH consists of practices that include both staged productions to large audiences of patients from across the hospital (and other adult companions, such as their families) and small-scale, intimate performances for individual children in selected hospital wards. Therefore, it is useful to articulate our broader understandings of the collaboration between theatre and arts and health, and the synergistic relationship between the child and the artist in the performance, as well as the particular learning that can be gained from this approach.

The structure of the book

Chapter One offers a conceptual framework of TCH practice, including a definition of theatre practice for children in hospitals and a description of TCH through existing research. This chapter's emphasis on sharing a definition and description of TCH aims to make a contribution to the field. TCH is defined as a hybrid due to its mixed nature, comprising of a combination of practices (performance and drama, storytelling with the use of soft toys, and relaxation techniques); cultures (the artistic and the clinical); skills (acting, singing, improvisation); and mixed research methodologies (traditional qualitative tools and practice *as* research). The definition aims to make the book equally relevant to everyone involved: artists, researchers and audiences in healthcare. At the centre of the definition is the role of theatre as an 'antidote' to clinical stress. I discuss TCH as a possible 'escape' from traumatic realities. Excited by the marriage of the two cultures, the artistic and the clinical, I share my thoughts about audience participation with children involved in one-to-one situations. I position TCH under the umbrella of applied theatre practices whilst I am arguing for a type of *learning* that differs from, but does not contradict, the social, political and educational learning and purpose of other applied practices. Part of this discussion is formed by reworked thoughts about the learning that Theatre-in-Education (TiE) aims for and the role of a different type of audience empowerment in clinical contexts. Some of the roots of these ideas can be found in my doctorate thesis (Sextou 2004). These ideas progress from my postdoctoral research and reflect on my continuous experimentation with children as audiences in non-traditional contexts, which has been a form of incessant investigation for over two decades now.

Definition leads the reader to the discussion of TCH audience participation as a phenomenon that develops within a dialogue between the artistic and the clinical. I am interested in exploring the relationship between the artist and the audience in hospital, how the dynamics in the artist–participant relationship change in clinical settings. The distinctive role of aesthetics in bedside performance in hospital and the type of participation that takes place in this live art are important to this discussion. It is important to explore what is expected of the child in hospital performance in relation to theatrical conventions and how the child responds to it. As Gareth White (2013) says in the introduction to *Audience Participation in Theatre*:

> The work becomes meaningful through its aesthetic, and this aesthetic – as a collection of proportions about what an artwork is and how to respond to it – if examined in detail can tell us much more about the meanings and potential meanings of the work than

an analysis that takes effects as the first line of investigation: in order to understand an aesthetic we must understand its media.

(White 2013: 11)

I, too, am interested in the 'aesthetics of invitation' in hospital performance, the process of practice and the problems associated with the 'distinctive aesthetics' of audience participation in clinical settings. In particular, I am curious to examine whether the child's role is crucially important to the theatrical event itself, and what to expect of each TCH performance. Is each performance a different work? Can we expect the performance to be owned by the artist? Is the ownership of the performance shared between the child and the artist? Chapter Two provides examples of incidents that happened in bedside performance that illustrate what happens in hospitals and suggest answers to these questions.

Just as White (2013) returns again and again in his book to the invitation of participation and the response to it, I return to the invitation of participation with attention to the details of the interaction between the artist and the child. Interaction addresses some important details that lead to important questions about the level of engagement in the fiction, the level of respect for the child's availability to participate, and the level of awareness of the responsibility of making TCH in a distinctive context. I am interested in understanding the child's role in TCH aesthetics, and how TCH is anchored in the artist–child relationship, but I am also cautious of the ethics of participation in TCH. Therefore, I give space in the book to discuss the risks of using stories of illness in the performance, risks of emotional responses. I wonder: how can the artist be objective about illness and audiences who suffer from it? Can they escape filtering their art through what they know about illness and how they understand it? Would the opposite potentially become a problem? To answer this intellectual suspicion, I suggest paying attention to ethics and consideration for the risks that are involved with devising, writing or adapting for audiences who experience illness. This is an exciting discussion that aims to offer the reader insight into the awareness of the TCH context and the ethical challenges of its artistic processes. However, the book deliberately does not attempt to make final statements about TCH ethics, which are by nature complex and sensitive. Rather, it aims to clarify the relationship between the TCH art form and illness and suggest some new ways of attending illness through the art form.

Emphasis has therefore been placed on discussing the concept of illness and the ability of the sick child to participate, bringing an inspirational element to the discussion. Stimulated by Havi Carel's (2012, 2013) stirring philosophical approach to illness, I am drawing on the existential experience of being ill and distant from one's body. Carel draws the attention of those who are not ill to the 'new identity of the ill person', an identity that is adopted by those individuals who feels restricted by their own body because of illness. Illness is often an experience of physical inability, a shift from 'I can' to 'I cannot'. The ill person faces a fundamental change to the way in which the body is experienced. A body restricted by illness affects the person's interaction with the world. This view is fascinating to me because the identity of the ill person is a label that many children often adopt during their stay in hospital. The children who experience illness often question the 'new' condition of their body: 'What is wrong with me, Mum? Why can't I walk?' and 'Why I am in pain? I can't play like other kids', and in some cases, 'Mum, am I going to die?' The (dis)ability of the child to do things as normal while they stay in hospital creates a circle of negative experience that follows patterns of passivity. 'I am in bed', 'I cannot move', 'There is something wrong with me', 'I cannot...' and 'I am not able to...' Promoting positive messages about the role of TCH as a participatory process in breaking the circle of inability and disability that children experience in hospital, I explore possible theatrical ways to liberate the child from medical labels that affect their trust in what they can do. I look into the details of what a rather experimental, unconventional actor–audience relationship can tell us about theatre in hospital. Two elements are vital to this discussion. One is the accidental as an opportunity for playfulness. The other is the transformation of the hospital into a 'stage'. Drawing on some ideas from Birch and Tompkins's (2012) work about the effectiveness of site-specific theatre, I give their theory a broader capacity to address the particular conditions and conventions of the hospital site-specific theatrical experience; how the hospital space works as a 'stage'; and how it affects the dramatic work.

Finally, Chapter One addresses the problematic boundaries and overlaps between TCH and drama therapy, challenging notions of illness, entertainment and cure. Drawing on Anna Seymour's (2009) analogy between life and performance and John Somers's (2009) discussion of dramatic activities that could be seen as therapeutic, I explore the identity of TCH in association with drama therapy. With recognition of drama therapy as a clinical process and TCH as an artistic process, I address the distinctions between TCH and drama therapy. Between the two, there is a scale of drama from explicit therapeutic aims to performance. The two ends of this scale have different goals and values. At the same time, I express my concerns over deliberately distancing what is considered therapy from what is not intended to be explicitly therapeutic. One of the consequences of this distinction is that making art through which the audience feels better does not become as valued as therapy because the artist does not define the work *as* therapy: drama therapists treat TCH in this way. In my discussion, I argue that TCH does not have explicit aims to personal change as drama therapy does, but it can be helpful to the child's wellbeing while they are staying in hospital experiencing illness and recovering from it.

Chapter Two is where the *kardía* (heart) of the book is. It draws on the conceptual framework of TCH practice in Chapter One, and analyses a specific example of bedside theatre practice. This chapter communicates research results with enthusiasm and confidence for the efficacy of theatrical interventions in improving children's experience of hospital life. It provides the reader with views that are left open to discussion and to further experimentation with art forms and approaches. It presents examples of bedside theatre in hospitals from a research study that took place in hospital wards in the United Kingdom. The practitioner-reader will appreciate this chapter for its lively tone and practical nature. This chapter aims to familiarize the reader with the distinctive features of TCH as these are observed and evaluated in practice. More specifically, I present my research about a specific type of TCH bedside theatre practice that was conducted with children and their families at NHS Trust hospitals in the West Midlands between 2010 and 2015. As practice is one of the unique strengths of the book (the other one is the passion for research), this chapter brings practice and research together. Paying attention to Armstrong and Aitken's (2000) observation that children undergo stresses of new and old unpleasant experiences in hospital, I investigate the impact of bedside theatre performance on hospitalized children's wellbeing. Armstrong and Aitken (2000) work with hospitalized children to prepare them for medical procedures. They have noticed that children who undergo surgical procedures experience pre- and post-operative anxiety, pain and negative emotional situations. Their research offers positive indications that play reduces the symptoms of anxiety and supports children during their stay in hospital. In this book, I evaluate the participants' perceived benefits of the theatrical experience in relation to emotional stress and anxiety. I present findings from both the pilot and the main study about bedside theatre as these are evaluated by children and their families, as well as findings from the dissemination phase about what the artist can learn from the performance. The learning is in relation to the distinctive aesthetics of audience participation, which relate to the clinical stressors that the child experiences in hospital.

As part of the analysis of the research findings, I also offer my semi-autobiographical reflections on situations and incidents in hospitals. I make no apologies for the fact that the analysis of practice depends much on my practical experience, background, learned disposition and personal value systems. Bedside theatre applications in hospitals are not used as 'prescriptions' for artists with a desire to cure the healthcare system. They are not used as recipes for successful applied theatre practice. My work, as all applied theatre practices, is by nature a developing, ongoing application that is open to change and improvement. Thus, the suggestions that the reader will find in this book are not conclusive. They are presented to inspire, to motivate and to facilitate discussion and further experimentation with artistic forms, approaches and processes in clinical contexts. What urges my writing is my zeal for researching practice. I am interested in how bedside performances have been perceived, conceived and commended by the child, the adult accompanying the child, and the artists. By extension, this will question whether actors can engage with the child in an intimate one-to-one performance. Are the artists able to treat the child as an audience rather than an ill person? These questions will form part of the analysis of the practical experience of TCH and the research results of the study in Chapter Two. A small part of this chapter grew out of articles on the impact of theatre on the wellbeing of children during their stay in hospitals (Sextou and Monk 2013; Sextou and Hall 2015). These articles were published in *Arts & Health: An International Journal of Policy, Research and Practice* and *Applied Theatre Research*. Each article has been reworked to contribute to this new chapter written especially for this book, with permission.

In this chapter, the reader will also be introduced to the importance of the artist's opinion in the development of practice. I do this by suggesting a mixed research methodology of traditional qualitative tools and elements of using practice as a research method itself, which provides the reader with the views of the children and the families in hospital wards. The study presents the expectations of the audience before the performance, and the experience of theatre during and after performance through the eyes of the audience. To illustrate my arguments, I use examples of performances, incidents and data collected from the audience, their families, the artists and selected hospital staff. I quote transcripts of the play as it developed moment-by-moment on the day in collaboration with the audience. Transcripts include improvised dialogues between the child and the artist during performance, as these were recorded on camera for the needs of the study. I describe and discuss both successful incidents of active interaction between the child, the artist and soft toys, and challenging moments of limited communication with the child due to a number of personal and medical factors in relation to the child's circumstances and health condition. These examples are used to explore the degree of child participation in bedside hospital performance and the effectiveness or failure of certain artistic choices about the usage of space, time and props. They indicate the need to utilize practice, learn from it and use the learning to draw conclusions as to what TCH can do for children in healthcare. Importantly, the description and analysis of these examples aim to raise awareness amongst the reader about the needs of children participating in TCH, and the ability of the artist to meet these needs through their artistic intentions. The experiences that reflect from the hospital wards back on this chapter also aim to inspire and engage the artist in a dialogue with their own theatre practice, approaches and processes in search of new dreams, ambitions and missions in healthcare.

In relation to this aim, I also examine the effectiveness of the interventions from the artist's perspective as well as from the views of hospital staff. I rate the artist's input as valuable to the analysis of TCH practice and as a way by which the reader gains insight into the learning that is generated through performance. Special space is, therefore, given to the artists' responses to the TCH experience and their reactions to performing with children in clinical settings. Quotations of their replies are used in the text as concrete examples to explain and illustrate the reception of bedside theatre interventions by the artists. This enables the consideration of thoughts, preferences, opinions, feelings and propositions in the analysis and evaluation of TCH. In relation to the data, ideas are witnessed, decisions are considered and conclusions are made about the possible effects of TCH on the lives of children in hospital as well as on the artist's personal and professional growth. By looking closely at the data, I make comparisons between the responses and learn to value the opinions of all parties involved in the study. The reader is provided with observations of practice and realizations that will hopefully give room for improvement, both artistic and professional. This possibility, combined with the particular circumstances in hospitals, has meant that I have felt free to experiment with different forms and make observations of how they work in practice with attention to the needs of children during the various stages of the study. The research presented here aims to make a positive contribution to further and deeper investigations into the role of theatre in healthcare. Readers will find this part of the book a useful point of reference when conducting their own projects arguing for a sense of purpose and evidenced value of TCH interventions. More evidence will be valuable in interconnecting the field of theatre as an art form with perceptions of the role of hospitals as institutions.

Chapter Three explores the role of the artist in discovering the philosophical meaning and importance of theatre in the lives of children in hospital, and the use of theatre in that context. Finding meaning in TCH is a real quest for each artist. Actors, artists, drama students and art researchers all have to experiment and discover how to integrate meaningful intentions in our artistic work within clinical contexts. Would it be wise to ignore the particular context within which art develops in our discoveries? Indeed, we need to make an effort to understand the demands of the context on our artwork and the ethical complexities of interacting with audiences who suffer with illness. This chapter is a personal journey of learning. I wrote this chapter to search for knowledge that would help the reader, and myself, to better understand self-wellbeing and gain fulfilment of purpose through TCH. I do not suggest, not for a moment, that this chapter will transform readers into happy, balanced, fulfilled practitioners with a complete sense of purpose and a full understanding of their potential in healthcare. I am aware that while this chapter opens a window of exploration for the curious artist, it only offers a short discussion of particularly challenging concepts such as illness, happiness, acceptance, empathy and compassion. As interconnections between the themes of happiness, acceptance, empathy and compassion can be found, I discuss them together. I have no intention to claim a detailed and in-depth analysis of their theories. That could be the content of another book. But I do hope that I will provide the reader with a base for thinking about these themes in relation to theatre in hospitals. This chapter aims to be a starting point for self-questioning and developing a more honest internal dialogue with ourselves as artists and human beings. This dialogue may reveal the real motivations, reasons and passions behind our interest in working with children with illness from a holistic approach.

Driven by personal interest in philosophy, I will offer Aristotle's (384–322 BCE) view on happiness (*eudaimonia*) and Heraclitus' (535–475 BCE) view on change as examples of seeing illness as a journey of change that is central to self-discovery, individual growth and learning for both the audience and the artist. Their theories are discussed in relation to what it means to be happy as an artist and to aim at happiness through artwork in hospitals. This is relevant to the argument of this book in that each child experiences illness as a change in different ways, though illness is something that they do not choose to happen to them. It is also relevant to the ways in which the artist learns from the experience of illness that happens to others. Children live differently through illness and they respond differently to the invitation to participate in hospital theatre performance. Illness as an experience of the child often leads the artist to question their past choices of making theatre for children. It often causes, in a good way, a change in artistic identity in which the previous experience of interacting with children as an audience in the main theatre is negotiated by a new, broadened experience of being present with the child together in performance.

While offering a definition of how the exercise of empathy founded on compassion is understood in psychology by Zaki, Bolger and Ochsner (2009), I also look at how these understandings connect with empathy in TCH more precisely. I will also draw on Gilbert's (2009, 2010) self-compassionate approach to life and therapy and suggest that these ideas warrant the artist a social role that has not been articulated. Compassion can be used as a vehicle for the study of challenging aspects of the artistic experience in clinical environments. I will argue that acceptance and empathy can be integral to a performance in hospital, as they facilitate a compassionate experience of hospital life. This argument relies on overlooked aspects of illness as life experience.

The final chapter reflects on the book and presents some concluding thoughts about the future of TCH. These thoughts aim to encourage a realistic consideration of environmental factors that might influence the growth of TCH in the countries where it already exists, and the emergence of forms of TCH practice in other social systems. The chapter does not make any predictions, rather it aims to raise awareness amongst readers about the conditions and support that can benefit TCH at the moment. It is also a valuable opportunity to make realizations about the need for further improvement of TCH provision. In a sense, the personal experience becomes shared and open to dialogue in this chapter. I share my understanding of what kind of actors we need in healthcare, aiming to offer the reader an opportunity for explorations and future planning about the actor in the healthcare profession.

Collecting evidence and experience to write this book has been a rich journey for me over the past few years. Inevitably, the book contains both evidence from the research study and personal accounts from my own understanding of audiences and artistic practices. It is my intention, however, that readers will be able to recognize the research findings as well as the processes, practices, concerns and examples that I offer here as an invitation for more experimentation with theatre practice in healthcare. It is my hope that it will speak to the hearts of people who care for children and support the arts, and it will contribute to the development of the field. This book looks at some of the opportunities available for the artist to use their art form with enthusiasm and knowledge and broaden their understanding of the role of the arts in the community. It looks at the connections between creative industries, drama and theatre studies, and the role of public health in bringing change for the better. It may take governments a long time to realize that TCH benefits children and complements healthcare provision. This book aims to contribute towards more complete and more thoroughly discussed realizations about the value of theatre for the improvement of child wellbeing in healthcare, in which the artists have expertise in performance, communication and interaction with the audience. I set out to explore how dramatic art transforms the experience of illness and to encourage a larger number of people, families, artists and health professionals to see the arts and patients differently. I hope that it will contribute to your learning and in turn improve the lives of children and their families in hospital. It is assumed that the contents of this book will be used with sensitivity, caution and care by artists, drama students, drama researchers, play specialists, teachers working with children in healthcare and nursing staff alike.

Chapter One

A TCH definition and more...

Applied theatre in hospitals

I position my TCH bedside methodology broadly under applied theatre. Applied theatre is an inclusive term used to host a variety of powerful, community-based participatory processes and educational practices. Historically, applied theatre practices include Theatre-in-Education (TiE), Theatre-in-Health Education (THE), Theatre for Development (TfD), prison theatre, community theatre, theatre for conflict resolution/reconciliation, reminiscence theatre with elderly people, theatre in museums, galleries and heritage centres, theatre at historic sites, and more recently, theatre in hospitals (Nicholson 2014).

> 'Applied' refers to an act that takes theatre practices out of the obscure black boxes and brings them back to the 'open air' [...] [It] should be understood as a contemporary theatre practice that has many different histories and varied rationales depending on where it is happening.
>
> (Thompson 2012: xix)

Thompson concentrates on the evolving process of applying theatre to community audiences and invests in learning about being human, being a citizen and being empowered to think and act in the particular moment and context within which theatre takes place. He also argues that the 'act of applying [theatre] is an unfinished process that encounters situations that are themselves evolving and not fixed examples of social practice' (Thompson 2012: xxi). But aren't all arts an unfinished process? Arts change over the years because humans change and environments change. Different styles of theatre and forms of theatrical applications outside traditional venues have been discovered, without which we would still be making theatre for middle-class audiences who can afford to attend.

From my research of applied theatre interventions in healthcare, I believe that theatre in hospitals *is* an unfinished process for many reasons. First, it encounters examples of an artistic practice that is continually evolving within the development of the arts in healthcare settings. This is the growth of the arts and health field that I discussed in the introduction. Second, TCII is the product of an unceasing experimentation with the art form in clinical contexts and environments, an artistic need to move on to new discoveries of the way theatre works in the community, investigating the needs of communities. As with all experimental practices, it desires answers. Questions created by the needs of hospitalized children, the specific demands of clinical space and time, the physical and emotional condition of the audience, the opportunities for making a difference in children's lives, and the occasional disappointment of having opportunities denied, are central to the experimentation with applied performance in hospitals. Third, TCH is an unfinished process of articulating the experience of hospital performance in words that make sense to those who have been involved in the experience, both the artist and the audience. The artist often struggles to find meaning in illness and pain: whether that is in direct relationship with family members or in professional relationship with audiences. Holding onto the principle, 'theatre for all, the sick, the poor and the sufferers', is a strong starting point, a creative motive, an enthusiastic beginning towards understanding theatre and communities in contexts of illness. Finally, TCH is an ongoing cultural process with potential to develop further from its strong interaction with children in hospital and the surrounding setting. The setting is an important aspect of TCH work but not more important than performance itself. Theatre that is 'applied' to community settings does not lack in aesthetic integrity (Brodzinski 2010). It is only fair to say that TCH, as all applied theatre practices, is rooted in the role of the space, the story, the characterization and the audience–artist relationship. At the same time, hospital performance develops in a continuing dialogue with the setting and the clinical context. TCH is always in transition and thus, perfectly positioned in applied theatre's unfinished businesses.

TCH is an interdisciplinary process. The act of applying theatre in relation to illness, like other research in this field, takes the artist into related disciplines including health and medical humanities, child wellbeing, the philosophy of illness and psychology. Primarily, the artist serves the arts and although they familiarize themselves with other disciplines, and learn from them and through them, they exercise learning from the perspective of the art form. The TCH artist uses knowledge from other disciplines to inform practice in hospital and create portable, child-centred, entertaining and relaxing performances that are offered to sick children while undertaking treatment. The objective of TCH is to harness theatre as an art form to improve child wellbeing in hospital while contributing to the wellbeing of those who care for them, such as their parent/carers and by extension, the wider family. The artist becomes a 'guest' in the house of illness but never stays too long. They enter the world of sickness for a while, bringing to the lives of children an air of normality that is associated with life outside the hospital, and they exit quietly – no applause and no 'bravos'. Working on the margins of the healthcare system is not necessarily a bad thing. 'One of applied theatre's strengths is in its status as the outsider, the visitor and the guest' (Thompson 2012: xx).

This viewpoint encourages me to say that the outsider artist works in collaboration with healthcare but does not serve it nor interrogate it, which reminds me of the role of the TiE practitioner who works in but does not serve the educational system. The artist's job in hospital is to reconnect the arts with wellbeing, which suggests a holistic approach to illness and healing that is rooted in ancient civilizations and systems of treatment and cure. For example, Hippocratic medicine treated the patient as a 'whole' (body, mind and spirit) and not just the symptoms of the disease. Hippocrates 'prescribed' massage, herbal diet, hydrotherapy, sea bathing (Osborn 2015) and theatre performances in the open-air Theatre of Cos Island in Greece to treat the body, the mind and the spirit. These experiences were enriched by worshipping and participation in religious ceremonies, and offered the patient a rounded caring experience and improved wellbeing. Although no claim can be made that my TCH practice draws on Hippocratic values exclusively, one sees a connection between believing in alternative supportive treatments and offering theatre as an alternative method of supporting patients. The TCH artist enters healthcare with the belief that theatre works as a complementary 'prescription' to medication and clinical remedies. Whereas many people in western societies speak with confidence about traditional medicine and how it works for the patients, TCH makes a holistic proposition.

Research evidence strengthens this view. Kostenius and Öhrling (2009) and Aldiss, Horstman, O'Leary, Richardson and Gibson (2008) argue that theatrical interventions can reduce child pre- and post-operative clinical stress and enhance their wellbeing. The TCH artist can use these findings to inform their practice. This perspective insists that there is no professional from within the healthcare system, no doctor, nurse or therapist, who can claim holistic practice because their practice is constructed around traditional medicine. Even if they do support holistic thinking, they are usually limited by medical regulations not to apply it to their patients. The visitor-artist faces no such limitations. The artist brings into healthcare a non-medical approach to illness and a system of values that is new to the clinical context. Those values – aesthetic, social, cultural, and ethical – may be incomplete and even irrelevant to the hospital context but they may generate an integration of artistic and clinical values (I oppose the imposition of artist values upon the clinical and vice versa) with aesthetic fulfilment. A commitment to these values explains why being a guest in healthcare is a good thing. TCH seeks to benefit children's wellbeing in ways that the healthcare system cannot achieve alone.

Those artists who engage in TCH, as many applied theatre practitioners do, are often motivated by the desire to make a difference to the lives of children through theatre. In that case, they may be elevated by idealism and altruism, courage and compassion. They come from outside the healthcare system to help and support children, give them normality and hope, bring a smile to their faces and change the ways they experience illness during their hospital life. This is the 'guest in applied theatre' position that I discussed earlier. What can be wrong with that? Nicholson (2005) suggests that working in a context (clinical) that is not theirs may create an 'uneven balance of power' between altruist (the applied practitioner) and recipient (the audience) and she argues that

Because practitioners often work in contexts in which they are outsiders, for all kinds of reasons their good intentions about 'helping' others in 'need' may be construed as patronising or authoritarian, contributing to keeping 'others' on the margins rather than taking centre stage.

(Nicholson 2005: 30)

From this standpoint, Nicholson (2005) discusses the reciprocal relationship between altruism and self-interest, between the artist and the community in applied theatre practice, and the effect of this relationship on the development of social citizenship. In its best collective form, applied theatre is offered to the community as a gift. It is, nevertheless, not always obvious why and how people need help and thus, what is intended to be beneficial for the audience often turns out to be more beneficial for the giver, the applied theatre artist. This is because the diagnosis of the 'needs' of others may fall into personal interpretation. The artist, for example, assumes that a child in hospital needs a performance for a reason. The artist might assume that one child needs the performance more than another does; a child with critical illness needs it more than a child who is in hospital for a short stay, but again this is only an assumption. In fact, the artist does not know which child needs the performance and therefore they rely on the children themselves to decide if they want the entertainment or not. The artist does not know what it is exactly that the child needs. Therefore, they cannot make any accurate predictions about the ways in which the performance will support each child. Altruism sometimes acts as a blind person who cannot see with their objective senses but can only perceive things with their minds. Moreover, because the blind man has a desire to see, his perception of what might be there can almost feel real. The altruistic artist can sometimes perceive the needs of the audience from such a personal and subjective perspective as if they were blind. They are passionately motivated to benefit children in hospital but can only perceive and interpret things through filters of personal understanding. However, altruist's authority to make interpretations of the child's needs and decisions about the work needs attention. In my experience, the artist occasionally perceives their role as rescuers who enter hospitals to show their ability to love and perform for those who are in need. However, the performance is clearly not a heroic act, and certainly should not appeal to the artist as a victory in the battle with the child's illness. Applied theatre practice is a process that may require bravery, care and compassion, especially in communities that have experienced suffering and trauma, but it should not be seen as a relationship between artists who act as heroes and audiences who are victims waiting to be saved.

Calvert (2015) summarizes deep-seated concerns about heroism in applied theatre work as these have been developed from provocations presented at the Theatre and Performance Research Association (TAPRA) Tenth Anniversary Annual Conference, 3–5 September 2014. Calvert discusses shared anxieties amongst TAPRA applied and social theatre working groups about 'the relationship between heroism [...] and the inflections of risk, bravery, care and compassion that identify the hero, and the tensions between individual and collective empowerment' (Calvert 2015: 175).

In addressing these concerns, applied theatre becomes an exercise in resolving the tensions of power and control between the practitioner and the audience, the individual and the community, the artist who is representing others and the others who are dependent on them as the representors of their own stories and rituals. Applied theatre practitioners should be aware of the idea of giving and what this 'giving' can teach them about the act of applying theatre to communities. We should be wary of egoism. Theatre should be a gift that the artist gives to themselves, a special feeling of completion and happiness, but it is also a gift to the audience. There should be no expectations of return or ownership. What a dishonest and dangerous image of the community artist that would be! Thus, the emphasis on altruism and heroism in a TCH context should be countered with an alternative view that rejects egoism and self-centred attitudes towards acting for children who are sick, and holds that the value of the work lies in encouraging the children to work together with the artist to make performance happen in the moment. This type of encouragement is complex, but suggests a shift in the power that a child experiences when they are iill, as the artwork is created and offered to the children with scope for activating them, engaging and involving them in it, at various levels. The notion of 'empowerment' in applied theatre and what it means in relation to hospital audiences is a good starting point for the discussion of the fictional as a deviation from painful realities. But first-place is given to the definition of hospital audiences.

TCH audiences consist of children of all health conditions during their stay in hospital and children of all age groups till early adolescence, from babies (months old to toddlers), and early years up to 12. TCH audiences usually lie in their beds but if their condition permits it, they may also move to the hospital's play centre, education centre and school or physiotherapy room, if this is the only other suitable space for TCH to happen. Very few hospitals have their own theatre and even then, some children are unable to leave their beds to visit another room where a theatre performance is taking place. So, often the artist resolves, with the support of the nurses and play specialists, to overcome this difficulty by performing bedside or in other hospital rooms convenient to the child. TCH's chosen audiences are considered by society as 'patients' but TCH 'disturbs' the norm and treats them as audiences. The artist invites them to collaborate and participate in a performance that is distinctive for its intimacy, sensitivity, generosity and respect for the person, the individual – not the child labelled as 'patient'. Every performance in hospital is different. Every artist takes a different ownership of the theatrical event in the space where it takes place. Every child embraces the opportunity to participate in the performance in different ways. In this way, the artist and the child get involved in different aspects of the play, taking away different benefits from it. This personal experience of TCH makes every performance unique, unpredictable and unrepeatable. It makes every child in hospital special, every participant exceptional.

Returning to the idea that TCH is a process of 'empowerment' in performance, I need to clarify that for ease of expression I use the term 'empowerment' throughout the book, but the meaning I give to the word is specifically related to the child's personal awareness that they have the power to participate in the performance. The artist by no means gives power to the child to play, but rather creates the dramatic conditions and playful atmosphere to encourage the child to use their own power and ability to play. In the absence of an English word, at least to my knowledge, that defines the power of being aware of having it, I cautiously use 'empowerment'. I spent a lot of time working on the concepts of applied theatre practice and empowerment in my doctorate thesis (Sextou 2004), from which I borrow some ideas for this book. Empowerment (in translation) has been used as a term for democratic audience treatment by Augusto Boal to describe his ideas about awakening critical consciousness. Boal is known for encouraging spectators to participate actively in performance and become actors (thus, the audience became spect-actors). He writes in his first and most influential book, *Theatre of the Oppressed*, that

> the liberated spectator (the one who discusses plans for change, makes decisions, tries out solutions and trains himself for action), as a whole person, launches into action. No matter that the action is fictional; what matters is that it is action!

(Boal 1979: 122)

For applied theatre practitioners, it has not been difficult to use Boal's notion that audiences need to be engaged in action, because applied theatre is about taking action in education and in society. Boal's techniques came to offer the applied theatre practitioner a kind of reassurance that they can make effective theatre that can change passive spectators into active participants an effective theatrical phenomenon. Empowerment develops by addressing communities' specific social problems, in order to be truly and deeply engaged with the performance and participate actively towards a solution of the problems presented. Boel's techniques are widely used in order to 'problematize specific issues', and help audiences relate the problem to their own lives, positions, values and attitudes in the same or similar situations by asking, 'what would or should I do if I were in the shoes of this character?'

Boal's theatrical practice revolves around social transformation and revolutionary theatre. He is, metaphorically speaking, a practitioner who asks his audiences to fall into overflowing rivers (social problems in particular contexts) and for his actors to assist in rescuing the audience. This makes his theatre extremely 'dangerous' and exciting for both actors and audiences because it makes those involved both interested in action and responsible for their own actions, which again is a political position with clear educational intentions. The unique value of Boal's interactive theatre has always relied on the fact that communities as spectators were educated through theatre by being required to rehearse their own lives during the performance and by putting themselves in specific dramatized situations through forms of participatory theatre. Boal (1979: 142) said, 'instead of taking something away from the spectator, evoke in him a desire to practice in reality the act he has rehearsed in the theatre'. That idea enabled practitioners such as TiE actor/teachers to act in the praxis of drama and communicate ideas and notions in groupwork (Jackson 1993: 28). The impact of Boal's work is evident in TiE programmes, and other forms of applied and social theatre that offer learning opportunities for the audience to experience situations of 'real life' in a dramatic context, and a way of living and exploring complicated and sensitive issues. Applied theatre is a process that takes theatre into new, broad, not didactic, forms of learning about a person's role in community life by raising their awareness of what they can achieve.

According to this perspective, therefore, the hospital performance provides a framework within which the artist encourages the child to participate in the fiction, investing in a positive change of moods and behaviours that may happen during and after the performance.

Helping the child to become less bored and more active while being ill is significant. TCH proceeds with realistic aims that can be achieved, and does not claim transformation of communities as applied theatre practitioners traditionally aim to do. Applied theatre work has been recognized for its ambition to 'learn from each other in the service of community', a collectivism that allows each member of the community to have a say, and question social reality in order to create local culture and identity in sociopolitical theatre programmes. I am fascinated by the mission of applied theatre practice to improve societies, but the trick is to be aware of the limitations of this method when defining TCH practice. Transformation is a big claim, and often it is also an unrealistic promise. This is because applied theatre practice is open to the unpredictable, the unexpected, and sometimes, the unmeasured. My intention is not to criticize the intentionality of applied practice. Rather, it is to orientate TCH within its range as accurately as possible and avoid laying claims for social change and major changes in children's lives where these do not exist.

Unlike other applied theatre forms, such as Theatre for Development and Theatre-in-Education, which use theatre towards social and political transformation, TCH uses theatre as a process of wellbeing. The expression 'political' here demands an explanation because it affects the analysis of TCH practice. Applied and social theatre 'borrow' from the climate of the 1960s – the 'political' difference and the 'alternative' culture – the notion of making theatre in different, liberal, radical, creative, unconventional and spontaneous ways. TiE's 'politics', for example, are concerned with systems of government; the process by which these systems might change; the active engagement of pupils (audience participation) in the practical processes of changing society; the relationship between the systems of government and the pupils' own ideas, which may oppose and develop or defend and sustain the sets of values and ideologies that already exist in societies. Therefore, to identify applied theatre as 'political' means that it is as political as any type of theatre can be. Graham Holderness (1992) notes:

> Theatre may be 'political' without becoming 'political theatre', in the sense that a play may represent political matters or address political issues, in exactly the same way as a play can represent love, or old age, or poverty, or madness; if, that is, the play performs that representation of politics in an objective way, without taking sides.
>
> (Holderness 1992: 2)

Within this context of 'political', applied theatre is political because it always deals with social values and specific dilemmas that, ideally, affect people's social ethos and attitude. Even when not dealing directly with 'hot' social issues, applied theatre practice embodies transformation and social change in the ways that it helps audiences become capable of researching, questioning, investigating and daring to oppose what they have been used to believing or doing. Above all, it is political, one way or another, either by reinforcing the pre-existed values and ideologies, or by questioning them for change. So, art and politics are inseparable. But are all applied theatre productions alternative? The question is whether all practitioners are treating audiences as active participants who are allowed to make judgements; are taking a brave step in dealing with controversial issues by, ideally, trying to be objective; are being sociopolitically conscious and aiming to encourage their audiences to analyse society; are raising a thematic range of socially sensitive issues to question preconceptions in society; are developing outreach to audiences from various social classes (including the working-class audiences 'neglected' by conventional theatre); are developing an artistic and aesthetic freedom while negotiating these issues with audiences in creative ways; are focusing on locality and acknowledging the importance of making theatre in the service of community; are choosing to perform outside theatre venues; are choosing to challenge boundaries and perform to prisoners, the disabled, refugees, the poor and the elderly – those forgotten by the governments; are intervening in social environments and making theatre with people who would not normally make theatre; and are believing in the human and social possibility for change.

Here, a 'yes' to the multi-scaled question above would be naive and unrealistic. We need to consider that applied theatre can still be creative in 'seeing freshly with new eyes and new understanding' with permission to 'look again, to reconsider, to find new connections between the actual and the possible, the given and the imagined, the personal and the social and to investigate alternative pictures of the world' (Jackson, A. 2007: 146). Indeed, applied theatre can still be effective without making big claims of radical, unconventional ways of working with communities. Applied theatre works on the margins of social, educational, cultural, and justice and healthcare systems, and, at its best, encourages community engagement; raises social and personal awareness; reconnects communities after traumatic incidents of crisis; comforts and improves a sense of belonging to a group of people with similar interests, passions, experiences and needs; reflects on the needs of communities and individuals; and initiates debates about the improvement of our societies. Applied theatre is, therefore, not a transformation, nor political change, nor social reformation, but something greater. It is a process in progress that involves our active participation in making, remaking, constructing, deconstructing, analysing, reviewing, questioning our practice, challenging our ideologies, and criticizing and recreating our lives whether we agree or disagree with change, whether we aim for change or not, whether we think ourselves capable of bringing change to ourselves, others and the world or not. It is a practice in exploration, investigation, imagining and hoping for a better world. Thus, not all applied theatre practitioners apply forms of theatre that strictly aim at political and social transformation.

This is to be welcomed and coincides with Michael Balfour's (2009) view that applied theatre practice is 'a theatre of little changes', a playful practice between the artist and the audience, a theatre with focus on aesthetics and a theatre that moves away from an emphasis on the need for sociopolitical change. Balfour argues that where aesthetics are central, the little changes emerge from the quality of the process that participants go through in making theatre, the quality of the open relationships that are established during the process, and the quality of the work that is created. Although there is no specific definition provided of these little changes, it seems to me that this term implies progress in experiencing theatre, community life and personal relationships with others in creative, inspired and safe ways within the dramatic.

TCH is also theatre of 'little changes'. It creates possibilities for the child to explore the aesthetic dimension of theatre in hospital settings through creativity, imagination and active participation. It makes no big claims for the personal and social growth of the child, but it does provide space that allows them to inter-play, interact and communicate with the actor. The child and the artist ideally meet together in the story and establish a relationship as an audience-actor in the fictional. The quality of the relationship and the process of engaging in the story are defined by respect and recognition of the child as important to the performance. When this happens in hospitals, it demonstrates a change in the routines and habits of hospital life. The child is not an inactive patient in bed anymore. Rather, the child becomes an active participant in a creative event located in a hospital. The child does not depend on actors to make decisions for them about the story. Rather, the actor invites the child to share ownership with them. This is an area that will come into the discussion of my practice again and again in the next chapter. The TCH artist is present *with* the child in drama, and both the artist and the child are part of the artistic process. That is what I call the quality of the process. Thus, the analysis of the artistic process matters to TCH because it helps us understand the effects of the aesthetic on children with illness.

To the eyes of the artist who lacks acquaintance with TCH, these effects may not seem to be changes at all. The inexperienced lack skills to *see* the quality in process. Besides, these changes can only be judged accurately within the process and the particular context in which the theatrical experience takes place (Prendergast and Saxton 2013). What is 'little' in one context may be a great achievement in a different context. A smile, a laughter, a song, a spontaneous gesture and an improvised word are not little things when they come from a child who is experiencing pain and stress. These are not indicators of little changes. In fact, these can be changes that make a great difference to the ways children deal with the ordeal they face during their stay in hospitals. This understanding broadens applied practice's prospects and potential. It expands its purpose and gives different meaning to change. A positive change in the mood and behaviour of a child in hospital may look less glorious and triumphant in the eyes of the activist-artist but it is magnificent, genuine and valuable in the eyes of the child.

Over the years of researching the impact of bedside theatre on children, I have come to realize some important components of this positive change: an acceptance of hospital theatre performance as a flexible medium that is not preoccupied by determined outcomes; an awareness of the child's illness as an aspect of life; an adoption of a more empathetic approach to hospital performance by the artist; and an awareness of the quality of the collaboration between the artist and the child and the ethics that are attached to it. For example, the artist recognizes that while the audience is in need of support and entertainment to improve their wellbeing, the children have the right to participate or not to participate in the theatrical experience. TCH is about respecting the child's unique situation and clinical condition.

This is particularly difficult as talking about illness and working with individuals who suffer from it is often a 'taboo' topic. People do not know what to think of illness, what to feel and what to say but this needs be overcome. TCH is a form of applied theatre that facilitates rich opportunities for maintaining optimism and self-confidence through creative participation in theatre. This is what I call the effects of 'empowerment' within TCH.

Hospital performance with children is an organic process in which the artist integrates the child's responses and uses them for the growth of performance. Far from performing to the child, the TCH artist is responding to the child's availability: what the child wants, what the child can do and what the child does in the moment. As they walk into the hospital room, the artist uses their perception to notice any specific tired, fatigued or lethargic moods in the child. Facial expressions, gestures and verbal communication offer the artist some indication of how the child is and how he or she is responding to the conditions in the room. These indications will guide the artist in facilitating the performance as a living and evolving experience with the child. The child becomes central to the synthesis of the actor–audience relationship and part of the making of theatre in hospital. This process has a certain degree of organic plasticity, a kind of elasticity based on improvisation involved in it. This means that although there is a script, the structure and pace of the TCH performance can be altered: making it shorter or longer than initially rehearsed, cutting or adding lines to the script, including or not including singing, using or not using puppets and props, and so on. The 'stretching' of structure and pace aims to create a flexible performance that is sensitive to the needs of the child. This 'stretching' requests the artist to be attentive and responsive to the child's ability and mood when they meet. Because TCH operates in agreement with the child that they will make the performance their own together, they are free to speak or not to speak during performance. They are free to act or not to act, to ask questions or to fall asleep, to bring their soft toys in, to interact and enjoy the performance too, or to stop the performance at any point and rest. Therefore, the TCH artist needs to be confident to invite the child to share control of the performance.

This is not unusual in applied theatre practice. TiE, for example, recognizes audiences as valuable participants in the evolution of the performance. I have been involved in TiE programmes all my life in the United Kingdom and abroad and from my observations of audience participation in hospitals I have come to realize that audience participation is challenged in hospital settings. Theatre-in-Education (TiE) empowers children to become active and critical learners through theatre in educational settings (Jackson and Vine 2013). TiE audience participation is used to help children to learn in alternative ways within an *aesthetic framework,* as Jackson (2007: 152) explains in his book, *Theatre, Education and the Making of Meanings*, one that 'allows actors and audience to meet on metaphorical ground'. He argues that it can be created anywhere in and outside a conventional theatre venue. If the conditions are right, if the focus and the purpose of the event are clear, if the artistic conventions of space and time are agreed, and if the physical space is appropriately configured, then the audience will be in a position to be open to the theatrical experience and gain pleasure, awareness and insight into the meaning of life.

I would add to this argument that if an aesthetic framework is effective, it creates opportunities for the audience to express their ideas and emotions in the fictional with safety. In TiE programmes, for instance, the art form provides audiences with the conditions to examine the implications of the issues they explore in drama enabling them to explore different perspectives of contemporary themes within the security of the art form (Readman 1993). Security is associated with the notion of how a theatre participant acts in protected and unthreatened fictional situations. Readman's position compels the artist to ask whether applied theatre is a practice that forces the audience to forget about their real lives and pretend that what they experience on metaphorical ground is true (when they know that it is not) and behave as if their real life of encountering difficulties and pain is not true (when they know that it is). Should the fictional be seen as a safety net protecting audiences from reality? Applied theatre should aim to offer opportunities for involvement in the fiction, which may enable the audience to transport to another location at another time and experience a story that may relate to their true lives. However, does it aim to erase or challenge reality? Can emotions become diverted? Can trauma in communities, the emotional pain of refugees, the nostos of immigrants, the anxiety of prisoners, and the fear of death in cases of children facing critical illness be forgotten? Should theatre aim to help the audience divert from reality for as long as the performance lasts or ignore reality? Are we comfortable with this role of applied theatre? These questions reflect some of my concerns about the meaning of theatre in hospital, the experience of illness, and the stress that is often attached to it; concerns that are commented on throughout this book.

My view is that TCH is a reciprocal experience of theatre *through* illness and the experience of illness *through* theatre. What I mean by this is that theatrical experience is used to help children experience their illness differently and not to ignore it. This is achieved by encouraging children to do things that they are not expected to do as patients (play, laugh, sing and even dance), and collaboratively enjoy theatre as a lived experience. All this liberates them from passivity and boredom. It is a moment-by-moment experience where one gesture, one line and one song, is leading to another. When this kind of empowerment is achieved in TCH performances, it enables the children to experience new ways of staying in hospital, something they did not know how to do before the performance, something that no healthcare system, doctor or nurse could teach them. Successful aesthetics can lead the people involved towards paths of theatrical experience and new types of learning.

One of the most significant things about this new insight into the world of ill children through theatre is the child's agreement to become involved in the artistic practice. When participation is achieved, the child is recognized for their ability to be creative, to respond verbally and physically. Each child brings something into performance that could become essential to the experience of theatre. All responses, all moods and all behaviours are valuable because they have something to contribute to a composition of new theatrical experiences, and by extension, to new experiences in the child's life. TCH places the child in the centre of the performance in dialogue with the artists, offering them confidence and self-respect. As the TiE practitioner acknowledges the child as a learner-participant capable of discovering new meanings in things, and motivates the child to become a confident learner in education, the TCH artist acknowledges the child as an active participant, and motivates the child to become more relaxed while staying in hospital. This means that the difference the artist makes in healthcare is not to make hospital a more interesting place for learning, but to make life in hospital more manageable. The child is present in illness, aware of their condition and informed about their treatment. TCH takes their minds away from aspects of the hospital experience that cause worries, such as the outcome of an operation and the results of medical tests. It relocates their attention away from physical pain towards the invitation to participate in the play. During performance, TCH disassociates their stay in hospital from illness but only for as long as the performance lasts. The artist has no intension of ignoring reality or persuading the child that illness does not exist. Other applied theatre forms, such as Theatre for Development (TfD), Theatre in Prisons and Theatre-in-Education, use theatre as a tool for individuals to explore choice and responsibility and become better thinkers, better learners and better citizens. Theatre for Children in Hospital uses theatre as a tool for children to explore better ways to experience communication, collaboration and enjoyment of life in hospital and become happier while they undertake treatment.

Theatre as an 'antidote' to clinical stress

TCH does not have a remedial agenda but I would use a metaphor from medicine and call it an 'antidote' to hospital life and clinical distress. I am using the phrase 'antidote' because antidotes counteract poisons and toxins in the body. Metaphorically speaking, TCH aims to reduce the influences of hospital toxins on the child and relax them. Toxins can be the clinical stressors that relate to physical pain, the impact of surgery, immobility, loss of control and disruption, the shock caused by the medical incident, the possible side effects of the medical treatment, the seriousness of the illness, and the emotional condition of the child. Toxins can also be the lack of privacy in a hospital ward, separation from significant others, the pressure on the child–family relationship, and the surroundings, such as having a small room in relation to a large number of people (Coyne 2006; Aldiss, Horstman, O'Leary et al. 2008; Kostenius and Öhrling 2009). The child in hospital has very little privacy. Hospital wards are communal spaces where any patient is exposed to anyone who walks in, from nurses and doctors to visitors. Beds are separated by curtains, which fail to create a personal physical space. The child misses normality, a sense of routine that offers stability in their personal lives. They miss spending time with their school friends and family. With all these changes going on in a child's life, it is not surprising that children in hospital experience anxiety.

Rebecca Crane (2009) argues that anxiety that is caused by clinical stressors is persistent and deep for hospitalized children as it occurs together with other emotional relapses. As a child experiences physical pain, shock, fear of the clinical professionals, fear of the unexpected related to medical surgery and the risk of operation. For children who have experienced stress and anxiety outside the hospital in the past, these moments of stress are moments of exposure because they are likely to put them at higher emotional risk. Thus, enjoyment and relaxation are important to these children to help them adapt to new situations, and take pleasure in creative activities and experiences. Peterson and Shigetomi (2006) also argue for the importance of child relaxation prior to and after medical or surgical procedures and the contribution of coping techniques to minimize child stress and anxiety. Just as antidotes counteract the effects of poison in our bodies, theatre aims to prevent the TCH child from staying in shock, fear or anxiety during their stay in hospital. Little could be more important to children in hospitals than the TCH 'de-toxification', resulting in less fear, less stress and more creative involvement in enjoyable activities. TCH is a non-pharmacological antidote, a theatrical relaxation experience central to the lives of children in hospital for which it is created and offered.

TCH is an exciting, welcomed family experience in hospital that connects the child with the parent/carer in positive ways. Through enjoyment of the play and laughter, children and parents/carers share positive moments in hospital. This book provides evidence to support this in Chapter Two. Over the implementation of the study, I learned that most of the time, the invitation to participate in performance excites and enthuses children. The announcement by the nurse that theatre is coming to the hospital ward breaks the hospital routine. It creates an atmosphere of excitement in anticipation of the upcoming performance. The nurse gives out information leaflets or theatre programmes for the child to read with their parent/carer. This information is aimed at encouraging the involvement of the children in the theatrical experience, while retaining the element of suprise. The element of surprise is a key dimension to TCH. Children know what the story is about but they do not know what to expect. There are cases of parents who are willing to stimulate their child's appetite and curiosity about the performance and they talk about the upcoming event with their child. When this happens, the child's imagination is stimulated. The children ask their parents questions: 'What is it going to be like?', 'What is the story about?', 'When are the actors coming?', and so on. Often children make guesses about the cast and their costumes, and they talk about the story while waiting for the artists to arrive. Some children even get ready for theatre. They put on their favourite set of nightwear and style their hair to look nice. Excitement, enthusiasm and preparation pave the way for the performance to take place in the hospital. Children recall these moments of theatrical experience and discuss them later. The memory of the lived performance often helps them to overcome the boredom and dullness of being in the hospital, especially if they are in for a long period of time. Theatre brings joy to those who need it most, an important effect of theatrical de-toxification.

There are other times when the invitation to the performance causes ambiguity related to the ways children perceive their role as patients. The child is expected to be and behave as a 'patient', a 'hospital resident', simply because the child is not present in hospital as a theatre audience. This time the theatre *goes* to meet the child in hospital. This initiative employs alternative and unconventional ways of connecting the arts with audiences outside of theatre venues. All this is new to the hospital culture. It is almost eccentric to be a theatre audience in hospital. Traditionally, children's audiences are encouraged to interact with actors, in pantomimes for example, and participate in performance (although mostly superficially). To interact with the actor in bedside performance is definitely an unusual expectation of a sick child. It is radical. It disrupts accustomed patterns of patient behaviour. It invites the child to participate in a theatrical event while being a hospital resident. By doing this, it aims to change the passive behaviour that children adopt in hospital into active modes of behaviour that children adopt as theatre audiences in participatory plays.

Havi Carel (2013), in her inspired writings about illness as a philosophical phenomenon, acknowledges the appearance of a new identity for the ill person, and a negative focus on the body in illness. She says, 'The primitive sense of "I can" becomes replaced by a conscious, artificial, mediated sense of "I cannot," or "I once was able to but am no longer"' (Carel 2013: 9). However, she also argues that illness can become the vehicle of personal growth. Her view is particularly valuable to TCH because it encourages us to see illness as an opportunity for changing our perception of the self through theatre. The ill child experiences the world as less joyful and full of limitations; they are expected to stay calm in bed and take their medication. Things can become more complex if we accept that most children have not previously considered theatre as part of the healthcare services, and may not have even considered it a part of their lives outside the hospital. Not every child is a theatre-goer and not every family celebrates theatre on a regular basis. For a child to see theatre for the first time and to see it in her pyjamas in a hospital bed can be a unique and unusual experience. The child does not realize that through participation in performance, she exchanges the identity of the 'ill person' with the identity of the audience/participant. The exchange happens almost unconsciously: it is a hidden benefit of the theatrical experience, and yet important to the child's wellbeing, but how does it work?

TCH aims to reveal a different path for the child to experience illness in hospital. Whilst the child may be in shock due to the new identity of the 'ill person' and the loss of the familiar, such as family, school and friends, TCH puts the child in a more privileged and stronger position. Through fiction, TCH opens the child to a stimulating theatrical experience intending to potentially become a *regulator* of their experience in hospital and a tool for replacing the sense of 'I cannot do' or 'I am ill' and 'I am in pain' with a sense of 'I can speak and laugh and interact' and 'I can have a good time while I am ill'. The child is encouraged to revise what they think of themselves as patients and act differently to what is expected in hospital. If the show is engaging and the trust between the child and the artist is established successfully, the child will participate in performance. Acceptance of the invitation to participate suggests that illness is not a synonym for sadness and monotony. You can have fun, happiness and joy when you are ill. Theatre in hospital is an art form and the role of art in healthcare, in my view, is to make propositions and create possibilities of experiencing illness, clinical stress and hospital life differently through art. This is another effect of de-toxification, relying on the affirmation of certain responses from participants whilst being aware that many more stress-related benefits for the whole family may be resulting from TCH in practice.

Illness causes stress and anxiety that affect the relationships between family members, causing additional emotional pain that is usually communicated back to the child. Critical illness becomes a destabilizing factor in families because the pressure on the child–family relationship depends on the seriousness of the illness and the length of stay in hospital. As a theatre practice that takes account of the stress of the parents, TCH aims to contribute to the improvement of family experiences of illness by offering the possibility of an escape from the effects of hospitalization. I am aware that this aim is easier said than done, but there is, I believe, a case of shared symptoms of hospitalization between children and their families that makes this discussion worthwhile. Illness has the power to affect the family and all those who witness the child being ill. Rockach and Matalon's (2007) research findings state:

> The stresses imposed by hospitalization may precipitate uncharacteristic behaviours and emotions in the children, which, in turn, may become a major source of stress for their parents […] especially when it is for a lengthy period of time and/or for a serious or life-threatening illness.
>
> (Rockach and Matalon 2007: 301–04)

This stressed state of parents is significant because it is that which creates a vicious circle of negative behaviours, attitudes and moods that may affect the child's psychology and wellbeing. Compas, Jaser, Dunn and Rodriguez (2012) reviewed the role of the child in coping with stress caused by serious chronic illness and the role of the family to better explicate adaptations to illness. They report:

> The role of parents' coping may be important to consider on several levels as parents may serve as resources to support and scaffold children's coping, parents may serve as important models of effective and ineffective coping for their children, and parents' who are ineffective in coping with the stress of their child's illness may contribute to increased distress in their children.
>
> (Compas, Jaser, Dunn and Rodriguez 2012: 478)

These research findings show that the challenges and stressors of critical illness are sometimes uncontrollable and help explain the parents' responses to the bedside performance. I am convinced that illness causes stress that affects the whole family depending on what the members of the family do with it, how they cope. Over the years, I have worked with children in hospitals who were trapped in overwhelming emotions that destabilized their wellbeing and affected themselves and their families. I have had parents saying to me that they cannot manage their emotions when they see their child suffering. I remember I was once waiting for my actors to finish their performances in the oncology unit when I witnessed an incident. Two nurses were trying to calm down a father who was finding it difficult to cope with his son's medical condition. He was out of control, shouting at the nurses, throwing threats and complaints at them. He was in denial while experiencing emotional pain. He was crying his soul out, 'I want my son back. I will take him home for the weekend. Do you hear me? I will take him with me. He is fine now'. The nurses had to call assistance to walk the father out of the ward into the waiting area. I was shocked, devastated and puzzled. What more is there for us, the artists, to do in order to offer parents like this father an opportunity to view their child participating in activities with joy, I wondered.

I have had conversations with play specialists in paediatrics who explained to me how not all the parents have the time to be with their children in hospital and how in some cases the mother is responsible for four or five other children at home. I have come across situations where the child was left alone in hospital for days because the father could not afford the petrol to drive 50 miles to and from the hospital every day to see his child. I have seen families not coping well with illness. In the case of these families, illness forces itself not only upon the child but upon the entire family life, compelling them to work around it, to deal with practical problems. Illness is not the problem here. The pre-existing difficulties in family relationships are the problem. Poor communication, loose bonds, lack of trust and insecurity in families can cause poor management of situations and decision-making that affects the ill child. Illness is something that brings disturbed family relationships to the surface of family life, rather than causes them. In cases of critical illness, becoming involved in the delivery of care requires very careful management of the lives of the children. Families can make a significant contribution to the child's wellbeing if they manage to live with illness, something that widens the scope of TCH and the arts.

Lucinda Jarrett (2007) argues that the arts are considered to be a way of taking control over illness, restoring the families' self-esteem and gaining confidence on a personal level. I agree that art is a kind of investment in family wellbeing when a member is seriously ill, but how difficult that is to achieve is another matter. The investment of TCH in family wellbeing may not be as profound as that of a child who directly participates in the performance, but it is powerful. In the same way that the child can be inspired to respond creatively to illness through theatre, the families of children in hospital can become more relaxed when they get a break as carers and see their children having a good time in hospital. They become better able to deal with their difficulties through their child's improved mood as a gift of theatre. TCH can become an opportunity to gain something from illness. 'One does not need to be ill in order to learn from illness' (Carel 2013: 11). Parents can benefit from seeing that theatre can change the child's attitude to illness for the better. In Chapter Two, I will discuss how Taikwando Kid's (pseudonym) dad felt happy because his child, who was suffering from cancer, was happy watching the play. 'A real bonus', are the words of another parent who acknowledges that theatre makes parents feel good and adds value to the hospital services in paediatrics. In this sense, TCH acknowledges the importance of the art process to children and its effectiveness on child wellbeing as well as on the wellbeing of the adults who care for them. The result is a product of collaboration between the artist, the child, the families, the art form and the healthcare system.

Of course, there will always be audience members, especially adults, who do not value the theatrical experience that is offered to their children in hospitals: adults who are disrespectful to the artist, probably out of ignorance, like some parents who interrupt the communication between the child and the artist. These audiences perceive theatre as a welcome event at the beginning and, then, they find it disturbing. Some parents need other types of attention and care. They find it too challenging to break the conventions of hospital routine, and although this is understandable, it is a waste of an opportunity to enjoy life and benefit from the support TCH can bring. Nevertheless, these responses are not for us to judge. Not all parents have the strength and the strategies to cope with difficult situations and I am sure that the reader will agree that it can be hard to be open to new experiences under immense stress. Parents are only humans and families are complex systems of relationships and behaviours. TCH may be the basis to begin a dialogue about the potential of theatre in family wellbeing in hospital situations.

A playful 'marriage' of two cultures, the artistic with the clinical in audience participation

TCH is the outcome of a collaboration between the art form and the hospital as a site where the audience is positioned. The artist alone cannot produce TCH unless the hospital operates as a host of theatre companies. Theatre that takes place in hospital functions in relation to, negotiation with and acceptance of the clinical context. The art, which the artists serve, interacts with the hospital, where the child is located. These are cultures of different stories, values and priorities. Where an exchange of stories, values and priorities is possible, there is a chance for TCH to emerge through a dialogue between the artist who enters the clinical culture and the audience who accepts the artist to interfere in their lives in hospital. In this dialogue, the artist and the audience are joined as 'partners' in a creative relationship. The artist's expertise and experience in the art form is combined with the child's expertise and experience in illness. I do not mean here that the artist plays to her strengths to be the 'perfect' performer and the child is trying to be the 'perfect' patient. What I mean is that the two of them can be a perfect match playing together in performance. The addition of a playful dimension to this process is significant towards the marriage of the art with the clinical because it fosters an atmosphere of happiness and energy. To explain the use of 'playful', first, I draw the reader's attention to the role of play in child healthcare.

Hall and Reet (2000) recognize that playing with children in hospital is beneficial to children, families and nursing staff. Additionally, Jun-Tai (2008), in her important work about child-play in hospitals, observed children during play to argue that there is no less need for the continuation of the skills of participation, imagination and discovery during illness and hospitalization:

Play produces comfort and reassurance at a time of unfamiliar and potentially frightening experiences. Play helps to coordinate developmental and learning strategies to help children understand their environment. The multifaceted nature of play contributes to the non-pharmacological approaches to hospital procedures; play is not just for passing time pleasurably or relieving boredom (though both are crucial for a positive experience within this setting).

(Jun-Tai 2008: 233)

These works demonstrate a profound understanding of the value of child-play in hospital settings. They suggest that playing with a child is a valuable methodology to reduce clinical stress. This statement strengthens my view that play is an important component of bedside performance. Children may not have strategies for controlling the embarrassments that haunt their role as patients but they do have experience of playing; they are experts in playing by nature. To benefit the child, we encourage playful use: of the script; of the moment adding an uplifting dimension to what the child experiences in the hospital; of movement; of objects such as props, soft toys, and so on. Play as an organic, non-static, process aims to manage anxieties that might exaggerate the feeling of isolation, fear, stress and negative emotions that a child may have in hospital. In performance, the child and the artist are invited to play together by using their imitation, creativity and imagination skills to communicate and interact effectively in a complementary role. The artist alone cannot make TCH. The child alone cannot benefit from TCH. They are both needed to combine their voices, narratives, moods, references and skills to create TCH. The act of playing together provides the participants with space that allows this exchange to happen. Then, TCH could be further defined as playful practice that is created, mediated and communicated by the artist through interaction with audiences of children who are undergoing treatment for their illness.

The reader is encouraged to think of TCH as the product of the dialogue between the visiting artist and the hospital inhabitant, a special type of audience participation that evolves in performance. This is not only because TCH's nature is defined by its participatory approach and the characteristics of flexible, inter-play practice but also because the participation of the arts in the lives of children with illness gives TCH clarity of purpose. To understand the purpose of participation in TCH, it needs to be seen within the distinctive context of the clinical space and its ideological meanings; TCH participation belongs to the world of healthcare and not to the world of theatre. This is a particularly interesting area which exposes us to a challenging discussion about the 'marriage' of clinical space with performance.

In TCH practice, the hospital becomes a 'stage' (Brodzinski 2010), one that can be extremely limited and intimate compared to any other stage in the theatre. In bedside performances, in particular, the stage extends no more than a few steps from the side of the child. To transform this tiny hospital space into a stage, in which both children and artists can participate in performance, the artist mediates between the fiction and reality by using the dramatic conventions of space and time. The space where the performance happens is usually symbolized by the artist as an imaginary location where the story takes place. Occasionally, installed artworks and a small but proper theatre set including lighting and sound is used to 'transform' the hospital environment into a theatrical space. However, the theatrical space is not something that is created in a hospital effortlessly. It takes energy and skills to reform the relationships between the site and the audience and make different meanings out of the space depending on the needs of the performance.

Allain and Harvie (2006) discuss social geography where the relationships between the artists and the audience are affected by social and ideological meanings of performance spaces. What are the ideological meanings of hospital space? It is important to note the illness-specific nature of the space: it is impossible to imagine a child living in hospital without considering their health condition affecting their role audience members. By extension, I would ask, 'is the ideological meaning of TCH illness-specific?' For a start, theatre in hospital as an art form exists within the dominant signs of illness: what the artist sees in hospital are children whose roles are immediately perceived according to the clinical context. The child in bed is so often connected with pain and disability. Emotions that arise for the artist when they visit children in hospital, especially if the artist is inexperienced, are emotions engaged with the environment around the children. The hospital, the artist and the child are all participants within the aesthetic of TCH. In simple words, they all belong to the experience at the core of the TCH practice and style of performance. The artists who participate in bedside theatre are surrounded by illness. How much the artist is affected by illness is hard to judge but the artist, as most people would, has a personal understanding of illness in relation to their experiences of life and wellness.

For many, a hospital is 'the kingdom of the sick'. This is a powerful metaphor that Susan Sontag (1978) used to criticize the language that society uses to describe illness. Sontag throws light on the ignorance, if not arrogance, of people, and their limited understanding of illness. She argues that we all have equal chances to become residents of the kingdom of illness in our lives and she is so right. This is almost inevitable. Illness imposes a label of 'disable-ism' that shadows the child during their stay in hospital. I borrow the phrase 'disable-ism' from Tim Mitchell (Mitchell and Snyder 2015) who talked about disability in film at the conference *Negotiating Space and (Dis)Ability on Theatre, Film and the Media* (Poland, September 2015). He discussed the devil of 'able-ism' and the social expectations for the disabled to match the image of the abled. He was inspiring in saying that society leads the individual to question their own body and the limitations that it forces upon them in everyday life. 'What is wrong with my body?' and 'Why can't I do things?' become constant questions that trouble the person. The identity of the ill and the label of disable-ism both affect TCH participation, but why?

This is a case where TCH depends on audience participation, and the audience's lack of confidence in participation depends on the reception of their role as patients. Illness is a challenge that affects our lives in many unexpected ways. I am sure that the reader will agree that the role of patient and the characteristics of disability are adopted almost automatically by someone the moment they walk into a hospital reception. The identity of illness becomes second nature. The question is what the artist can do with it to improve the child's confidence and moods while they are ill. I am aware that the theme of illness and what we can do with it in TCH comes to the discussion again and again but this is because of its importance in this type of theatre. To understand the effects of the hospital's involvement as a site for audience participation, and of the potential of TCH to inspire participation, we need to understand this paradox. The artists enter the hospital with little power to change the ideological illness-specific meaning of the site but with the ambition to use it as a space for artistic interventions.

There is a confusing paradox here but it also carries a serious meaning. The artist wants to use the hospital for a purpose other than the purpose for which it was built. The artist is faced with the responsibility to manipulate clinical space and the surrounding atmosphere, and transform it into dramatic space; they offer the child the possibility of 'seeing' the space differently through the dramatic. By doing this successfully, the artist changes the purpose of hospital from a medical care provider to an entertainment provider. The artist gives a whole new purpose to TCH; the purpose of 'renovation'. Theatre is used to 'renovate' the hospital experience and help children feel better during their stay. It aims to offer the child experiences that do not relate to the illness itself. This answers the question of whether TCH should be illness-specific or not, and it is important to remember it: children simply do not like being ill and staying in hospital. According to the 2007 Economic and Social Research Council (ESRC) report on children's perceptions of hospital space, children value personal space and privacy and often experience hospital wards as boring and isolating. A hospital can be dull for a child, although it is a busy working environment. And although theatre is not seen as important amongst other clinical priorities, we should recognize the need to make alternative use of the hospital to make children feel less bored and isolated. Whether we can use the hospital site efficiently in practice to transform the walls, beds and monitors of a hospital into an environment that would stimulate an aesthetic experience is another matter.

Birch and Tompkins (2012), in *Performing Site-Specific Theatre*, argue that site-specific performance operates differently from performance that takes place within a theatre because it seeks to match form and content (and place and space) more finely than performance in a conventional venue. They see the form as encouraging an investigation of how the audience might understand 'site' as less fixed or less specifically geographical. If we are to accept this claim, it has consequences, again, for our understanding of TCH participation. From many years of experience I have come to believe that, the audience is an integral part of the clinical 'site'. Children in hospital do not experience the space as visitors, as the artists do. Especially, for children with terminal illness, the hospital is their home. They spend more of their lives in hospital wards than in their own bedroom. This makes a big difference to how a child-patient perceives and 'owns' the clinical space compared to any other spectator who participates in site-specific events. As the TCH artist enters the hospital ward and moves closer to the child's bedside to perform, it often seems like they enter the child's private space. The bed is the child's fort. No one should get close to it without a serious sense of respect, responsibility and discretion. However, as it often turns out, the child's fort is constantly 'attacked' by adults. Children in hospital are rarely asked if they want doctors, nurses, and visitors in their space, if they want to allow them to be close to them and let them be seated on their beds.

To illustrate my argument, I turn to an episode that occurred while waiting for the link nurse to collect participation consent forms from the children and their families in the cardiac hospital ward. I am standing outside the room. It is a small room with only one bed. I see a girl around 6 sitting on the bed. She is waiting for a heart operation to take place on the following day. She is also waiting for the artists to get into the room for the scheduled bedside entertainment. She looks calm but I am sensing that she is anxious about the medical procedure the next day. She is not relaxed. She is looking around the room and biting her nails. A woman, possibly a friend or relative of the family, comes in. The visitor brings balloons and a bag of unknown contents. I cannot see everything from where I am standing. The child seems to enjoy the visit until the woman sits on her bed. A pink Disney duvet that her mum must have brought her from home covers her bed. By the time the visitor sits on the bed, the child starts getting annoyed. She becomes moody, she is pulling off her duvet and she is positioning her teddy bear on her bed next to her feet. To my eyes, the girl's change of mood, her movements and the use of her toy are all indications of efforts to own her space. I begin to worry about many things at this point. How would the child respond to the artists? Will she be defensive of her space? Should I tell them not to get too close to the bed? I am hoping that the girl will be in a better mood later on.

This incident and many others that I have witnessed during my research, tells me that children in hospital develop their own relationship with space and that we, the adults, struggle to understand it because we are not participants in the hospital experience as the child is. This means that performing site-specific theatre in a hospital would never be the same experience of space for the artist as it is for the child. The artist wants to create a fictional life by using the site, real hospital walls, doors and monitors, in performance. But the child experiences real life within the site and within these hospital walls, doors and monitors. The child has its own personal reality, its own sense and ownership of the hospital space. The physical space on her bed and around it is a replica of the child's personal space, a private zone. The child is part of the site and the site is imposed on the child as part of its identity. The way in which the TCH artist enters the child's space requires attention for the way it affects the child's privacy and ability to engage with others in the space.

One approach to the problematic usage of hospital space in performance is the use of symbolism. Symbolism comes from the Greek word 'συμβολισμός', a noun which derives from the verb 'συμβάλλω' and means 'I put together', and 'I contribute'. In the discussion of hospital space, the use of the word symbolism is significant. It contributes a different meaning, purpose and functionality to the signified space. It transforms it into something that has not been associated with the real meaning, purpose and function of the clinical space. The language of symbolization is one of the oldest languages we have, and persists as an important feature of theatre. Transforming hospital wards into spaces for dramatic action is not a simple re-organization of sets of furniture, but a greater intervention in the hospital culture. Brian Way (1981: 87) argues that 'theatre can rise above life not merely repeat it, and much of the transcending lies within the realm of the symbolic'. He also says that theatre audiences between 5 and 9 years old respond well to symbolism. This information is particularly helpful to the discussion because the symbolization of the hospital space by young children is central in transforming the hospital ward, or part of it, into a theatrical environment for the needs of the TCH performance. The physical location can become a dramatic space where amazing things can happen in a productive kind of theatrical practice. Brought together, the elements of dramatization and symbolism offer the potential for the TCH artist to adapt the performance to the unusual and limiting characteristics of the hospital. The nature of the communication between the children, the actors and the circumstances of their meeting are enhanced by an imaginative and symbolic use of the hospital space that can transform it into an imaginary 'as if' location.

The artist invites the child to negotiate the usage of the space. In simple words, the child is asked how they visualize the hospital room, what they want the space to become, and to imagine the room changing. From my own experience, I can confirm that children usually suggest imaginary locations that they are familiar with from fairy tales and video games, such as valleys, castles, spaceships, galaxies, planets, oceans and mythical lands. These are the products of their imagination, what they choose to create in their minds. The imagined symbolic location (valley, spaceship, ocean, mythical land, etc.) becomes the 'home' for theatre to unfold. The artist enters the space assuming that the child will welcome the characters and that the two worlds of fiction and reality will inter-play for a while in the 'space' between the child and the artist. The child and the artist will play together. The artist generously involves the child in making decisions about the performance. This is an action of artistic generosity because it removes some of the artist's power to make decisions for the art form. But it also recognizes the child's right to make decisions about how to transform life, especially life that is in a difficult stage, into art. Way's (1981) theatrical 'magic' is not worked on the child but *with* the child in hospital. In TCH, theatre works its magic gently, slowly and respectfully to the child: the structure is flexible and the artist is attentive to suggestions. Theatre provides the potential to experience the hospital as a different, alternative space through symbolism.

Other examples of theatre projects in clinical settings improve our understanding of the symbolic usage of space in hospitals and support the definition of theatre as an imaginative intervention in healthcare environments. 'Hospitalworks', for example, a collaborative theatre project created by Theatre-Rites, Polka Theatre and Theater der Welt, was targeted towards children between the ages of 3 and 6 in the Mayday University Hospital in London in 2005. In collaboration with installation artists, Hospitalworks transformed hospital rooms through performance, object puppetry and installation. Theatre-Rites created a unique performance that turned the hospital environment into a playful, interactive and enchanting place suitable for children of that age group (Theatre-Rites 2005). The company paid close attention to the details of hospital life. They structured the piece around the role of nurses and doctors , as it is seen through the eyes of children and communicated by the artists in creative and inspirational ways. This project is an example of using a mixture of imagery techniques together with performance, puppetry and sound aiming to inspire young audiences in hospital and normalize their stay. The contribution of imagery in performance gave the site a new identity through the symbolic.

In Steven Berkoff's interview by Richard Eyre, it is argued that the body of an experienced actor becomes the set. As Berkoff puts it, 'It has to be symbolic, so that the audience is fascinated with the trick, with the idea, with the symbol, because the human imagination feeds on symbolism' (Eyre 2009: 290). The audience becomes excited to see something that needs interpretation such as two bodies becoming a door. Symbolism offers audiences opportunities to see the potential, to accept the possibility. I have seen it happening in hospitals too. In 2008, I directed a play for the National Theatre of Northern Greece. The play was an adaptation of an old story from the Greek storytelling tradition, which was originally known as 'The Princess's Ring'. We presented it to young children in regional hospitals. The story revolves around the unexplained and unfortunate disappearances of a ring and the adventures of a troubled young princess who searches for it. In this search she finds her strength through a journey of maturity and mental growth. When I first read the story I thought, 'what *is* the ring in a children's hospital ward but normality and stability'. The loss of the ring could represent the difficulties children and their families experience because of illness. Children lose normality in their lives when they are in hospital. The appearances of the ring could symbolize the hope that things can go better despite all odds: time after time the ring was found and brought to the princess by a boy, an owl and a fish! So I had the three actors (two women and a man) each playing a range of different parts including a bird, a tree, a princess, a storyteller, a boy, a fish, a thief and a prince. The actress's body became a tree. She stretched her arms wide open and wrapped her shawl around her shoulders to offer shelter to the princess's body. What a wonderful image: two bodies in one shape. This is something quite similar to child pretend-play where young children develop their ability to transform objects and actions and to take roles in drama (Bergen 2002). The ring was lost many times in many different ways yet it always managed to return to the finger of the princess. Every time the ring returned to her she exclaimed, 'Oh, my much loved ring has come back to me! I know I can survive this for hope has not been lost'. Hope always speaks for itself. Children in the audience appreciated the symbolic meaning of the ring. In after-show discussions, they said that their favourite part was when the princess cheered up because 'she was so happy she had found her ring' and 'she was brave when she had her ring'. They also, of course, enjoyed the happy ending – the princess finds her prince, the love of her heart, and they live together happily ever after. Symbolism in this hospital performance was a window of hope that opened from the marriage of the artistic with the clinical.

The artist–child synergistic relationship

One of the greatest experiences of all in the life of an artist in healthcare and one of the greatest lessons that I have learned from practising bedside theatre is communication and collaboration with the audience. The artist is required to understand what the child needs in that moment from the artist, and make appropriate choices to add a creative dimension to this reality. Negus and Pickering (2004), in the preface of their book *Creativity, Communication and Cultural Value*, point out the idea that creativity is 'a relational process' between the artist and the viewer, reader or listener. They argue that 'creativity involves the communication of experience, a dynamic which can take various forms and characteristics and which certainly does not imply a sender/receiver or decoding/encoding type of communication' (Negus and Pickering 2004: ix). Later in their book, they explain that 'the communication of experience entails a relationship which brings together the addresser, the addressee and the created expression of experience that passes between them' (2004: 24). Negus and Pickering acknowledge a significant value in the interaction between the participants of the creative event, as a basis for sharing and understanding creativity as a form of communication.

The bedside theatre study that I present in Chapter Two reveals that the TCH experience is one that the artist and the child create together. The story evolved from the collaboration between the child, and the characters of the play. This is invaluable to both the child and the artist. The child shares the experience of being in hospital with the artist, and the artist shares the experience of being with a child who lives in hospital. The sharing of the location as an experience is an opportunity for communication between the child and the artist. Sharing in hospital could be interpreted as synonymous with sadness, pitiful weakness, passivity and a desire for assistance. All these can be part of the experience but, primarily, sharing in performance equates with playfulness, a desire for joy and a celebration of life, all of which help improve the child's experience of being in hospital. The medical professionals would probably smile at hearing this but I do think that smiles and laughter are evidence of a change in the child's mood for the better; an experience can make a big difference in patient wellbeing and satisfaction. Studies on the theatre experience of children in hospitals shows that laughter related to humorous incidents during performance involves positive psychological, emotional, social and behavioural aspects that assist the child in facing their difficulties (Rokach and Matalon 2007). I have seen children's faces light up and children laughing during and after the performance. Some children communicate with the artist verbally and even physically by simple gestures; they become creative in responding to the characters, they use their toys in practising relaxation techniques during performance, they become more creative, they breathe better and they smile. They change roles from passive patients to active participants. And although this is not always predicted or promised, it happens. When it happens, it should be seen as a great gift of creativity that involves the child's communication skills.

The 'fruit' of communication with the audience as a creative process in hospital wards merely depends on the audiences' freedom. The ways theatre 'speaks' to each child in a clinical setting is difficult to foresee. Each child receives the same invitation to communicate with the artist, to be together in the story as an audience. However, not everyone responds in the same way. Each child responds differently and, therefore, bears a different fruit. Why is it so? The story is the same, the artist is the same, and the invitation to participation is the same. Why do they not all produce the same outcome? Why is each performance different?

The answer lies neither with the story nor the artist, although the artist plays a major part in the process; rather, it lies with the collaboration between the artist and the child. Both the artist and the child are free to make choices. Both can tolerate the sharing of wishes and choices. What takes place between the child and the artist is a collection of these choices which lead to creative personal moments. One of the benefits of creative participation *is* these moments. They are a creative product of relational process, a product of communicated experience, a product of collaboration. Collaboration means that the artist and the child are together in the aesthetic experience and together in illness during the theatrical intervention. This is a situation different than being alone in illness. Someone can be surrounded by many people and yet, feel alone. During the performance, both the artist and the child are present in the moment together. They both accept the dramatic as a condition. They both know that they are present in a story. The 'present' is defined by the dramatic time. It is fictional but it is 'real' in a sense that the artist and the child as participants in the fictional are real people, with real lives and real feelings and emotions. The different reality of theatre is what people call 'the unreal'. In theatre, the 'unreal' is lived *as if* it was real. When the child lives in hospital in a new imaginative dimension, then, there is a possibility for some kind of 'change' of their experience. The hospital is not the hospital anymore. For some children this condition offers and escape from the anxieties of real life that leads to a world of dramatic illusion.

Oyebody (2012) discusses theatre from the perspective of the psychiatrist and points to the role of theatre in helping the audience step out of reality when reality causes suffering. He writes,

> In drama, illusion is at the heart of the narrative. [...] nothing is what it seems [...] time is compressed, a sense of reality is suspended. [...] It is dipping in and out of the fact of reality – remaining aware of the decay and dilapidation of existence, of the pain and anguish that it causes.
>
> (Oyebody 2012: 63–64)

If the audience can 'escape' at the theatre it is because people have a break from reality during the performance. The audience experiences the illusion of 'what it seems to be', and leave behind 'what it really is' for as long as the play lasts. Somehow this is an investment in the art form, an investment in the hope that when the play is over nothing will still be the same and things in life will be better than how they were before the play began. TCH audiences need to be encouraged to find a middle way between fantasy and reality, between entertainment and struggle, between relaxation and challenge. At the theatre we experience a depiction of life, aspects of it portrayed in a dramatic form. At the hospital, life might be unsettling and difficult to cope with. Theatre's role is to elevate children from unsettling realities through the world of imagination.

Although the TCH artist is not deployed to alleviate suffering and sickness, they invite the child to step out of reality, to have a break in which the child and the family will avoid discussing illness while enjoying the performance. Each hospital performance is a journey from reality to fiction and back to reality. This is a special relationship between the real and the fictional that adopts the notion that the fictional is a deviation from reality and an 'escape' from it (Somers 2003). 'Nothing is what it seems' in performance. TCH audiences have an opportunity to imagine that they are in a fictional location during the performance where they can have fun. Theatre in hospital, then, aims to give the child a different perspective on how to see their illness, using their imagination. The artist learns to negotiate what is suitable for the child and how to break from reality, if the child agrees to enter the fictional. This is one of the lessons a TCH artist first learns, that the child is what matters. So one comes to the answers about the dramatic illusion through the child.

This is not as simple as is suggested. Sometimes the performance becomes a complex endeavour and the artist soon learns from previous experience that differences arise between what the children seem to be capable of doing in the performance because of their condition, and what they actually do when the performance begins. Over the years I have realized that the child's condition may include pre- and post-operative stress and medication side effects. There are children who feel sick, children in a lethargic state, children with varying moods, limited ability to concentrate and lack of willingness to watch the play, like children who had recently come out of intensive care and were tired. I have seen children being quiet, still and low in concentration. Children who are seriously ill or have had a bad day are most unlikely to attend entertainment. They are most likely to lose concentration and communication with the artist. Nevertheless, there are other children with a very good focus and balance between how they use their energy in moments of quietness and excitement in the play. Sometimes, by fortunate coincidence, the child is awake, willing to watch the performance, in a good mood and willing to interact with the artists verbally and physically. I have seen tired children becoming engaged in the action of the performance and stepping in to speak to the characters and smile. It is never too obvious why and how this happens but it indicates that the theatrical experience can be lived in hospitals. And it is never too easy to achieve. It will take the artist time and effort to engage the child in the story. Once the child knows that she is in a dramatic world, she may release herself into the fiction with confidence but only if the child is well enough to attend and play actively. There are, of course, limits as to how long children can sit awake and participate consciously during a performance, but while children are patients, TCH aims to enable them to bring awareness to their role as spectators and to respond to the performance to the best of their ability. The child is challenged to respond to the artist and give back to the artist's generosity.

Way (1981: 35) has no doubt that the depth and extent of the response does not really matter and 'is never as important as sincerity', which will often depend on the actor's confidence that the play will work and the child will respond. This view tells us what to expect of TCH and why audience participation is not a one-way responsibility. It points to the inter-play of child and artist: where the child commands the attention of the artist, the artist responds to the child through the symbolic use of space and objects in the art form (play), and the child responds back to the artist at a level of symbolic meaning through intellectual, verbal and physical 'language'. This journey cannot be travelled alone by the actor. The participation of the child in the performance is important to the making of meanings about the story, its content and its relation to the child's life. It is the child that makes the performance happen. I have seen children in cardiac wards with tracheotomies not being able to speak but they still fully communicated with the artist and responded to the play through facial expressions. Some of them nod, give smiles as a sign of enjoyment, and some others close their eyes as a sign of relaxation or tiredness. Some children point to musical instruments with their fingers out of curiosity and others reach out to touch puppets and colourful props. Children sometimes ask the characters questions about the story and expect some very good answers. Others pop out of bed to shake hands with the actors and use their teddy to hug the protagonist, and sometimes they even have opinions about the outcome of the story and make their own suggestions about what should have happened in the end instead. Such responses occur out of 'synergy' that develops between the child and the actor in hospital settings. The size of these responses may be the product of small but sincere efforts to be present and active in performance.

Ethical concerns

Together with synergy, TCH inevitably comes to include artistic ethics and emotional risks. These appear in combination with illness as a theme that is close to the hearts of the child and the family who participate in performance. Therefore, the selection of the story, a story to tell *to* and *with* children in hospital, is most delicate. Will the story be site-related? Whether the focus of the story will be on illness and recovery or not needs to be decided. Do stories of illness make the audience feel sad, weak and vulnerable? This is a particularly difficult conversation because it opens up TCH to ethical concerns and the emotional risks that are inherent in participating in stories of illness in TCH. My worry is that stories of illness can potentially attack the child emotionally. While the artist performs in hospitals, they need to be aware of the risks of causing overwhelming emotional responses.

Prentki and Preston (2009), in their edition of *The Applied Theatre Reader*, add a dimension to audience participation. They note their ethical considerations of 'using' people's stories in participatory theatre. They are interested in how every effort is essential to maintain the privacy and dignity of the individuals as the artists built their confidence in their ability to artistically and truthfully tell others' stories. Privacy is challenged here, they say, but what seems to remain is the possibility that these stories will become meaningful to the audience as they were meaningful to their previous owners. This can be very true especially in educational contexts such as Theatre for Development (TfD) and Theatre-in-Education (TiE) where the audience is offered opportunities for learning through questioning, decision-making and resolving problems of personal importance as well as global concern. A story that portrays a similar experience to the life of the audience could be meaningful to them and appropriately effective to the theatrical event. After all, the aim of most of these socially applied theatrical interventions is that of serving the needs, problems and resources of communities. I have tremendous sympathy with this form of educational theatre but I do also think that privacy can often be challenged.

In his essay, James Thompson (2009) debates the whole subject of social theatre and trauma. He argues that the problem lies with the arrogance of some theatre practitioners to 'help' the audience transform their lives by inviting them to speak about their memories of pain and memories of traumatic experiences that should continue to be kept personal. Thompson (2012) also defends the significance of privacy, the right of the audience to remain silent, not to tell their stories, not to give permission to share with the others memories of personal experiences. His strong voice searches for 'alternatives to the rhetoric of trauma', for a new repertoire for social theatre, a repertoire that respects the memory. Inspired by Thompson's (2012) view about the significance of privacy and sensitive approach to stories of suffering, I am wondering about the risk of using stories of illness in TCH. Is a story about illness a safe story to tell to a child in hospital? A story about illness could be 'meaningful' to a hospitalized child but 'meaningful' easily and mistakenly can become painful in TCH. Telling stories of illness to children in hospital holds the risk of engaging the child deeper in situations of clinical stress. Illness should be respected and recognized as a living experience, but telling a story about illness in search of a connection with the child – as an effort to engage them in the story – is an approach that can potentially cause more suffering. Who cares about the meaningfulness of theatre, if making meaning causes grief?

I remember when a colleague from a Primary Education Teacher Training course gave me Hoban's marvellous story *Jim's Lion* (2001) to consider it as a possible story for TCH. The book is about a boy with cancer who is facing death. In his dream, he discovers a lion in his heart who teaches him the strength not to become afraid of death. I was touched by the story and how the author approached the experience of terminal illness with sensitivity and the use of symbolism. The lion symbolizes strength and courage in the midst of difficult times. At the same time, I was cautious not to use the story for TCH because of the emotional risk inherent in the story. The risk is that a story like this might not increase the child's confidence as it should aim to do, but rather recreate and reinforce their fears and anxieties about their illness. It is possible that the nearer the story sails to personal experience of illness, the more challenging it becomes for the child to engage without discomfort. It is possible that if something in a performance is too close to the bone for a child, it triggers a painful emotional experience for them.

White (2013) introduces the idea that emotion plays a significant part in audience participation that arises from triggering phenomena. This is important to an understanding of interaction and emotion in TCH performance. It is possible that the performance reminds the child of his/her condition, and by doing so exposes them to unpleasant experiences of being in the hospital, such as feeling anxious about the operation, and fearful about the progress of their illness and its effect on their lives in the long term. The question of what effect an ill character would have on a sick child and how the child would relate to characters, such as Jim and his terminal illness, is one that cannot be answered easily. And yet, the risk of reinforcing traumatic experiences of illness through Jim's condition needs be diminished. My understanding of how children feel during their stay in hospital is not perfect but I am sure that the reader will agree with me that life introduces the child to illness in the most direct way through traumatic experience – and it does not need fiction to help it do so. TCH is a medium of joy and relaxation, a possible escape from the anxieties that emerge from illness. If the performance is painful, an emotional challenge for the child, then the artist has failed in their aim to bring joy to the lives of children who suffer from illness. A performance that talks about illness offers an overdose of this reality, something that can be harmful to the child's emotional state.

Prádier (2011) argues in his work about theatre and compassion that 'emotional sharing' in performance is subject to risks that encounter personal distress as a reaction of the spectator to an 'overdose of reality'. He then explains that 'the emotional contagion is a very intense and powerful form of "emotional sharing". But it is also clear that this may break the limit of "pain *fictionally* true" and fall into the "*real* pain caused by fiction"' (Prádier 2011: 435, original emphasis). In TCH, pain and discomfort are not desirable responses. The TCH artist needs to be aware that illness and hospital are interconnected phenomena, and that their task is to break the cycle of pain, isolation and stress in this space. In my practice, the art form is used as a vehicle to distract the child's mind from the ordeal they face and improve their ability to remain calm and optimistic. Every contact with the child, every choice of a story to tell in hospital, and every process of writing a play for hospital includes the TCH artist in making decisions based on ethical considerations. Is this not a great responsibility?

In the conclusion of *Applied Theatre: Bewilderment and Beyond*, Thompson (2012) acknowledges the importance of ethics as a generator of theatre in communities:

> Theatre is implicated in the ethical struggles of the zones in which it exists. It does not sit above them. Every action performed, game played, question asked, story told and scene witnessed includes the theatre practitioner in an active ethical debate.
>
> (Thompson 2012: 168)

This argument has particular value for TCH. TCH is created and developed by the artists with attention to the needs of the audience. In reflection on many days of intellectual debate, ethical questioning and examination of various options, I have come to a realization. The artist is responsible for selecting the stimulus for the play; making decisions about the collection of stories; using them in performance; deciding on the goals of the play; choosing the tools of delivery; addressing the stories to the child; giving out an invitation to engage the child with the play; being attentive to the child's mood; being respectful of the child's condition; and being sensitive to the child's response to the invitation of participation. These responsibilities involve the artist in a complex ethical debate. The artist has decisions to make about the play and its meaning, about the role of the artist in a power-control relationship with an ill child, and about the style of performance. These can be difficult because the artist, deep in their heart, knows that lack of attention to the child's mood, lack of respect and sensitivity to the child's condition, lack of ability to respond to the accidental in performance, and lack of ability to engage the child in fiction can put both the child and the artist at emotional risk. One of the risks that is involved in telling stories of illness is that the child will relate to it. The challenge for the artist is to search for examples of stories that do not relate to illness, stories that may give birth to 'alternative repertoires', stories that disconnect the child from the site and the dominant messages of illness. This is a difficult job because it requires sensitivity and attention to the child, the context, the site and the complexity of ethics.

At the same time, writing stories or plays based on real stories for TCH can be a learning curve, a journey of research and excitement for the artist through experimenting with forms and ideas in a collaborative process (Jellicoe 1987; Oddey 1994). Devising for theatre in healthcare calls the artist to focus on exploration, articulation and gaining awareness of self-awareness (Brodzinski 2010). The artistic work is devised from either the articulation of imaginative stories or the adaptation of existing stories, myths, fables, rhymes and poems. Devising or adaptation is, I suggest, an integral dimension of TCH. I have been thinking a lot about devising for theatre as a medium of creative exploration and some of my ideas are published in 'Devised drama, Shakespeare and creativity: Practical work on *Othello*'s pathos' (Sextou and Trotman 2013). In this article we argue that the artist is engaged in the exploration of different ideas, cultures and environments. Heddon and Milling (2006) discuss devising as an activity that can be used to help the artist challenge the dominant literary-theatre tradition, which focuses on the director's interpretation of a script. The opinions of the artists are considered as vital to making collaborative rather than individual decisions about the work. As well as being a process that enhances democratic relationships in a theatre company, devising also enhances creativity. Devising advances the actors' physical, mental and practical creativity by giving shape and meaning to an unstructured idea through representation. Actors are, then, empowered to think, to be critical and to make artistic decisions about the content, style and form of the performance through collective experimentation with forms and ideas (Jellicoe 1987). Devising has been widely used in imaginative site-specific and community-based theatre performances that are 'staged' in alternative venues, reflecting a wide range of interests, needs and practitioner abilities. Imagination is an advanced form of synthesis, a combination of ideas and explorations of possibilities that demand decisions to be made in order for the devised process to emerge. The story becomes the result of the artist's creativity, imagination, composing capacity and sensitivity. The fact that the artist is called to make decisions about the theme, the characters and the plot, adds to the artist's responsibility for the possible implications of the story to the audience's wellbeing. The positive side of this responsibility is the inherent opportunity to question stereotypes about illness.

For example, the artist may want to interrogate how illness is experienced by people and how the ill person is perceived by society, how people with a condition are treated by others and how audiences should be approached. These questions are very important to devising because they address deeper illness and stigma-related questions in our society. Through investigation the artist needs to understand the concepts of illness and wellbeing, how people experience these and how the artist relates to these views. By doing this, the artist gets closer to finding a personal meaning in the facts (people's stories) and creates possibilities for the fiction through personal reflections and interpretations. This can be a particularly challenging process. It is challenging as it may bring the artist's personal biases and prejudices about an illness to the surface while writing for audiences who suffer from it. In the devising process, the artist is a central figure, one that filters the stories through personal experience and thoughts. Filtering stories is an ethical debate too. But I know many artists including actors and playwrights who, despite the responsibility, would love to work on TCH projects, to see the world from the sick child's point of view, to see how the child sees things. What an adventure that would be!

Despite the delicacy of the subject, in several instances, theatre companies engage with patients who offer their stories, personal memories and critical viewpoints on hospitalization in the development of a scenario or a script. Nine children from the Dialysis Unit of Evelina Hospital School in Guy's & St Thomas's Hospital in London have contributed to creating site-specific theatre that was produced by the Unicorn Theatre company and toured in schools (Sextou 2011). The children attended workshops led by the theatre company to explore themes and characters and create dramatic stories. However, with all the success involved in a process like this, a performance that is based on stories of illness may be problematic if it relates to traumas of individuals, and vulnerable communities (Thompson 2005). This needs to be considered when the performance is addressed to audiences with similar experiences to the characters of the story. The Unicorn Theatre Company was sensitive to ethics and chose to tour the show in schools rather than take it back to children in hospitals, where the story initially derived. Again, I believe that if a child feels close to an experience of illness, they will also be uncomfortable watching a story close to that experience. So, when the artist provides the child in hospital with a positive theatrical experience that is not related to illness and trauma, they are more likely to build up a sense of wellbeing. This is achieved through a redirection of the child's attention to situations other than illness with the minimum exposure to emotional distress.

TCH and therapy

No TCH definition would be complete without considering its place in relation to therapy. TCH is not defined as therapy in its precise sense. TCH is an artistic activity which does not aim to either prevent or enhance recovery. It makes no clinical promises for healing and claims no curative principles or results. However, TCH and drama therapy are not contrasting practices. There is a shared recognition that they have much in common with techniques of facilitation and, thus, the borderline between TCH and drama therapy can be blurred.

In Sue Jennings's edited collection, *Dramatherapy and Social Change: Necessary Dialogues* (2009), some drama therapists recognize the theatrical art form as central to the therapy process. John Somers recognizes that 'applied drama has the maximum potential for therapeutic affect' (2009: 194). In Somers's scale of drama activities, from those with therapeutic intent (drama therapy) to theatre performance, there is a range of activities with wellbeing potential. He writes 'The area in between, especially on the left of the continuum, [drama therapy] is inhabited by a great range of drama activity that has explicit or implicit aims to change. Many of these changes could be seen as therapeutic' (Somers 2009: 193). The use of 'therapeutic intent' can be interpreted as close to 'pure' therapy in a clinical practice. The activities placed in the area close to theatre, the so-called performance-based interventions, are interactive projects of pedagogic structures supporting wellbeing. In the Charter for Arts, Health and Wellbeing (LAHF 2012a), Rosie Jackson also recognizes that the purposes of arts projects in healthcare range from expressive, restorative, educational to therapeutic, addressing both clinical and social factors of health. Jackson argues that educational projects aim to raise public awareness about health and wellbeing, and improve the lives of individuals and patients who suffer from long-term and terminal illness. And yet, I think that drama practice that is not defined by an explicit or implicit therapeutic intention cannot claim the benefits of drama therapy. Drama therapy *is* a clinical practice that aims to bring positive change and post-traumatic growth to the life of the individual (client). Drama therapy aims to work preventively and enhance recovery (NAAHW 2012). The main aim of drama therapy is to focus upon process rather than theatre product (Jones 2007). Thus, in my definition, TCH is better positioned as theatre with a wellbeing potential.

In trying to understand the broadly speaking 'wellbeing potential' of TCH, we need to gain insight into its focus away from the curative goal and process. The 2013 Arts and Health South West (AHSW) *International Culture Health and Wellbeing Conference*, organized by the South West Regional Body of the National Alliance for Arts Health and Wellbeing, presented examples of a range of arts practices in health, with either direct or indirect relation to therapy. I was fascinated by the works presented at the conference from around the world and the collection of practices and approaches to the arts in clinical settings. Some of these works had a clear therapeutic intent and others had less obvious connections to healing. Some set out to reach educational objectives while others used the art form for entertainment. For example, The Heroes' Journey in Cancer project was not described as therapy. It was an educational arts project exploring the potential of the collaboration between the art form of storytelling and psychology to meet each other's goals. To meet the needs of the project, Joseph Daniel Sobol used storytelling to help oncologists hear their patients' cancer narratives that are often critical to their own understanding of their illness. The focus of the project was on the art form offering opportunities for useful understandings of the child's psychology and improving the hospital experience. 'Voices from Behind the Fence', on the other hand, was classified as an arts therapy project. Tony Gammidge used objects in his artwork to create narratives of mental illness. His focus was on deploying materials and sources available to participants to introduce strategies of recovery, relief, meditation and coping with personal issues (AHSW 2013). An example of a process-led art therapy project for children in hospitals was Art for Life, a community arts mentorship programme by Reed, Kennedy and Wamboldt (2014). They employed artist-mentors from art, dance and movement and music backgrounds to help chronically ill children develop new coping skills. This project illustrated that the arts have a therapeutic function and that the arts can be, indeed, an essential part of our hospital services.

All three projects were effective in their own ways; they aimed at patient satisfaction and improved wellbeing, either directly or indirectly. However, if I had been asked to position TCH in relation to the projects, I would say that TCH is like none of them, though it could be placed somewhere in between them. This is because TCH positions the child in the role of the audience, not the patient, otherwise it faces the risk of focusing on the 'healing' aspect of therapy. I am keen on not making promises of this kind. At the heart of TCH is the aim to support children and families during a difficult time, but it makes no promises for curing its audiences of illness, or discovering their ability to cope with illness (this would be drama therapy), but one of enjoying life while they are ill. Thus, the role of the artist is not the role of a child's therapist in times of vulnerability.

Although not technically defined as therapy, the ability to enjoy life during illness can be in itself 'potentially therapeutic'. Van de Water (2012: 143) uses the term 'therapeutic' broadly in the analysis of the Beslan project. In 2004, 334 people, of whom more than half were children, died during a terrorist act in a school in Beslan, North Ossetia, in Russia. The project that followed aimed to help the people of Beslan to re-win a lost sense of happiness and introduce creative forms of 'being' through theatre. Theatre processes and creative activities were followed with children in a community in crisis to relieve the trauma of violence. The Beslan project demonstrates that theatre 'has the potential to make a difference' in children's lives and the community as a whole (Van de Water 2012: 143). What interests me in this project is that the goal of most of the activities was not directly curative. 'The goal was to restore relationships and bring families together working on one project. It is of note that the artistic leaders maintained that they did not do anything special or therapeutic, just the work they normally do' (Van de Water 2012: 166). The experience of art created (almost unintentionally?) a 'restoring' environment for the children and families involved and a space for relaxing from the stress of the terror through artistic methods. We may never really understand how the arts exactly do this but when it happens it is not to be ignored. The case of Beslan is horrific and it leaves me speechless and emotionally affected but I am fascinated by the courage of the artists and the participants in the project. Their work fights back against the loss of innocence, the loss of happiness, the loss of security and the loss of hope. In my eyes, this is an example of bravery and determination; a successful artistic intervention.

However, there is some scepticism about the therapeutic role of the arts outside of a formal framework of therapy. By this I mean that the artists should be careful with their ambitions where there are situations of fear and despair, such as situations of critical illness that involve fear of death, loss of happiness and loss of hope. The desire of the artist to help the child should not be overpowered by the ambition to cure them. I have seen some children in oncology, usually the older ones who had an awareness of their illness, who hardly looked at the artist and hardly spoke; they did not smile and stayed there quiet with their own thoughts. I do believe in the power of TCH as a potential strategy to give children and their families joy. But, given the seriousness of the child's illness and the terrible feeling of fear in facing the possibility of death, can theatre claim a psychological therapeutic effect unless it uses therapeutic processes? In my understanding of drama therapy, therapists develop sessions with the child to cope with thoughts and emotions that the child might experience while being in difficulty. Drama therapy deals with patients suffering from psychological illness and treats them as 'clients'. To Emunah (1994: 8), drama therapy's focus is on 'the intentional and systematic use of theatre process to achieve psychological growth and change', a focus that is rooted in psychotherapy. But TCH is primarily an art form. Theatre as an art form that takes place with children in difficulty focuses on the dramatic outcome, the depth of characterization and audience participation that can be achieved during performance. The audience should know that performance is not necessarily associated with problems associated with suffering. TCH is not a systematic approach to facts such as trauma.

Both TCH and drama therapy relate to illness through the use of imagination, although in different ways and with different purposes. This may sometimes cause confusion. For example, for drama therapy, imagination is the vehicle in which to travel the journey of life, explore the happenings and the relationships that take place in the individual's personal journey. Roger Grainger (1995: 130) argues, 'The distinguishing characteristic of Drama therapy is not its underlying psychopathology [...]; the unique property of drama therapy is its use of imagination. [...] For drama therapy imagination is the raw material of transformed reality'. Grainger (1995) recognizes that this is a fascinating use of imagination, which demands the profound involvement and concentration of the individual; a greater degree of self-exploration, and a commitment to long and sometimes painful processes of discovery about one's self, which can be greatly rewarding in the end. There is no intention here of using imagination to re-open wounds and explore the child's past in TCH performance. This attitude would be against the TCH principle of distracting children's minds from painful situations related to illness. Instead, imagination is used as a vehicle to engage the child within the fictional frame of the theatrical performance. The artist aims to involve the child in the dramatic conventions of time and space, aiming to establish make-believe situations that are non-illness-specific. At this level, TCH carries the ambition that the active use of the child's imagination in performance benefits the children involved in it. It makes them feel imaginative, creative, innovative and artistic. Imagination helps to set the dramatic, lets the story emerge, connects with the fictional, and eases the experience of participation and communication within the protection of the imagined. For all concerned, theatre in hospital is active, not passive, and although it takes place in an environment of illness, it engages with patients as audiences.

Because both TCH and drama therapy use drama in contexts of illness and practices of cure, TCH often falls into misinterpretations and mistaken understandings. In simple terms, people confuse TCH with therapy and while TCH is less interested in therapy, its processes are expected to be therapeutic. I would encourage the reader to see TCH as being as important as therapy. Although some cannot understand why theatre has a different value in different settings, it does. TCH is defined by the constantly evolving experience of being an artist, sharing experience with the child as audience. Through TCH practice, we learn to appreciate the power of theatre as an art form, the role of the artist in healthcare, and the benefits of volunteering and building partnerships between academic institutions and healthcare organizations; we learn that devoting time and love to TCH is a skill in itself that can be developed through constant effort, passion, motivation and hard work; we learn that it is impossible to benefit ill children through theatre unless we accept their condition as a phase of change and pay attention to the individual, not the ill person; we learn from the child's and family's perspectives that TCH is appreciated for offering considerable benefits to the child's wellbeing; and we learn that it is possible to discover more about ourselves as human beings through TCH, even if we have to care for others when the common intention in our society is to care only for one's self. In the next chapter, I will discuss how caring for others through the arts can not only make a difference to the beneficiaries but also to the artist's personal fulfilment and growth.

Chapter Two

The distinctive features of TCH practice and research

Background information of the study

This chapter argues that new evidence has contributed to an increasing interest in research that addresses theatre interventions in child healthcare. Researching TCH is particularly useful in bringing knowledge, experience and insight when theatre's role in hospitals goes beyond the traditional roles of the audience and the artist. TCH is a new practice compared to other applied theatre practices in the community, and urges our efforts to evaluate and create new ways of looking at the living experience of hospital life through the art form.

In search of an appropriate and efficient approach to the evaluation of TCH practice, experimentation with various methods is required. The critical departure for the methodology that I present in this chapter is in the proposition that applied theatre requires a mixed method approach to prove its efficacy in the absence of 'hard data' (Balfour, Bundy, Burton, Dunn and Woodrow 2015). TCH needs to find a combination of more traditional qualitative research methods and tools (i.e. interview, observation and journals) with an arts-based approach (i.e. performance as research) to investigate the impact of the performance on the participants through reflection. The two together, traditional and arts-based research methods, seek patterns of meaning that contribute to a better and fuller understanding of TCH. I clarify that the methodology I used is not about using theatre in research as a one-way process of generating data. It is intended to be a reciprocal process between the researcher, children and their families. I value practice (bedside performance) as central to the study and I recognize children as both audiences and judges who are fit to criticize our practice. Central to the methodology of the study is a short theatre performance based on *A Boy and a Turtle*, a story for stress-free kids written by Lori Lite (2001), which was performed bedside to children on a one-to-one basis by two actors. Consent from the author of the story was secured prior to the starting date of the study for the needs of the project. Performance is vital to the methodology and it is difficult to separate it from the research. This is because of the significance of the participatory nature of TCH within research. This study is about evaluating theatre *with* those involved in performance in hospital. In the absence of 'hard data' to prove that bedside theatre performance is an effective methodology in clinical settings, I adopt a mixed method.

In this chapter, TCH practice should be understood within the distinctive features of clinical contexts. Those artists who have experience of working with state health systems are aware of their confusing labyrinth-type structure and bureaucratic processes. They can understand how challenging it can be to conduct arts-based research in healthcare, through a medium that is governed by artistic values, priorities and objectives that the NHS and other health organizations often do not understand. The NHS, as other health systems, is an organization governed by clinical values, priorities and operations. The NHS Research Ethics process is an example of a difference in priority. Before the study was conducted, approvals were gained from the NHS Research Ethics Committee, the Specific Site Research Development Offices (RD) in hospitals, and the Research Ethics Committee (REC) from the higher education institution that employs the employs the researchers. As the chief investigator of the study, I went through a separate research ethics process for each stage of the study and gained in total nine REC certificates, three for each stage. My experience concludes that the Research Ethics process in the NHS is efficient for medics but not sufficient for artists, simply because NHS REC processes are clinical and our work is artistic. Therefore, part of the challenge for the artist-researcher is to be responsible for reducing any possible interference the study could have on the hospital operation while protecting their own artistic approach to research. This means that the researcher is responsible for designing the study and structuring the theatre work to create rich artistic opportunities for the participants who relate to a non-artistic context. Despite how petrifying the request of working with the NHS may sound, I see it as an opportunity for experimentation, a learning curve for the artist-researcher in healthcare. To understand how the artistic can occur ethically within the clinical to fulfil the needs of the study, the researcher first has to examine how the NHS could affect their artistic principles and objectives. Appendix Five offers a ten-step guide for applying for NHS Research Ethics Approval.

Understanding the clinical context

To better understand the NHS context, we worked with key people in hospitals, hoping that our conversations would clarify the things that we need to consider in our practice, such as hospital routines and scheduled treatments, staff arrangements and suitable times. Thompson (2012) argues that applied theatre is the product of negotiations between practice and the community context within which it develops.

> Every circumstance to which a theatre project is applied will similarly make its own demands for the adaptations of practice. [...] Understanding applied theatre requires an examination of how a context affects, makes demands upon or constrains at the same time as exploring how that practice adapts to or resists these determining factors.
>
> (Thompson 2012: 108)

The participants of the present study are a community of children in healthcare in NHS sites. The determining factors are the practical restrictions and hospital routines that take place in the hospitals where the study was conducted. By being responsive to the demands of the NHS, I became exposed to the request of adapting practice to clinical priorities. For our part, my colleagues and I were committed to our research objectives, but in keeping good relationships with the hospitals, we were also willing to be as flexible as possible. Therefore, the study was conducted in collaboration with the hospital's arts managers, and nurses who were involved in a preliminary, exploratory phase of the study. I, then, used my understanding of the hospital operations as a guide to the design of the study.

I visited hospitals prior to the study several times and observed the environment where the children participate in the research. Visits were time-consuming to organize with the hospital administration staff, which was disappointing at times. However, they largely benefited the project and my understanding of how the hospital context affects, makes demands upon and puts constrains on TCH practice and, by extension, on its evaluation. I visited the hospital during busy times and quiet times. The children are more settled during quiet periods, such as after teatime (5 p.m.+) and before the night's sleep (–7 p.m.). The medical treatments are out of the way and most of the visitors are likely to be gone. I also observed that most visitors arrive in the daytime (10 a.m. – 12 p.m. and 1 p.m. – 5 p.m.) and they usually leave the hospital at some point in the evening. To adapt the performance to the routines of the hospital, the arts managers and I agreed to bring the performance to the child between 5 p.m. and 7 p.m. These adjustments are practical adaptations necessary for the smooth implementation of the study. I realized that very little physical space is available for theatrical activity in the hospital wards but there are other rooms where theatre can happen, such as playrooms in paediatrics, education training centres and physiotherapy rooms where the space is better. Despite these options, the performances took place bedside, in order to offer each child special attention and individual care through the arts and make theatre accessible to children who could not physically move out of bed. Jarvis (1992) has drawn upon the role of individual care with children who suffer from chronic or terminal illness as one of immense importance to patient–nurse communication. Similarly, I felt that the provision of individual bedside performance would help the child to experience the benefits of participation and collaborate with the artist and use their imagination, engage with the fictional story and characters, do the breathing training together and relax.

During my visits, I was also hoping to gather information about the children's cultural background in hospital and their level of understanding of English. Birmingham is a culturally diverse city with established significant ethnic minorities, communities, and immigrants. I was interested in how one-to-one participatory bedside theatre might work for children who do not speak English as their first language. Balfour, Bundy, Burton, Dunn and Woodrow (2015: 76), in their book *Applied Theatre, Resettlement: Drama, Refugee and Resilience*, reflect on their drama research, which involved newly arrived children, their teachers and the community. In using process drama to support refugee settlement processes, they wonder how process drama might work with children as beginner language learners. Embedded within their work is the principle 'Language is power and as such is a key aspect of resilience'. They use the language of metaphor and symbolism and the language of the body (gestures and facial expression) to explore artistic ways of communication with the children and their families through interactive forms of dramatic activity. By doing this, they aim to give children confidence as language learners. Inherent in their objective is that this confidence in language will also give the children control over language, power over situations and help them overcome social inequalities.

Similar to their approach and with respect for the child, I wondered: would children with limited understanding of English respond to the bedside performance? Would the artists have the skills to overcome language and cultural barriers? I should note here that there was no intention on my part to differentiate between the audiences based on their language-efficacy. In this instance, to facilitate the gathering of data and make our research possible, only children and families with a good level of understanding and communication in English were considered as research participants and were invited to participate in the interviews and questionnaires. However, every child in the ward and their parent/carers were invited to become potential audiences. Indeed, I was determined to offer bedside performance as a form of entertainment to all children in hospital. After all, TCH is a flexible participatory approach. Language barriers are a factor in performance but they should not come between a sick child and the arts. I was looking for ways to overcome any problems relating to language by using the experience of the nurses who interact with children and families from non-British backgrounds every day. And so I asked the nurses how they communicate with children and their families with diverse cultural backgrounds and language skills. I also had informal discussions with the arts managers in the hospitals and various play specialists. They explained to me that there is always a way to communicate and collaborate with the sick child, even if there is no shared language. I had no doubt that the language of body, metaphor and symbolism were effective artistic methods of communication with children in performance, but hearing from those who work with children on an everyday basis that communication with non-native children was possible was reassuring.

My visits to the hospital helped me to better understand the conditions within which the performance would happen but most importantly, to develop new ways to respond to these conditions with respect to all audiences. How to respond to what the children need can only be judged for each child separately during the performance. It cannot be accurately diagnosed in advance and it cannot be predetermined accurately. This requires a better understanding of the practical limitations of involving children in TCH research.

O'Connor and Anderson (2015: 47), in their book *Applied Theatre: Research: Radical Departures*, propose Applied Theatre as Research (ATAR). ATAR is a methodological model with practice central to evaluation. O'Connor and Anderson argue that communities are involved in a 'symbiotic research experience'. 'Symbiotic' is rooted in the Greek word 'συμβίωση', which means living together, and it employs skills and values of collaboration and democracy. ATAR involves communities in the design of the research, its evaluation and in the representation of the data in a new art product (i.e. film, documentary, performance, etc.) which they disseminate back to the communities. In other words, ATAR is the employment of arts in public service. Performance, as defined in the book, is a form of agency. Ideally I would like to employ children's ideas in creating the bedside performance, but the complete 'symbiotic experience' that ATAR argues for is not always achievable in hospitals. 'Symbiotic' research can be deeply engaging, creative and productive but it can also be time consuming and problematic in clinical settings. Because of the strict NHS REC regulations on access to the children on a regular basis, and due to time restrictions set by the hospital R&D (Research and Development) department, children did not participate in the actual design of the study. Instead, they were involved in the pilot study and the main phase of the study (the evaluation of the performance), which required fewer visits and less time with children and their families.

By the completion of the main phase, I felt the desire and the need to create an improved performance based on our analysis. I considered the views of those involved in the study since its beginnings to remake the performance and communicated it back to children in hospital. I wanted to give something back to the children for what they taught me: to be brave, courageous and optimistic in the battle with illness. This is such a great lesson. It 'inverts the common research practice of entering a community mining data from "subjects" and then leaving the community without offering anything in return' (O'Connor and Anderson 2015: 61). Therefore, I proceeded in the dissemination phase, which represents the learning we gained from the views of children and their families. Their comments and recommendations about the suitability of the story to specific audience age groups; the use of relaxation practice in performance; the impact of one-to-one participation on children's moods; the role of soft toys in communication; and so on, were used in further experimentation with the art form in *Breathing with Love*, improved TCH piece that evolved from the evaluation of previous phases.

From a phenomenological perspective (Thomas and O'Kane 2000), encouraging children to participate in evaluation helps us better discover how children think, how theatre can integrate into the worlds of children in hospital and be of best use from the child's perspective. What is important to the methodology is that we seek to understand what children think about theatre that is created for them and to be encouraged to rethink theatre and childhood. The first stage in doing so is to incorporate children's perspectives alongside adult accounts to gain insight into the children's world through their voices, worries, claims and interpretations (Clavering and McLaughlin 2010). We recognize the children as accomplished judges capable of reflecting on our practice. The allowance for interface reflection increased my efforts to encourage the children to express their opinions, and make recommendations about the performance where possible. At first, I thought that the children would reflect on what they saw and how they experienced it, but I was wrong. It is easy to assume that children's judgements reflect information about the object, which in this case is the performance, but actually there can be many factors that might affect their judgement. In the case of judgement, 'value might be assigned to the person's own cognitions and inclinations' (Clore and Huntsinger 2007: 398). Cognitions and inclinations in TCH practice may include personal understandings of theatre, feelings and emotions; taste or preference; sense of humour; good or bad mood; physical and emotional conditions such as pain, stress and anxiety; a desire or resistance to engage with the play; medical news on the day of the performance; and more. All the above are possible factors that can affect the child's experience of theatre and consequently, their judgement. These may vary from child to child and from moment to moment. Whether the play is liked or disliked by the children is always the product of a relational processing of the performance according to some of these factors. The researcher needs to be aware of that. To me personally, despite their changing moods, feelings and emotions, children can appreciate or depreciate the work we create for them better than any adult. It is the children who are fit to criticize TCH because the children are significant members of the context in which the performance is aimed and offered. Thus, children are central to the methodology of this study.

I would like the reader to know that I attempt no analysis of the lives of the children who participate in the study. But I do consider their ability to participate, their enthusiastic responses, and their imagination and creativity. I seek to create opportunities to explore the complexities of practice through the eyes of the child. Therefore, the focus of the examination is on the possibility that something that works for one child in hospital may not necessarily work for another. It is the opportunity to negotiate the practice and make theatre that meets the children's needs, and not just meet the needs of the researcher, which excites me. This possibility, combined with selected forms and approaches to meet the particular demands of the hospitals, has meant that I have felt free to experiment with different forms and make observations of how they work in practice. In this study, the children are informed prior to performance that they will be both participants in performance, and participants in evaluation. They know that their involvement will contribute to the improvement of theatre practice for children in hospital. The researcher also knows that the contribution of the child in performance will not only improve the human experience of the child in hospital but it will provide research with material for reflection.

The study: Methodology

The study examined the delivery of a bedside theatre-based initiative in a clinical environment and its impact on the wellbeing of children, their families and the professional growth of the artist. The complete study was conducted in three phases: the pilot study, the main phase and the dissemination phase. The pilot study and the main phase took place at the general pathology, cardiac and cancer wards at Birmingham Children's Hospital (BCH). The dissemination phase took place at the paediatric ward of the Heartlands Hospital, Heart of England. Both are NHS hospitals situated in Birmingham, UK, and provide both general and emergency healthcare to children in the region and beyond.

Bedside theatre was developed originally to liaise with groups of link nurses in different wards. Link nurses played the role of contact points for the research team to make arrangements about the times of the performances and the number of children who agreed to participate in the study. They were important to the smooth running of the project, allowing liaison with one primary member of staff per ward. This helped to integrate the project within the ongoing hospital routines and allowed the negotiation of necessary changes to performances following unexpected medical concerns. Link nurses were appointed by the arts manager in agreement with the ward managers, dependent upon staff capacity in the selected hospital wards. They also distributed leaflets and collected participation consent forms from children and parent/carers. The research team designed audience leaflets with information about the project for children and families. Leaflets and research tools were piloted with a group of children and parents in the same clinical setting to ensure that the language and terminology used in the interview questionnaires was comprehensible to this age group (Bryman 2008). Selected final-year drama students and drama graduates presented bedside performances. Objective and fair selection criteria helped to ensure recruitment of the best students and professional drama practitioners for this project (General Council of the Bar 2012). Criteria included excellence of understanding applied theatre in health and wellbeing environments; evident work placement experience as artists in healthcare; and advanced acting and oral communication skills. The pilot study and the main phase were funded by the W. A. Cadbury Trust and the Grimmitt Trust, local charities that operate in the West Midlands in the United Kingdom. The dissemination phase was awarded a grant by the arts department of Heartlands Hospital, Heart of England NHS Foundation Trust.

The research project was created according to the rationale that children who go under treatment in hospital should benefit from theatre performance to improve their wellbeing during their stay. The project addresses the following goals:

- To examine the potential of enjoyment of theatre, and the relaxation and distraction from illness inherent in the delivery of bedside theatre performance for the benefit of the child and the family while staying in the hospital.
- To investigate bedside theatre as a potentially important strategy for preparing children for procedures and maintaining optimism during pre and post-operative stress and anxiety.

The research was interested in answering this primary question:

Can bedside theatre performance, integrated relaxation exercises in the performance, distract the child from their illness, offer moments of creativity through entertainment and relax them whilst in hospital?

It is anticipated that if the child is enabled to use their imagination to enjoy the intervention and relax, then these benefits can also be passed on to the parent/carers and their families through seeing their child stress-free. The research initially aimed to explore the children's and parent/carers' views on the following questions:

How does bedside theatre affect the child's hospital experience? Can bedside theatre on bedtime stories offer sick children special care, satisfaction, relaxation, stress management, comfort and joy in hospital? Can the participation of theatre improve the child's mood and contribute to the development of their cooperation with parent/carers and nursing staff? Do children enjoy bedside theatre? Do parents feel that their children benefit from bedside theatre and how?

The research participants were children and their parent/carers enrolled voluntarily via parental discussion with the link nurses. No previous experience in drama or theatre was required to enrol. Children in oncology were long-term patients (over ten days) while the most frequent length of stay for children from the cardiac, paediatrics and general pathology ward was three to five days. Six children between 5 and 12 years old and six parent/carers participated in the pilot study and another thirteen children and thirteen parent/carers participated in the main study, with the children aged from 4 to 10 years old. The decision to set the limit at 4 years of age responds to the need of making clear distinctions between the 'real' (hospital life and what comes with it) and 'fantasy' (the dramatic conditions) during performance. 'By age 4, young spectators know full well various distinctions between fantasy–reality and false beliefs' (Maguire and Schuitema 2012: 150). Distinctions would make symbolism and metaphor possible to happen in drama, and by extension, they would create conditions for a possible 'escape' from a painful reality to a more pleasant imagined world through theatre. There were, however, parents of two children under the age of 4, one was 2½ and the other was 3, who asked to have the bedside performance. It felt right to offer it to them as opportunities to experience theatre in hospital do not occur every day.

A small group of the children and parents had English as an additional language but this did not exclude them from participating in the study, as the level of understanding and communication in English was good. Other children in the same hospital room who had decided not to participate in the study were, however, able to access the performance from a distance as they remained in their beds. There were direct (children participants) and indirect audiences (parent/carers, visitors and hospital staff). The total number of direct audiences who participated in the pilot study and the main phase was 38, of which there were 19 children and 19 adults. There were also two children under the age of 4 who watched the performance but did not participate in the study. The number of indirect spectators who participated in the study was 42. Indirect audiences were further increased during the dissemination phase but they are not recorded here because they did not participate in the study. All the names used in this chapter are pseudonyms chosen by the children. Evidence is contained in the personal responses of children and parent/carers to the experience of participating in the performance. These are recognitions of what happens in theatre practice taking place in clinical environments.

The aims of the study were addressed through selecting mixed qualitative methods (Wisker 2009). Data was collected prior to performance through a short pre-performance questionnaire; during the performance by observation and video recording; and after the performance by a post-performance standardized interview. The questionnaire was conducted with the children and the accompanying adults on the day of the performance before the bedside was presented to the child, to gain some context for their later responses (Scott 2004). The questionnaire aimed to collect the views of the participants on what they were experiencing, which was important for gaining insight into the possibilities and limitations of TCH as perceived by the audience. The short questionnaire covered topics such as how long the child had been in hospital, their general feelings about their treatment and their expectations from the performance. Post-performance face-to-face interviews with children, parents or carers took place on the day following the performance, with the social sciences researcher aiming to understand their personal responses. The interview style was informal, following a simple semi-structured format using open questions (Bryman 2008). The children and parents were mainly interviewed alongside each other (Mayall 2008). Data was collected in words describing opinions and feelings, in contexts that cannot be converted in statistical form but are essential to understanding the individuals' views (Greetham 2009). Data was recorded on a Dictaphone and transcribed by the researchers within one week of the collection date.

While the study reports on a qualitative evaluation of a bedside performance for children in hospital, it also reports on the nature of the process and the complexities of performance in hospital sites. To capture the atmosphere in performance and the child's responses to performance I used qualitative observations of the children's responses to the performance while they were participating in the story. Observing child–adult interactions on the spot under specific circumstances offers contextual data on settings and individuals (Regents of the University of Michigan 2013). Data was collected in recording sheets with space for narrative descriptions (Fawcett 1996), and using digital cameras to try to capture the details of child behaviours, child facial expressions, gestures, body and verbal communication during participation, and the atmosphere in the room where the intervention took place. Digital data was destroyed after the completion of the study. Observations combined with interviews and journals collected from the participant artists, aimed to create a fuller and deeper understanding of how TCH practice works to the benefit of children in hospitals. Performances were presented exclusively to each child by two artists to provide opportunities for observation of each child's physical and verbal reactions to performance, and to generate children's and adults' reflections on the performance. Relevant medical data, such as the children's pulse rates, pulse ox levels, blood pressure and comments regarding sleep quality, were also collected in the main phase by link nurses. Collections of medical data took place on the day of performance (prior to and post the performance) and on the following day when there was no performance. Medical data were collected to examine the performance's impact on the physical condition of the child but proved less important within the context of this study. Clinical tests, measurements and results reflect a different approach to data generation in arts-based research. Medical data have limited methodological value in understanding the art form, the complexity of the participatory experience of the child, and the artistic experience in TCH.

We discussed our data collaboratively to engage with the nature of arts-based interventions with children as a form of interdisciplinary exploration of wellbeing

(Atkinson and Rubidge 2013). We made notes on our collected data, which was analysed using simple descriptive statistics for the pre-performance questionnaires and grounded theory analysis techniques (Strauss and Corbin 1998) for the post-performance interviews. We combined these with detailed observations of the event (performance) to compare our findings and explore the areas of similarity and difference within the scope of the study.

The last phase of the study, containing *Breathing with Love,* was evaluated by the artists, who reflected on their own learning during the rehearsals and performances at the hospital. The artists revisited hospitals to perform the improved version of the play and this time they were involved as participants in self-evaluating the experience of performing with sick children in clinical settings. Valuable responses from the artists reflecting on both the process of reworking the play and the performances that took place in hospitals were collected in journals and questionnaires. This research aimed at revealing critically important findings about the artist's experience in hospital, which enable us to better define their role and responsibilities as theatre practitioners in healthcare. Korogodsky (1978: 16–17) notes that respect to the child-spectator generates recognition that theatre is an act of responsibility, an act of civic involvement. The assumption here is that as artists experience more performances in hospitals, their understanding of what it means to use theatre to support the community with respect and sensitivity will develop into a particular responsibility as a citizen-artist. For artists who have not experienced TCH performance in the past, such as the ones who participated in this study, these performances in hospital wards are opportunities to improve responsibility towards community audiences.

From the artists, we will learn how children in hospital were integrated into their creative work, and what the artist learnt from the child about young audiences in hospitals. The danger of not paying attention to the perspective of the artist is that they become excluded from the evaluation of TCH practice. The artist-researcher is part of the aesthetic of the practice in hospital and they engage with the work methodologically. Without the artists it would not have been possible to conduct TCH practice and explore how children in hospitals engage with theatre in some of the most challenging 'dramatic' conditions. Evaluation of the artist's experience is crucial to TCH because it offers the members of the company an opportunity to develop a self-critical approach to their work regarding these main three areas: learning, responsibility and awareness of their role in the community. Evaluation also helps the artist gauge the impact that the production was having on the children from the artist's perspective, which is separate to the impact the production was having on children and families from their own perspective. The artists' quotes in the research enable reflection on the theatrical experience and the experience of community.

Ethnographic research methods (Greetham 2009) were used, including two journals – one for recording the experience of the rehearsals and one for the experience at the hospital – and a questionnaire. These user-friendly documents were distributed to the artists electronically in advance. There were two categories of questions: those that examined the artist's volunteering experience and those that sought their perspective on what they learned about and through TCH. Analysis consisted of comparing the artists' independent views, and of assessing observation notes by the author about the artists' training when they rehearsed, and their touring experience in hospitals. All the questions were open, in order to probe the artists' response to the process of creating TCH and to question what they had learned from participating in it. Attempts were made to quote artists' comments verbatim. This was a qualitative analysis based on the following criteria: volunteering offered the artists opportunities to extend their practical experience in clinical environments; to engage the child in performance and use the art form to relax the child; to contribute to the improvement of theatre applications in the community; to contribute to the improvement of a compassionate healthcare system through the arts; and to contribute to the improvement of theatre practice *as* research. Learning from the project included gaining improvisation and acting experience in confined site-specific settings; gaining community experience; gaining better understanding of applied theatre as a subject; using the dramatic form in clinical settings; exploring their role as community artists; and engaging with young audiences in distinctive contexts. The project allowed the artist to drop out of the study, if they wished. Not all the artists performed but they all participated in the TCH production and gained from the overall experience. There were some of them who worked backstage, helped with props, took notes of the rehearsing process and were present during the performances in hospital.

I led the rehearsals and observed all the performances that were taken into hospital wards during this 5-year study. This remarkable journey, growing an embryonic TCH project into a touring study, puts me in the position to provide comments about the development of the artists' skills and understanding of TCH. It also enables me to provide a view of the artists' reactions to the patients' responses to the play, their participation in performance and their appreciation during the study, and to produce recommendations that inform TCH practice.

Feedback from the arts managers; the lead nurses, who were responsible for patient satisfaction and participation; and the nursery nurses was also collected through journals and informal discussions. The contents of these discussions are not considered as data but they are used when necessary to provide the reader with the full picture of what happened in the ward. The people who were involved in this phase had special knowledge of the children in hospital whom they had spent time with. Their 'specialized knowledge of the research population' (O'Connor and Anderson 2015: 64) not only provided informed feedback to the artists but it also communicated advice in the planning of future research.

This part of the book sets a background of using theatre-based research approaches for children in hospital. It should be perceived as a proposed methodology with evidenced outcomes. The efficacy of the project will be considered in terms of the knowledge gained from the theatrical experience in specific clinical NHS settings. However, the evidence offers the reader tools and information that can be applied to new experimentation with arts-based research methodologies in TCH in various clinical settings and health systems worldwide.

Findings and discussion: TCH practice comes alive!

The bedside performance, *A Boy and a Turtle* celebrated a flexible structure and participatory one-to-one style open to adjustments and improvisation, in order to reach children and engage with them in moments of difficulty and clinical stress. An actor played the Boy and an actress played the Rainbow. The Boy brought a soft toy with him to play Mr Turtle. We used a pillow-sized soft toy – a turtle with big brown friendly eyes. Soft toys are commonly used in healthcare to reduce stress; help children to adapt to hospitalization; decrease fear, anxiety and frustration; and facilitate communication between the child and the healthcare team (De Lima, Azevedo, Nascimento, and Rocha 2009). Throughout the study we used two turtles, one brown with a green shell and one pink with a red shell, to suit the preferences of the children. We realized from the pilot study that boys over the age of 7 are not very keen on interacting with a pink turtle, whereas girls of all ages between 2 and 12 absolutely love it. I have to clarify here that there was no intention to reinforce sexist stereotypes about toys and colours through the play. Indeed, as soon as we realized that there were preferences of colour, we offered the child the option to choose between the brown or pink turtle before the performance. By offering the option to choose from two turtles, the artist gives the child some kind of authority over the performance. It gives them some kind of ownership of the event.

We worked in the rehearsals with shared ownership in mind. Appendix Two offers the shape of our rehearsals at a glance, aiming to provide the reader with a structure to work with, especially if TCH is unknown to them. We treated the story as a pattern for an evolving participatory experience with the child rather than as a solid final text that had to be learned and followed religiously. The two actors were allowed to play around with the script. The original script, an adaptation of the bedtime story, is available in Appendix One. The reader may want to compare the script with the dialogues that emerged in practice, as they are described in this chapter, and see for themselves how the script was altered each time to meet the needs of the performance. The artists improvised their moments in between their cues to respond to the child's needs; developed short dialogues with the child; animated soft toys as puppets; and encouraged interaction with the child. However, actors rehearsed the play extensively. We reworked it many times and integrated suggestions that came out of improvisation. The aim was to make the script their own: It was important to the success of the performance to offer the actors some ownership of the script and give them permission to improvise their lines in dialogue with the child, and consider unpredictable incidents, such as noise, medical emergencies, sudden cancellations and other distractions the actors may face when they perform outside the main theatre. At the same time, it was important to the success of audience participation to offer the children some ownership of the play in order to engage with the story and improve their confidence in participation. Therefore, the artists were prepared to expect the unpredictable in performance.

The performance incorporates a warm-up, the play and a closure. Warm-up consists of informal improvised conversations which take place bedside between the artist playing

Timmy, and each child. These conversations aim to break the ice, build trust with the artist, position the artist in the space that is used as the 'stage', and gradually engage the child with the play. 'Chit-chat' conversations with children about clothes, film heroes, music and other non-important and non-illness-specific topics were conducted to introduce the child to a new relationship with the artist. This also aimed to allow the artist to spend some time with the child and invite them into the dramatic world.

With sensitivity to the child's privacy in hospital, Timmy enters the room with respect for the child. He asks the child's permission to stay in their space and relax with them. Timmy waits for the child to respond and improvises the next step depending on what the child says. In all cases, the artist bears in mind the need to establish a relationship with the child. In this relationship, the artist acknowledges that the child 'owns' the space around their hospital bed and that he looks for a verbal consent or gesture from the child to find his way into that private space. If the child welcomes Timmy, then the next step for the artist is to position himself in relation to the child in the space. How close the artist will be to the bed is to be decided by the child. In a sense, the artist tries to encourage the child to have control of the situation. The child is given the freedom to either let the artist approach or block him outside of their space and, by extension their world. By achieving this, the child not only decides when and how they will invite the artist into their space but also when and how they will let him into their private hospital lives. And by doing this, without knowing it, the child also decides the dimensions of the 'stage' where the play will unfold.

After the first introductory conversations, improvised dialogues with the child continue, aiming to involve the child in the performance. If the child's response is positive, the artist will continue. If the child is tired, the artist will find an excuse to end the intervention. He will yawn, admit tiredness and leave the child in peace. The artist needs to be flexible with the performance in such a way that differentiation between each performance, depending on each child's mood and response during the performance, will be available. Van de Water (2012: 135), in her discussion of Rable's notion of 'Children's Theatre', mentions the importance of keeping the child's interest alive during performance: '[The artist should] feel the audience; find the same breath as the children'. The TCH artist may want to consider using their inherent intuition and communication qualities to feel the audience in their acting. The artist often uses their intuition to respond to the child in the moment; for example, to let the story flow if the child responds well, or bring the performance to an end, in case of a hospital emergency, if the child feels tired, or if they fall asleep.

The following transcripts from our filming illustrate the above and show some examples of what happened in hospitals when the artists entered the hospital room and how they responded to the child's mood when they first met with the child:

TIMMY: Hello, Mr Spiderman! *(The boy is 6 years old. He has chosen his own pseudonym for the needs of the study. It is of no surprise that he also wears Spiderman-style pyjamas)* I am Timmy.

CHILD: *(Silence)*

TIMMY:	That's a nice suit you are wearing, Mr Spiderman.
CHILD:	*(Silence, but a smile lights his face)*
TIMMY:	How did you know you are my favourite hero?
CHILD:	*(Keeps smiling)*
TIMMY:	I have always wanted to meet you. Today is my lucky day! Can you do some cool stuff with your webs?
CHILD:	I can stand on the wall.
TIMMY:	You have impressed me now. Can you really do it?
CHILD:	I can.
TIMMY:	Of course you can.
CHILD:	Can you do it?
TIMMY:	Me? No! How could I? Besides, can't you see? I am soaked. It's pouring outside. Typical weather for a summer! British summer in Birmingham. Where is my beautiful sun? *(Pause)* I got off the bus and a big splash covered me. Look! I am like a cloud. I am so wet that I'm pouring raindrops on the floor. *(Pause. Timmy looks around)* It's nice and warm here, can I stay with you to dry off?
CHILD:	*(Silence)*
TIMMY:	Please? I will play my guitar for you.
CHILD:	You are making a watery mess.
TIMMY:	I am so sorry. I didn't realize. There is water all over the floor. Oops! I'm terribly sorry. I'll be on my way home right away!
CHILD:	You can stay.
TIMMY:	Thank you! You're ever so generous. Mr Spiderman, is it OK with you if I sit here? *(Timmy points at a chair by the child's bed)*
CHILD:	Yes.
TIMMY:	Am I too close to you?
CHILD:	No.
TIMMY:	Shall I move closer to you?
CHILD:	*(Nodding)*
TIMMY:	Perfect! *(He takes out his guitar and plays a musical tune for about one minute)* How can I ever thank you for letting me stay? Oh, I know, I will tell you a secret. Do you keep secrets? I met a very special friend on my way to you …

It is clear from the extract above that the child walked through the passage that connects reality with fantasy successfully. Walking the road from a real situation to the acceptance of the dramatic is not an experience that happens automatically. It is a 'ritual' experience with a starting point and an ending. The actor in our project needed to help the child to step into fiction and together with the child set the foundations for the transformation of the clinical space into an imaginary location. Therefore, the actor invited the child into a fictional situation by saying, 'I am so wet that I'm pouring raindrops on the floor'. The implied question to the child was, 'Can you *see* it?' The child accepted the invitation to the fictional and replied to the artist, 'You are making a watery mess', implying, 'Of course I can *see* it'. In this moment, both the actor and the child are in agreement. They both passed from reality to fantasy by accepting the non-real (Timmy is wet and there is water on the floor) *as* real. This is a typical dramatic convention that allows the artist to mediate between the audience (child) and fiction, encouraging focus from the strength of theatre. The child in the example engaged with the fictional in preparation for the story. From now on, the actor has to maintain the fictional as a condition for drama to unfold and continue with enthusiasm for the duration of the interaction with the child.

Next, Timmy tells the child that after school he walked through the park and stopped by an oak tree while it was raining. There he waited for the rain to stop. We had a discussion about the symbolic meaning of rain during our rehearsals (Appendix Two). What does rain represent for the artist? Timmy does not like the rain but Rainbow is keen for the rain because, as she says, 'Rain allows me to be!' Rainbow is critical of things that we may not necessarily like (the moody weather) or may not necessarily understand their existence of in our lives (illness), but which are needed, and may bring a positive experience out of the difficulties. Timmy tells the child that when the last drop of rain fell from the sky, he met a new friend, a bright Rainbow. At a level of symbolic meaning, the positive experience out of rain for Timmy was his friendship with Rainbow. He would never have met her if it was not for the rain. At the same time, by telling a story about a rainbow, we were hoping that the children would identify with the actual experience of seeing a rainbow in the United Kingdom, especially in the West Midlands – a district that is known for its wet weather.

In the rehearsals we also discussed how the Rainbow got into the hospital and how much she is aware of what a hospital is and why children stay in their beds. First, we decided that Rainbow came through the atmosphere led by her promise to Timmy to meet him again. This might sound simplistic but it serves the needs of the play to bring the two, Timmy and Rainbow, on 'stage' bedside. Who Rainbow really is and what the character represents raised more questions in the group. Is she a woman, a goddess, a fairy queen or a natural phenomenon? This was a delightful discussion but a difficult decision to make. All options were interesting in that they brought a variety of qualities to the role including beauty, powers of healing and kindness, innocence, magic and excitement. It was decided that Rainbow represents a natural phenomenon and although 'she' is portrayed by an actress, she is not a human. Therefore, she doesn't know why people are in hospital and she doesn't know about illness, pain, treatments, fear, worries, etc. It is possible, we thought, that in the eyes of the children Rainbow will appeal as a beautiful girl dressed up in a bright costume. We did not expect the children to be able to read the subtext of the role but some of them may do. It was important to us as artists to create Rainbow as a non-illness-specific and non-illness-related character. '"She" is as naive and innocent as most little children', the actress says. This approach helped the actress to play Rainbow as a playful character freed from connotations of pain and suffering. It aimed to take the child out of their situation for a while through their interaction with a character that does not belong to the clinical context.

We provided opportunities for the artist to initiate a conversation about the colours of the rainbow. The artist takes the opportunity here to engage the child verbally in the story by asking questions:

TIMMY: Have you ever seen a rainbow?

CHILD: Yes.

TIMMY: What was it like?

CHILD: It was like an arch with many colours.

TIMMY: That's right. Wasn't that wonderful? There are seven colours in the rainbow. Let's name a few: blue and green for sure.

CHILD: Red.

TIMMY: Yes, red, orange, yellow and purple. Are we good to carry on?

In this incident, the child is responding well to the artists' invitation to participation. They 'play' together. And so the artist continues:

TIMMY: Rainbow is a great dancer. Do you want to meet her? Well, first we have to make up a song to call her so that she knows that we are here. What about this *(Tries a few notes… Music)* Tell me when you see her.

CHILD: She is coming!

RAINBOW: Hello.

TIMMY: Hello, Rainbow. *(Voice-over music)* Where have you been hiding?

RAINBOW: I have been waiting behind the seas for the rain to stop and come out.

TIMMY: You are a beautiful rainbow. You should come out more often.

RAINBOW: Thank you. *(Pause)* Who is he?

TIMMY: This is Mr Spiderman.

RAINBOW: That's a beautiful name. Hello Mr Spiderman. I am Rainbow! Do you like my colours? All the other rainbows are jealous of me because I am the most beautiful rainbow ever. But you know what my favourite thing is of all? *(Waits for response)* I love the rain!

TIMMY: I don't like the rain. I love the sun! I want to relax in a field with the warm sun playing my guitar. *(He stops playing his guitar)*

RAINBOW: I like the sun and the rain. Do you want to know why?

TIMMY: Why Rainbow?

RAINBOW: Because when the sun comes out after it rains, my colours are the brightest and everyone is pointing at me because I am so special. Rain allows me to be.

TIMMY: Oh Rainbow. *(To the child)* She thinks everything is about her! Shall we tell her about us and how I got here today?

CHILD: He came to dry off from the rain.

RAINBOW: Oh yes, he was all wet when I met him. Good job you found the hospital Timmy, *(To Timmy)* have you been here before?

TIMMY: Yes, I have been here many times. I have made some good friends. *(To the child)* Shall we tell a story together?

RAINBOW: Can I be part of the story? I want to be part of the story.

TIMMY: I want to be part of the story too. Do you want to be part of the story, Mr Spiderman?

CHILD: Can I use my webs?

TIMMY: Of course you can!

RAINBOW: Great! Let's begin.

Some children are more enthusiastic and less shy than others. They want to get up and get out of bed, talk to the characters, touch the Rainbow's colours and play with Mr Turtle. The artist needs to open their performance to the audience and meet the child with the same level of enthusiasm by allowing them to interrupt their lines and add their own lines to the script. In a way, the artist and the child rewrite the script together moment-by-moment. An artist reports:

> During my visit to BCH I performed on the oncology ward to a young boy. He responded brilliantly and enjoyed the story a lot. He even began shouting out the colours before I had told him what came next, which was wonderful because it proved that he was engrossed in the story and wanted to hear more.
>
> (Journal, 31 July 2013)

In other situations, the children are not as responsive as in the example above. The following extract between the Rainbow and Tinker Bell (a little girl, 2½ years old, in cardiac) captures the possible difficulties of engaging a very young child:

TIMMY: Shall we tell Tinker Bell about the water? *(Music)*

RAINBOW: Yes, the water. *(Pause)* Let's imagine that there is a pond, a calm blue pond with little yellow and white daisies around the edge of the water, and purple butterflies that flutter in the air. Do you like butterflies, Tinker Bell? Just like you they can fly!

CHILD: *(She is smiling)*

RAINBOW: …And swimming across the pond is a duck followed by all her baby ducklings (quack quack) while the birds above are tweeting (tweet tweet). And then underneath the calm blue water is a little golden goldfish swimming across the waters. And above it all is a clear blue sky. It's a beautiful day today, isn't it Tinker Bell?

CHILD: *(She is nodding)*

TIMMY: And the grass…!

RAINBOW: Can you smell the grass, Timmy?

TIMMY:	I can smell the grass. Can you smell the grass, Tinker Bell?
CHILD:	*(Silence)*
RAINBOW:	Don't worry, Tinker Bell. I can't smell the grass either. My nose must be blocked. But I can feel the warm sunshine against my colours. I can feel the sunshine warming up my hair. It's lovely! *(Timmy plays his guitar... Music)* I'm ready to tell our story.
TIMMY:	I am ready to tell our story too. Are you ready to tell the story with us, Tinker Bell?
CHILD:	*(She looks at her mum, she turns in her bed and covers her face with the pillow)*
RAINBOW:	Oh, Timmy look, Tinker Bell is tired. We all get tired from time to time, isn't that so, Timmy?
TIMMY:	Yes, definitely. *(Yawning)*
RAINBOW:	Why don't we let Tinker Bell go to sleep now and come back when we all feel better?

By stepping away at that point, the artists follow their intuition of the child's needs. They remain in role and integrate Tinker Bell's reaction into the play as gently as possible. Their approach communicates to the child words of comfort: 'It's OK. It's normal to feel tired'. The artist knows that it is not always possible to engage every child in performance for reasons that sometimes are out of their responsibility. No artist can ignore the effects of strong medication on hospitalized children. No artist can maintain and reinforce the fiction in the clinical environment when a child is poorly. It would not feel right to force a performance on a child who does not want it, a child who cannot enjoy it. The artist reports:

> We were taken to the cardiac ward to perform to a little girl of the age 2½. Her mother requested we performed to her even though she was younger than the audience age we requested. She was unable to speak because she had recently come out of intensive care, but when Stefan began to play his guitar to her she responded really positively, as I approached the bedside and began to tell the story. However, the little girl was more intrigued by the guitar; as the story went on, unfortunately she felt unwell and began to get distressed so we had to stop the performance. This gave me the chance to use my improvisation skills and not break my character as I gently stopped the performance; I received positive feedback from the child's mother on how I handled the situation.
>
> (Journal, 19 July 2013)

Video recordings show that the little girl in cardiac started responding well, but after a few moments she had difficulty keeping her body upright and her eyes open. The child's face tells me that Tinker Bell was not only tired. She seemed to be in pain. Her mouth was compressed and her lips were pulled back. Prkachin (2009) assessed facial expressions of young children as pain indicators. He argues that Charles Darwin was right to assume that closely compressed mouths and retracted lips are evidence of silent pain expression.

Prkachin argues that the facial expression of pain connects the internal experience with social influence. This is a fascinating argument because it acknowledges pain, both physical and emotional. It values pain as an existent experience by suggesting that pain is communicated through the body in a way that the unspoken is expressed and is no longer hidden. This means to me that what is expressed is shared and it should not be ignored by the artist. Prkachin (2009) interestingly sees the need for the artist to be able to capture the sense of suffering through representations of the face and portray it. The artist in hospital surely needs develop skills of 'reading' pain indicators in order to understand how pain behaviour is processed and act on it with sensitivity and discreteness. Assessing pain by facial expression in a TCH context serves to understand how the child feels during performance. A child in pain uses their face as a non-verbal pain behaviour. The face serves to communicate the fact that pain is being experienced. A hospitalized child's face, then, is a behavioural source of evidence about pain. Tinker Bell's compressed mouth could not have been ignored. My interpretation of Tinker Bell's behaviour was that she was suffering but did not know how to express it verbally and because of that, she experienced additional stress. She would probably not know how to define the expression of pain, but the physical expression of pain was evident. This is how I captured her suffering in the absence of language communication.

Elaine Scarry (1988), in her book *The Body in Pain*, argues that pain often resists language; it can be inexpressible. Pain is difficult to put into words, no reason to disagree with that. Scarry argues that children usually use their facial expressions to speak what they cannot express. It seems as if words do not come easy to the child, as if the child cannot find the way to make others see what they go through. Tinker Bell did just that. She was too young for the play and too tired and she chose to stay in silence, a rich silence. Rainbow cleverly did not ignore the signs of tiredness and pain on the child's face. Instead, she used her ability to 'read' the silence as a place in time when many things were happening in the child's internal world, including pain and discomfort. Rainbow adopted a flexible and open position to the performance, resulting from the artist's understanding of the performance's implications on wellbeing and artistic integrity. The artist did not lose sight of her responsibility for the child's eventual positive experience of theatre in hospital. The artist was aiming at an entertaining, enjoyable, relaxing, calming and uplifting experience for the child but the experience cannot be strictly planned. Some moments can be more difficult than others, some moments request more empathy to deal with them than others, but this is part of the artist's learning too.

Fortunately, there were achievements within the performance as well, including the positive reaction of the parent. The mother appreciated the respectful response to Tinker Bell's attitude. She explained that the child was waiting for an operation; she was on strong medication which made her mood lethargic. She also had to go for a procedure for which she was quite nervous. The mother thanked the artists for their tactful approach to her daughter's not very polite reaction. The artists explained to the mother that there was no reason to apologize for her daughter because it is no one's fault. They also reassured her that there would be more opportunities for Tinker Bell to see theatre soon when she gets out of hospital. The 'failure' of engaging Tinker Bell in performance was a success of judging the moment correctly: being sensitive and attentive to the child's needs, and being flexible with the performance.

After the first introductions between the Rainbow and the child, the two actors and the child agree to share a story about their adventures. The artists invite the child to make a decision about the imaginary space.

TIMMY: Are you ready to go with us to a special place?
RAINBOW: Don't be silly. We are not going anywhere. I like it here.
TIMMY: I like it here too. It's nice and warm but why do we have to stay here if we can go anywhere we want?
RAINBOW: And how are we going to do that?
TIMMY: By using our imagination!
RAINBOW: Imagination? Is it a medicine?
TIMMY: It's better than any medicine!
RAINBOW: How does it work?
TIMMY: Well, our brain is a brilliant thing. We can use it to think of wonderful places or things that we can then visualize as if it's a dream.
RAINBOW: Can we do it now?
TIMMY: Sure we can.
RAINBOW: How do I do it?
TIMMY: Just close your eyes and think of a nice place.
RAINBOW: I think of the park where we met Timmy. The rain has just stopped.
TIMMY: (To the child) Easy peasy!
RAINBOW: (To the child) Let's do it together then.
TIMMY: Ready, Mr Spiderman?
CHILD: Yes!
RAINBOW: Let's close our eyes and imagine that we are going to the park.
TIMMY: Hold on a minute. I think we should let him [the child] decide where he wants to go. Do you want to follow Rainbow to the park, Mr Spiderman?

At this stage, the visualization of a fictional location aims to help the child 'escape' from the hospital environment through their imagination. The child's capacity to imagine a fantasy world, engage with it and live within it during performance, needs our attention. Fisher and Williams (2004) argue that

What imagination does is to enable the mind to represent images and ideas of what is not actually present to the senses [...] In short, imagination is the capacity to conceive possible (or impossible) worlds that lie beyond this time and place.

(Fisher and Williams 2004: 9)

This has a particular resonance with the creative opportunities offered to the children in the context of this book. What imagination does is to enable the child's mind to represent images of a location other than hospital and create a different external reality to their everyday real world. This is the 'escape' that I mentioned earlier. In reality, the child is physically present in the hospital but in the fictional, the child can be present in a fantasy world that is less familiar, less attached to negative experiences of pain and discomfort. Through imagination the child enters 'the impossible', such as a walk in the park. The impossible can be a situation that is not realistically possible given the health condition of the child. Imagining here involves pretence, supposition, hypothesizing and empathy (Trotman 2010: 130). Supposing that a walk in the park is possible opens a new world of possibilities for the child in drama. These are possibilities about things that 'never were, but which might become' (Eisner 2005: 108). These are things that might happen during performance. In a way, theatre in hospital becomes the process and result of fusing reality and fiction into one entity. What I mean is that intimate bedside performance in hospital is a combination of two different places in one situation. For example, the real place (I am in bed in paediatrics), and the imagined place (there is a park somewhere with fresh grass) blend into one situation (I am physically in my bed in paediatrics but I imagine that I am resting on the fresh grass in the park). The fictional situation almost invades the physical space in hospital, making the hospital space shift into a fictional space and creating a mixture of the two worlds. The child is aware of their life in hospital and they step into a visualized life outside hospital. This is an act of elevation above the ordinary, an act of liberation. Being encouraged to make the choice of space and time is key to the engagement of the child in the conflation of the two worlds and vital to the liberating experience of stepping into fiction in hospital. Therefore, we set the child free to make propositions of what they want to include in their image and visualize an imagined location of their preference.

There is evidence that demonstrates the effects of visualizing favourite places in reducing children's pre- and post-clinical anxiety. Pederson's (1995) experiment with children and teenagers (9–17 years old) who participated in imagery activities during cardiac catheterization reported lower anxiety after the relaxation practice. Cardiac catheterization is a medical procedure used for both diagnostic and interventional purposes. Children who undergo cardiac catheterization present pain-management challenges to nurses, but the children who participated in the study displayed fewer distress behaviours while being in the imaginary condition. Pölkki, Pietilä, Vehviläinen-Julkunen, Laukkala and Kiviluoma, (2008) also report that the imagery trip can be used to reduce children's post-operative pain in a hospital setting. The children who participated in imagery practice after they had undergone appendectomy or upper/lower-limb surgery reported having significantly less pain than children who did not. The interveners in both clinical trials above demonstrate the use of imagination and visualization practice as a clinical procedure aiming to relax the child's body and mind, both pre- and post-operative.

Our goal was not clinical but we also involved children in imagery and let the children brainstorm about the play's location. Imagery in our experimental work is used as a method to create both theatre and relaxation. Each child decided if the location would be a park, as it is in the original story, or not. Imagery practice was integrated in the performance aiming to relax the child while entering deeper into fiction. We encouraged the child to choose one of their favourite places. Whether there should be a pond or a lake, grass or fields of barley, streams, trees and flowers, birds, fox nests, horses and cows in the park, is to be decided by the child. Most of the time, the child would go where the Rainbow wants them to go. Sometimes, children demonstrate their strong preferences in ways that force the artists to stretch their improvisation skills to adjust to what the child imagines. An example comes from Buzz Lightyear, an 8-year-old boy in paediatrics. He was wearing a space-ranger pyjama set from *Toy Story 2*. He also kept a laser 'weapon' on his bed.

TIMMY: Do you want to follow Rainbow to the park, Mr Buzz Lightyear? [The child expressed very little interest in walking to the park in the company of a Rainbow. This was probably too 'girly' for a boy. Instead, he was eager to use his toy weapon in performance at any cost] That's OK. Have you got any idea where you want us to go?

BUZZ LIGHTYEAR: I want to go to Neptune.

TIMMY: How fascinating! Where is Neptune, do you know Rainbow?

RAINBOW: Is it in the sky?

BUZZ LIGHTYEAR: It's a gas-giant planet far from Earth.

That boy used the opportunity he was given to choose the location. It was difficult for the artists to resist such an imaginative proposition. The two artists possibly assumed that a trip to Neptune would help that boy break from reality better than walking in the park, and they accepted the boy's suggestion.

TIMMY: That's amazing, Rainbow! What do you say?

RAINBOW: I am in! Let's go for it!

TIMMY: At the moment we reach Neptune I am sure that we will find the place mesmerizing. We will get some rest [he means the breathing practice] and instead of laying down looking at the stars we will be laying down gazing at our beautiful Earth.

RAINBOW: Oh how wonderful! I will get a chance to brighten up my colours! Yes, rest will do me great good. What do you think, Mr Buzz Lightyear?

Something extraordinary happened here. The artist allowed the child to take control over the dramatic situation and let him play the game with his rules. This is a great example of appreciating the child as an equal player in the performance. To let the child guide the story in a different direction to what the artists had rehearsed is also a brave decision. As a result, the story was entirely adapted to a space adventure. As for the laser 'weapon', the child used it as a prop, a lighter that guided the three of them safely in their journey to Neptune and back to Birmingham. This example not only shows the artist's flexibility to integrate the child's wishes in performance, but it also offers evidence that shows the value of offering the child the freedom to make choices. What the artists had in mind for the imaginary location of the story did not matter. What mattered was to adapt the performance to the child's wishes. This example shows that there are no limitations to a child's imagination and no rules about what the location of the play should look like. Each 'stage' became a different 'park' in our study.

An artist notes about the use of imagination in performance:

> I had never had experience with hospitalized children before this experience and I have learnt that children need to find ways to feel safe, calm and comfortable within an environment that can be very scary and alien to them and in which they may find themselves alone without their parents/guardians for large periods of time. I think it is very important for children in hospital to have distractions from the reality of the hospital and to be able to use their imagination to help them even if they have to stay in bed and are unable to get up and play with other children.
>
> (Questionnaire, August 2013)

Once the space is symbolized and the two actors together with the child imagine themselves in the fictional space, the Rainbow becomes the narrator and Timmy starts playing his guitar. In cases when the child accepts the park as a location, the Rainbow suggests that there is a pond in the park. To continue the narrative thread presented to the child, the Rainbow involves more details about the location to help the child visualize the 'stage' as a calm and serene setting.

TIMMY: A rainbow danced at the water's edge. *(Rainbow dances)*

RAINBOW: A turtle on the other side of the pond also noticed the rainbow. *(The music goes on)* The boy removed his shoes, shut his eyes and put his feet into the water and imagined that the colours of the rainbow that filled the pond could also fill his body. *(Rainbow lifts Mr Turtle from the prop box and animates it. The child looks amazed)* The turtle, curious about what the boy was doing, also put his feet into the warm water and shut his eyes. The boy drew a breath of warm air in through his nose and felt all the stress of the day slip away. *(Timmy stops playing his guitar and the Rainbow passes Mr Turtle [puppet] on to him)*

TIMMY: Hello, Mr Turtle. Say hello to our friend. *(From now on Timmy will animate the turtle and change his voice to differentiate his character from 'Mr Turtle'. He improvises a short dialogue with the child as Mr Turtle)*

MR TURTLE: Hello. Nice to meet you.

CHILD:	Hi.
TIMMY:	The turtle also drew the warm air in through his nose and gave a gentle sigh as he let the air out through his mouth. *(Rainbow will demonstrate her colours [one at a time] by using the fabrics that are stitched on her hat with gentle movements and a soft voice)*
RAINBOW:	The boy imagined that the colour red was flowing up from the pond into his feet, making them float like petals on the water.
TIMMY:	The turtle also felt the red flow into his feet and he started to drift toward the boy.
MR TURTLE:	Oh yes, I can feel the red flowing into my feet. Can you feel it too [child's name]?
TIMMY:	Shall we do the breathing together now [child's name]? Do you want to try it with the turtle? *(Demonstrations follow with the child repeating the practice)*

At this stage of the performance, breathing and repetition plays an important part in the story as it focuses on the effects of breathing on body and mind. Our practice borrows elements from breathing practices to balance the nervous system and relax the body. When the hospitalized child's pre- or post-operative stress overwhelms the nervous system, the body is flooded with chemicals that wear the body down. The breathing response puts the body and the mind into a state of stability. The play aimed at just that by incorporating the breathing practice in the play. As can be seen in the examples of practice I offer, we use several repetitions of the breathing practice. The characters repeat their lines again and again and they invite the child to imitate and repeat the breathing practice again and again too. Lines like, 'Shall we do the breathing together again' and 'Well done!' help the child follow the practice, relax their bodies and minds, as well as shape a positive memory of the play.

Reason (2010) discusses repetition in children's theatre from an artistic perspective. He examines active audiences and the establishment of a memorable theatrical experience. He argues that repetition of lines and imitations of actions seen in performance shape the child's memory and make the performance a long-lasting experience:

> [...] As with this kind of verbalization or re-enacting, children frequently structure their memories of a performance around favourite instances or moments, which might be considered favourite instances precisely because they can be re-enacted and taken ownership of. It is the potential for repetition, and the repetition, which makes them successful as much as anything inherent in the moment itself. They become favourite moments in particular because they can be re-enacted [...] with friends and therefore mark a shared and stronger group experience.
>
> (Reason 2010: 28–29)

In the play, Timmy, Rainbow and Mr Turtle re-enact a short scene where a colour visits the child's body and fills it in with warmth. Each colour has something different to bring to the experience but the mode of practice is the same: the same gentle movements, the same soft voice and the same lines with varying degrees of child input. Children can be reserved at the beginning but they become more confident in breathing during the play. Mr Turtle and the repetitive breathing practice become central features in the play around which the characters build their dialogues and the children structure their memories of the performance. The use of the turtle soft toy as a central feature aims to introduce a position, the role of mediator, between the child and the adults – connecting the worlds of childhood in hospital with the artists and sharing the experience of performance between the two, the child and the artist. Repetitions of breathing with Mr Turtle were an investment in the hope that the child would re-enact the breathing with their parent/carer when they need to relax. It is hoped that these favourite moments of breathing with the turtle will provide helpful assistance to the child before and after a clinical procedure or surgery.

RAINBOW: The boy felt the red turn into orange as it travelled up his legs. The orange allowed his legs to relax and let go of all their tightness.

TIMMY: The turtle also felt the orange travel up his legs as he drifted closer to the boy.

MR TURTLE: Oh, I liked that. I feel quite orangey now!

TIMMY: Me too. I feel good. Are you [child's name] feeling good too? *(Waits for reply)* Shall we do the breathing together again [child's name]? *(Demonstrations follow with the child repeating)* Very good. That was a good try. What do you think, Mr Turtle?

MR TURTLE: I think [s/he] is great. I want to do it again myself.

RAINBOW: The boy felt the orange turn into yellow as it warmed his stomach and chest. The yellow filled his body with an inner glow.

TIMMY: The turtle also felt the yellow warm his body as he drifted even closer to the boy.

RAINBOW: The boy felt the yellow turn into green as it touched his heart and poured into his arms and hands. The gentle green filled his heart with love and made his arms feel like blades of grass swaying in the breeze.

TIMMY: The turtle also felt the green touch his heart and pour into his arms and hands as he drifted still closer to the boy. Shall we do the breathing together again? *(Demonstrations with the child repeating)* Well done! You are becoming an expert now!

MR TURTLE: I am becoming an expert too! Green is lovely. *(Dreamy voice)* I feel so relaxed now.

RAINBOW: The boy felt the green turn into blue as it explored his neck and jaw. The blue felt peaceful, like the ocean rising with the tide.

TIMMY: The turtle felt the blue explore his neck and jaw as he drifted even closer to the boy. Shall we do the breathing [child's name]? Are you ready? What about you, Mr Turtle? *(Waits for reply)* *(Demonstrations with the child repeating)* Well done [child's name]. You look very relaxed to me now.

RAINBOW: The boy felt the blue turn into purple as it swirled around his head. The purple washed all the thoughts from his head, leaving his mind completely still.

TIMMY: The turtle also felt the purple swirl around his head as he drifted so close that his head touched the boy's hand. Hey there, Mr Turtle. You are so cute.

MR TURTLE: Thanks Timmy. Shall we do the breathing together once more with [child's name]? *(Demonstrations with the child repeating)* Excellent! Well done!

RAINBOW: The boy smiled, and together the boy and the turtle felt the rainbow's colours embrace them in a soothing white glow.

TIMMY: In their newfound oneness, they knew that they had experienced the wonder of colours! Oh, I feel completely relaxed now.

At this point, Timmy passes the turtle to Rainbow and starts playing a relaxing tune on his guitar. A minute or two of music follows to let the child enjoy the relaxation.

RAINBOW: And I am very happy that my colours were part of the play! Would you remember us when you do your breathing exercises [child's name]? Remember Mr Turtle. *(The Rainbow gives the child a memo card showing Mr Turtle and the basic breathing exercise instructions)* The sun is out now, I've got to go.

TIMMY: I'm all dried up now. It's time for me to go too. Thank you for letting me relax with you [child's name]. I enjoyed relaxing with you. Did you have a good time? *(Small talk with the child about the performance; the favourite characters and colours. Timmy says goodbye to the Rainbow and Mr Turtle, who leave first. He then improvises a dialogue with the child before he departs playing his guitar)*

Sometimes little children fall asleep at this phase of the intervention, showing that the whole experience of theatre through imagery, visualization and breathing can lead to a calming physical reaction. An artist reports:

John [pseudonym]: He was too tired whilst he was falling asleep.

(Journal, 19 July 2013)

The benefits go beyond the researcher's ability to observe the experience. We understand that children will continue recalling the experience after the end of the performance, as evidence from the post-performance interviews shows. As one participant reported:

Erm, there was a boy and a turtle, and a rainbow dancer, and the rainbow made the boy relax and at the same time the turtle was drifting in towards the boy [...] And every time the colour went into the boy's body, the turtle got closer and closer to the boy.

(Taikwando Kid, male, aged 9)

The older children (ages 8–9) could verbalize their responses more coherently than the younger children (ages 5–7), but the researcher identified from responses that all the children could remember the characters and bright colours used in the play, and remembered doing some breathing exercises with Mr Turtle to help them to relax. Remembering details of the performance shows that the children paid attention to the play. This finding matches the video recordings, which also show that children remained concentrated on the characters' voice and body projection and kept on facing the performers throughout the show without turning their heads away. We trust that all children were attracted by the performance and distracted from the clinical environment as long as the performance lasted. Three children (two boys and one girl) said that the performance actually made them forget that they were in hospital. As one stated:

> Erm, cos it was like my own imagination, I was in my own little world. Erm, because it makes you feel relaxed and ready for bed.
>
> (Taikwando Kid, male, aged 9)

Three parents in oncology and cardiac wards reported that the performance had a positive impact on their children in relation to medical procedures the following day. These children were Bodge (aged 9, oncology ward), Rose (aged 5, cardiac ward) and Belle (aged 4, cardiac ward). Bodge's parents recalled that he normally has difficulty taking his medication. However, the day after watching the performance, with some prompting by his parents, Bodge remembered the words and actions of the turtle instructing him to breathe, enabling him to relax and take his medication with little difficulty as the extract from the interview with his parents demonstrates:

> Mum: Think it's encouraged him more to take his tablets more because he's more... he's been more what's-a-name, ain't he *[looking at Dad]*.
>
> Dad: Liked psyched up.
>
> Mum: Took a lot more deeper breaths cos we said take deep breaths a little bit more.
>
> Dad: Cos he's been so wound up, you know.
>
> Researcher: So you think it's helped him to unwind and be less stressed?
>
> Mum: Calmed down a little bit.
>
> Dad: Helped him unwind and relax.

One of the nurses confirmed that Bodge always had trouble taking his medication and that she had noted it seemed to have been much easier for him the following day. Similarly, Rose's mum reported that the following day Rose had to go for a procedure for which she was quite upset. As Rose's mum stated:

> To be honest with you, later on, Rose had to have a procedure done and we did keep saying, do you remember what the turtle told you, just breathe slowly, try and breathe

slowly and she actually did remember, albeit she was quite upset at the time she did try and do the breathing, you know, so it actually helped.

(Mum of Rose, female, aged 5)

When asked if she felt Rose would remember these activities for her next procedure or her next stay in hospital, she said:

I think if we say breathe how the turtle told you to breathe… there you go [Nods in the direction of Rose, who is demonstrating the breathing exercises]. See, you remember, don't you? [To Rose] In through your nose and out through your mouth, that's what he said wasn't it… very good!

Several participants demonstrated the breathing on the following day of the performance without being prompted to do so.

[Interviewer: What else do you remember?] The breathe, er… [Demonstrates] The turtle showed me how to do it.

(Lightning McQueen, male, aged 4)

There is more evidence from the study that children recalled the theatrical experience and used the breathing exercises which were repeated throughout the story. Belle, a young cardiac patient, not only followed the turtle's breathing instructions for as long as the performance lasted but also recalled the breathing practice on the following day.

A nurse also reports what she collected from a child aged 8 about the performance:

It was brilliant, lovely and really, really nice. It had emotions and the breathing helped me when I was a little bit nervous.

(Arts and Music Monthly Report, Heart of England NHS Foundation Trust, June 2014)

Some parents also reported that their children used the breathing exercises that the turtle taught them when they felt stressed and before they went for a pre-operative cardiac procedure. The children recalled breathing as part of the overall theatrical experience. Post-performance interviews indicate that they also remembered the characters of the play, which shows that the artistic context was effective. It made the breathing a lasting memory of happy moments which turned out to be a useful relaxation pre-operative tool because it linked it to personal theatrical experience.

The importance of these findings surely relates to the benefits of relaxation for children with critical health conditions, who experience pre-operative stress from their illness. These testimonies may help explain why bedside theatre incorporating relaxation practices can afford wellbeing benefits with cardiac and cancer patients after the performance has ended.

Some of the children emphasized relaxation as a major benefit of the performance. It seems possible that the combination of increasing relaxed feelings balanced out the emotional impact to some extent.

Both children and adults who participated in the study described a range of positive emotional responses, from feeling excited at the beginning by the artists' presence to feeling more relaxed together with the artist towards the end of the performance:

It was funny all the way through.

(DonkyKong, male, aged 8)

It made me feel very happy inside… and it did make me feel calm as well.

(Pikachu, male, aged 8)

I think she felt quite special.

(Mum of Daisy, female, aged 8)

All of the children seemed to think the parent/carer watching the performance with them enjoyed the performance as well. This was echoed by the parent/carers' comments, even though two of the participating fathers felt that the performance was a little young for their children. Most of the parents said that they enjoyed the performance because they could see their children enjoying it, as the quotes below demonstrate:

Cos it made Bodge smile and we haven't seen a smile on his face for two days. So he enjoyed it, I enjoyed it. It helped Bodge relax and for him to relax I was de-stressed.

(Mum of Bodge, male, aged 9)

I was happy, I was relaxed that at least it relaxed him a little bit otherwise he just gets stiff [relating to his illness].

(Mum of Stephen, male, aged 8)

It relaxed her, calmed her, took her mind off what's going on around her.

(Mum of Belle, female, aged 4)

I thoroughly enjoyed it, I felt totally relaxed.

(Nan of Lucy, female)

The performance met the parents' expectations of entertainment. These replies show that parents and family were having a good time with the child. What was also evident from the early stages of the study was that the need of the parents to relax and free their minds from anxious thoughts about the child's health for a while gave them a fine excuse for encouraging the children to have the bedside entertainment. Allowing parent/carers to be present during the performance, and watch the child participating in it, also demonstrates how theatre in hospital provides opportunities to gain a feeling of normality as a whole family. It also helps the parent/carers to make sense of the way TCH operates on the level of a child through personal experience. In relation to the fact that the performance was delivered at the child's bedside, the relaxation value of our one-to-one methodology was appreciated by the parent/carers, especially in the cardiac and oncology wards. They most appreciated the fact that it was an individual performance which made their child feel special:

> It's special and different, it makes you feel an individual and – you know – you're not just another child in a bed, somebody's specifically come to see you.
>
> (Mum of Rose, female, aged 5)

This also shows the high suitability of the individual performance for children at high risk. Restricted mobility, low immune system and the side effects of medication meant that children from the oncology and cardiac wards could not get easily out of bed to attend a theatre performance addressed to a large audience elsewhere in the hospital. Bedside theatre offers equal opportunities for them to experience the performance despite their condition as individuals who deserve to receive personal attention and care. Some of the parents also felt that their child would have benefited from seeing it even if other children had been around. Molly's mum responded:

> I really like the individual attention, I think that's really nice but I think you could do something to a small group of children... a lot of it is just about getting away from stuff in hospital so although you might not get the relaxation aspect so much in a group setting, it is still a distraction for them having the play, and maybe at the end do the breathing... I think both could work but I did like the fact that it was just at the bedside.
>
> (Mum of Molly, female, aged 6)

Other suggestions included using more actors and having the performance in a room dressed up like a real theatre. I spent a lot of time thinking about this recommendation. My interpretation of this comment is that gathering as an audience could give children and the family an option to watch the play with others and socialize before and after the theatrical event. It is a primitive need to share and interact. It is human to like others knowing what you go through, to share the experience of illness – much better than suffering in silence at least. TCH seems to be a good reason for gathering and sharing, an opportunity for human interaction and comfort. This picks up on another key finding that relates to the parent's need for socialization with other parents while their child is critically ill in hospital. Despite having fairly low expectations of their own enjoyment, many of them identified additional benefits for themselves. To acknowledge the parents' feeling of isolation, the provision of performances to larger groups of children in the hospital was considered. We subsequently scheduled a series of performances at the Play Centre of Birmingham Children's Hospital for the second half of 2013 to run parallel to performances in selected wards in the same hospital. Mixed audiences of patients (4–9 years old) and their parents/carers were invited from across the hospital wards to watch an adaptation of the bedside story performed to a larger group. The audience had an opportunity to meet the characters after the show and play with Mr Turtle.

Some parents of children with chronic illness also suggested that the play would have been more helpful during a later stage of the child's long-term recovery. This is a valid suggestion because it offers scope for investigation about the impact of relaxation on chronic-illness management inherent in our bedside theatre methodology. It is important to emphasize that medical research by Miller and Harris (2012) reports that children should be involved in taking responsibility for illness management. The authors argue that children need to develop decision-making autonomy and use of information and advice assisted by the family to cope with pain management. The idea of introducing breathing practice to children during performance while the parent/carers are present is similar to the notion of 'training' children in using breathing in pain management. A lack of relaxation elements in the play I believe would lead to limited relaxation effectiveness. The ambition to repeat the breathing seven times with support from Mr Turtle is what provides confidence in using the bedside theatre practice, incorporating relaxation techniques to increase the child's autonomy in managing pain. In the pilot bedside theatre study, it was found that performance incorporating breathing practice helps children relax and distracts the mind from pain. It is, therefore, possible that the provision of bedside theatre at a later stage of the child's treatment could support illness-management strategies. This could happen by allowing them to recall the theatrical experience, refocusing upon the dramatized story and the breathing exercise as a pleasant strategy to manage their physical pain.

The performance, whilst raising a lot of positive elements, did also note some negative points. One child (aged 8) who participated in the pilot study felt that it was a bit too 'girly'. This comment was possibly related to the pink-coloured turtle. We considered this comment in the development of the main phase to use brown turtle soft toys with green shells for the children who preferred it. The same child also felt that it was a bit too 'young' for him. His father also echoed the same concerns. Similarly, another father also felt that the performance was too young for his son, as he stated:

I thought it was a little bit young for Taikwando Kid if you see what I mean, sort of say 5, 6, 7ish, sort of that age.

(Dad of Taikwando Kid, male, aged 9)

We considered this feedback in amending the age group of children who participated in the main phase. We opened the performance to younger children (4–5 years) while we were still keen to offer the play to both older and younger children. Maybe the play was not age-appropriate for Taikwando Kid and therefore, he did not fully engage with the play. It is also possible that his reaction was affected by his personal condition. According to the link nurse the child had had a number of tests on that day and he was tired. Tests can become emotional moments that affect both the child and the family. However, Taikwando Kid and his father were very enthusiastic to see the performance. They also had the option to withdraw from the study or stop the performance at any stage but they did not. Although the play was too 'girly' for that boy, he enjoyed it and so did his dad. Taikwando Kid's dad said:

> Well, it was just you know, cos he [nods in direction of son] was happy watching it so that made me happy cos he was happy.
>
> (Dad of Taikwando Kid, male, aged 9)

The overall impact of the performance on each child varies because many factors influence their participation. Some of them we can understand and others are beyond our understanding. The most obvious is the physical condition of the child. The painful treatments, bad news from clinical results and the fear of the inevitable in some cases of terminal illness also influence the child's mood and affect the child emotionally in the difficult moment itself. Emotional stress, then, has implications on how they receive and respond to what is offered to them. There is no sense that these moments present children with problems that can be resolved through performance. However, there is evidence that critically ill children with emotional distress benefit from the presence of actors in hospitals. Evidence holds that our bedside theatre intervention carries some specific benefits for children in oncology. Four artists and a nurse recognize the importance of bedside performance and breathing for a child with terminal illness:

> It both pleased and humbled me to see how happy [child's name] was considering that she was recovering from chemotherapy. It showed me that these children are children and even through their illness they had found happiness and playfulness, like all children of their age.
>
> (Journal, 19 July 2013)

> Just as we were leaving his room he told us that he was going to practise the breathing exercises in the bath before bedtime. Hearing this was proof that what we were doing was in fact helping the children in the hospital.
>
> (Journal, 31 July 2013)

> We then got our opportunity to perform to a girl called Mary [pseudonym], her mum Alice [pseudonym] and Mary's friend David [pseudonym]. Mary was really responsive to the performances and was even showing the turtle how to do the breathing exercise. What impressed me was at the end of the story her friend, David, came back from the toilet, having missed the whole breathing exercise, and she even showed him how to do it with encouragement from Mr Turtle.
>
> (Journal, 19 July 2013)

The child was very interactive with the story from start to finish. As we left he informed us that he would intend to do his breathing in bed. This was most rewarding and showed the power of the performance.

(Journal, 19 July 2013)

Good to see the way the students captured his attention considering he is 2 years old. He flapped his arms around and mom states he does this when he is excited. The actors were able to adapt to his level and keep him interested throughout the performance.

(Nursery Nurse, June 2014)

The felt experience of relaxation and enjoyment during performance is certainly one of the beneficial roles of bedside theatre for children with cancer. But this does not come without continuous effort to adapt what the artists are doing to suit the individual needs of the child and their specific levels of low energy and mood. These are typical side effects of strong medication but they can also be caused by upsetting incidents in hospital life. The following incident illustrates the above and shows some of what happened when the artists visited the oncology unit in the hospital on a bad day.

It is 5 p.m. A boy in the oncology ward had passed away in the morning. The audience is a boy (aged 5) with leukaemia. He is in the same room – opposite beds – as the boy who died. Together with other children, parents and nurses from oncology, he had released balloons in the playground earlier in the afternoon (2.30 p.m.) in memory of that boy. Our audience member is now in his bed waiting for the scheduled performance. The artists are in the staff room with me. We are discussing the possibility of cancelling the performance but first we want to check with the child and the family. It is their choice to decide if they still want it and not ours. A link nurse speaks to the child and the family. She comes back saying, 'They want you to do it!' The artists feel that this will be a difficult one, difficult for the child and difficult for themselves. The artists and I have a conversation about their own feelings, emotions and needs. I ask them if they would be happy to do it and explained to them that they must take responsibility for their emotional wellbeing first. I say, 'You do not have to if you do not want to. We can always rearrange it with the nurse and come back for this child on a better day later this week'. They both reassure me that they are fine and they feel it is important to offer relaxation to a child who needs it most on a day like this. I admire them. They decide to enter the room together. This decision was probably based on their own need to face any challenges together. It was a clever decision that shows a sense of solidarity and a need to support each other in performance. Together they could use their intuition to feel the needs of the child. Together they could sense his availability or unavailability to participate in the performance. Together they could judge the moment better than doing it alone. Together they could improvise on the script to make the child feel comfortable within the play. Timmy and Rainbow walk into the room. I am standing outside the room filming. The two approach the child's bed. The atmosphere is heavy.

TIMMY: Hello [child's name]. I'm Timmy.
CHILD: *(Silence)*

RAINBOW: That's a nice Teddy Bear. It must be very soft! Do you sleep with him?

CHILD: *(Silence)*

RAINBOW: I sleep with a soft turtle. I bring her with me everywhere I go. I have it with me today. Do you want to see her?

CHILD: *(Nodding)*

RAINBOW: Do you think that Mr Turtle would like to come out, Timmy?

TIMMY: I think so, yes, but first I will play a tune for him. *(He plays his guitar)*

RAINBOW: *(Slowly, she takes Mr Turtle out of the basket moving it slightly to create the illusion that the turtle is dancing)*

CHILD: *(He is staring at the turtle but gives no verbal reply)*

RAINBOW: Mr Turtle is our friend. *(She animates the turtle and changes her voice)*

MR TURTLE: Hello, Teddy Bear. I am Mr Turtle. Nice to meet you!

CHILD: *(He is not responding verbally but he takes his Teddy Bear and moves it towards the turtle. Sad, the boy expresses his greeting through his Teddy Bear, shaking the bear's hand in response)*

MR TURTLE: Look Timmy, Teddy Bear is saying hello to me!

TIMMY: *(He is playing a musical tune while the turtle is dancing)* Would you like to dance, Mr Teddy Bear?

The artists also acknowledge that the invitation to explore ways of engaging the child through the use of Mr Turtle was tremendously helpful. In engaging with the turtle, there was more opportunity for the child to be carried away into the story and enjoy the performance.

> One child was particularly nervous [...] However, once the performance began he calmed down and, despite not being as responsive as the other children, did participate with the breathing exercises. [...] I believe that the puppet actually made him more comfortable watching the performance rather than just being spoken to by two performers.
>
> (Journal, 26 July 2013)

> He responded brilliantly and enjoyed the story a lot. At one point he even got his own toys involved!
>
> (Journal, 26 July 2013)

The incident shows how the artists responded to the difficult moment when they met with the child in an emotionally challenging atmosphere. Releasing balloons in memory of a child is in itself a strong emotional moment! It is a moment of right of ownership by the children in that ward. The child had the right to do with that experience what he wanted to do. That did not necessarily mean that the performance had to be cancelled or postponed for a 'better' day, but it meant that the artists had to look for ways to be together with the child in a sad situation. The boy in the incident above was obviously not in the mood to talk, but his sad mood did not prevent him from participating in his own way. When the artists seemed to be failing to connect directly with the child, they ingeniously used the soft toy to engage the child in an improvised play. Soft toys became communicators between the child and the artists. 'Indirect communication, perhaps using a doll or a soft toy, may be successful with the shy or wary child as this diffuses the focus from the child and introduces an element of play and therefore normality' (Burnard and Campling 1994: 162). Mr Turtle succeeded in diffusing the focus from the child and he diverted the child's attention from the sad incident that happened earlier that day to a joyful moment. Mr Turtle did to not let the child's mood affect his whole day. The performance was shorter than usual, as would be expected, but it worked successfully. The artist invited the child to participate in fiction through Mr Turtle. The child accepted the invitation to participate through his Teddy Bear. The two toys danced for a while in a humming tune to help the child and the artists to calm the tension and relax after the stress of the day. To the eyes of an outsider this 'performance' would be a failure, but to those who understand the distinctiveness of the clinical context, this performance was an achievement. For the child, his response was not the result of refusing to participate but the result of sensitive handling of a situation that involves a critically ill child.

Another example of successful communication between a child and Mr Turtle is an incident that took place in intensive care. Paediatric Intensive Care Units (PICU) in hospitals aim to provide children with the highest level of medical support, intensive therapies, continuous monitoring of things such as heart rate, and certain medication. Some children stay for a day but others stay for weeks or months after surgery, which might be a frightening experience for kids. We visited a boy, who had been in PICU for a week, and his mother.

It is 5.15 p.m. The room is different to other rooms in the hospital. Because the child needs extra-special care and support with breathing and feeding, there are machines and equipment around his bed. The room is quite hot, possibly because of all the equipment, and extremely small. There is only one recliner chair in the room for the parent/carer in case they want to sleep in the room overnight. The space between the child's bed and the chair is limited. Because the space is so small I decide to stay outside. Only the two artists go in. The door is closed but I can film through the glass. I am restricted to film without sound but I am hoping to capture the child's facial expressions and physical reactions to the performance on my camera. Despite the serious condition of the child there are no signs of tiredness on his face, no signs of withdrawal, but he looks bored and inactive. I cannot hear what they are saying but I am in a position to see that the pace of the performance is slower than usual. The artists explained to me later that they gave the child time to get used to their presence in the small room and let him dictate the pace.

The two artists said:

It was like performance in a submarine. No space, no air. It was such a confined and private space.

(Journal, 5 August 2011)

I really enjoyed performing by the bedside because it made the performance more intimate and 'special' for the child and it contributed to the exercise of imagination. This is why space was not a concern for me.

(Journal, 5 August 2011)

Artists also report that they developed skills in physical movement through paying attention to the child. They learned that 'what they communicate about their characters depends upon how they move; they seek some conscious control over the body-image they project' (McConachie 2013: 345). They learned to recognize where and how to stand, when and how to shift from one side of the bed to the other without blocking the nurse's way for emergencies and without invading the child's private space. The artists paid respect to the child's privacy. The child was given options to choose the distance between themselves and the artists before the beginning of the play. The child's agreement removes tension and so offers less chance for the child to feel 'attacked' in their private bed space. Although it does not completely resolve the 'problem' of space with all that is encountered, the intimacy of the space leads to the emergence of a particularly intimate performance. And so, this is what happened in PICU that day.

During the breathing practice, the child uses his Lion (a soft toy) to interact with the turtle. Together the Lion and Mr Turtle are having a shared experience of breathing and moments of relaxation. The child repeats the breathing with the Lion each time Mr Turtle demonstrates it. I am watching from a distance through the camera and I can see two soft toys becoming the protagonists of the play. The child is using the Lion as his extended body, letting him play from behind the protection of this toy. He is communicating through his toy. It seems to me that he is using the Lion to set the limits between the artists and himself. He chooses to be involved indirectly. By doing this, he probably feels more secure to participate and through participation, he is finding a sense of achievement and fulfilment.

Reflecting on the incidents in oncology and PICU, I realize that our one-to-one performance set the context for active participation. The success of *telling* the story together is the result of the child and artist's willing collaboration in the process of the performance. In both cases, the child-patient stepped out of his role as 'the ill person' and took over a more active role. Through performance he became a participant, a 'puppet player', and this is not a small thing for a critically ill child. The incident in PICU engages me deeply because it tells the story of a child who has been isolated in one small hospital room surrounded by equipment for over a week. It is the story of a child who knows that he is ill and sees his ill body supported by machines. It is the story of a child who cannot do things as other children can, a child who has adopted the attitude 'I cannot' and 'I am not able to' because I am stuck in bed. It is the story of an isolated, lonely and bored child who finds a window to 'escape' from the heat and the noise of mechanical ventilation in the room. It is the story of a boy who uses his imagination to relax by a calm pond in the park. This story highlights the value of Theatre for Children in Hospitals. It shows how theatre can create a safe atmosphere where the child becomes active and creative. As theatre in hospitals means more than simply offering entertainment, but rather is a striving for child empowerment in illness and improved wellbeing, this incident is evidence of empowerment and activity. This experience may have not changed the child's life but it offered him an opportunity to be actively and interactively responsive to a theatrical event in the midst of the endless passive, lonely and boring moments of hospital life.

Clearly much of what is quoted in this chapter demonstrates that particular emotions emerge into certain kinds of situations in hospitals. These situations are challenging for the child and also for the artist. There are moments that require that the artist remains calm and professional in order to distance themselves from the emotional tensions involved in hospital life. The incident below illustrates how particularly demanding it is to remain in-role during moments of distress. An artist reflects back on one of these moments:

> When we first went into the room the child was quite shy and introverted but did seem to want to engage in the story despite this. We were interrupted by a nurse who came in to inject his medicine through an IV drip. He did not want this to happen and became very distressed and distracted from the performance. We tried to maintain the performance; however, he was not responsive to this and was becoming more and more upset so we left the room until the nurse had left. This happened two more times and each time the child became increasingly upset and angry with the nurses as he did not want to have the drugs. He always wanted us to return to the room to continue with the story but he was increasingly upset each time we went back in. It was difficult for me as a performer to stay in-role throughout the whole experience as at times it felt inappropriate to continue as he was clearly distressed and disinterested in watching the performance and it was hard to detach myself personally from wanting to physically help him outside of the dramatic context.
>
> (Journal, 4 July 2014)

According to a nurse, the mum had to leave the hospital to look after her newborn baby and, having no other choice, she left the child in the hands of experienced nursing staff. The artist above came close to how the child felt: alone. The artist felt sympathy, which is different to empathy in the form of compassion (Gilbert 2009). Sympathetic feelings are automatic to the situation. She did not put any special effort into connecting emotionally with the child and feeling sorry for him. It is possible that her motherly instinct was alarmed and unsurprisingly, she wanted to help the child outside the dramatic context. This was a sympathetic response from the artist to the situation but the artist knew that she had to keep a professional distance from the incident. There is no doubt that sympathetic feelings can make it difficult for the artist to remain in role throughout the performance. Artists can easily be 'knocked out' of the dramatic convention and out of characterization. It is only human to want to 'rescue' a child from a difficult situation, the pain and the despair. The artist in this example knew that she was not meant to be there 'for' the child (sympathy) but 'with' the child (empathy). Her commitment was to be there in-role and although she found it not an easy situation to handle, she remained in-role. The artists must be clear about their role in healthcare. No matter what the situation is, the artist's role is to remain in-role throughout the performance but it does not always follow that the performance should continue. Despite the 'must' of remaining in-role, sometimes the performance has to end. The artist here could not ignore the child's desire to have the bedside entertainment. It did not feel right to reject him. It was the artist's personal choice to continue the performance when the treatment was complete. However, I understand that situations like this in hospitals can be a great challenge for the artist because they are confronted with experiences involving distressed children. How the situation is going to end is often unpredictable. For the artist in our example, the ending was a great reward.

> However, by the end of the performance he did join in with the breathing exercises and was happy to take the card with the picture of the turtle and the breathing exercises on it. I felt that at that point the performance was most effective as we could link what we were trying to do with his personal experiences by telling him to try the breathing exercises the next time his medication was being administered. I think that although he did not get the full experience and did not possibly take from the performance everything that we intended, I do think that us being there after the medication was administered was beneficial for him. He was on his own, upset and unwell, and I believe that having us as a distraction from the situation he was experiencing did make a small difference to what he was going through.
>
> (Journal, 4 July 2014)

In a way, there is an indication of recognition that the presence of the artists in the room was positive to the child. This is how it was perceived by the artist. It is possible, however, that the artist reflected on the event from her own need to make a positive meaning out of an emotionally challenging experience for her. It is difficult to diagnose the truth in her reflection but this does not make her judgement untruthful. I was present to witness the child's interaction with the artist. I saw his change of mood for the better when the performance was delivered to him. He was uplifted and he smiled!

However, I continue asking myself if we, as artists, always know how to protect ourselves from emotions. The artists sometimes throw themselves into the deep end of emotional situations taking place in hospitals while waiting to see how the event is going to end. The artist who experienced the above incident was courageous. She did not avoid the task (though this is not always a recommended practice). She waited to see how she would 'survive' the challenge of being there in the room while both she and the child were finding it hard to connect with the fictional. My concern was that the conditions were far too challenging to maintain the aesthetic of theatre. The child for most of the performance remained out of reach. Although the artist tried to connect, the child could not stay in the fiction for long. In the absence of a theatrical atmosphere created by light, sound and music, and in the presence of emotional tension and fear of the treatment, it was very challenging to establish, maintain and reinforce the fictional. The child's anxiety, the need to continue with the treatment and the artist's difficulty to remain in-role were all factors that caused the abandonment of the dramatic frame. I am aware that there is no absolute 'perfection' in performing in healthcare, simply because there is no absolute perfection in anything we do. We are just humans and it is wise to be able to admit it. It would be unwise to be unsatisfied with what I have witnessed and how I have learned to be *with* and connect *with* the child professionally.

We also learned that hospitals are spaces with distractions, constraints and demands which can affect the quality of the performance and the impact of the work on child wellbeing.

> The biggest difficulty for me in the play was coping with the noise in the room as the TV was turned up very loud and music began to play on a Tablet. Further issues emerged such as being able to signal the Rainbow to enter due to noise making it hard to hear. I believed the entrance in this performance did not go as clean as it should have done but the boy still responded well to the story on the whole when we left him to his relaxation and returned to the cardiac ward.
>
> (Journal, 26 July 2013)

This quote demonstrates how noise in the hospital environment causes distraction in performance. Reactions by the children to noise will often be followed by tension, bad moods and loss of concentration on the play. Noise is not the only distraction. Visitors often create problems for concentration on the performance and affect child participation. An artist comments:

> I really enjoyed performing on the [cardiac] ward but did find that the amount of adults visiting the child that we were performing to were a distraction/hindrance for the child in the sense that she was always looking for reassurance from the adults about getting involved with the performance. Sometimes she did seem slightly embarrassed at having the whole attention on her but I do feel that this was aided by the presence of so many adults around the bed.
>
> (Journal, 30 July 2013)

Of course, what the artist describes occurs partly because the focus of the adults is on the child and the focus of the child is not on the play but the adults. In other cases, the problems arise from parents who do not collaborate with the artist. Another artist describes a situation around the child's bed:

> One girl had her family all around her. There were seven adults and three children so we had to ask if some of the adults wouldn't mind waiting away from the bedside because the performance is for the child. I found this performance one of the most difficult. The child's mother got her iPhone out and began filming the performance without our

permission. She kept holding the phone in front of the child's face distracting her from the performance. We managed to keep the child engaged for a while and she joined in with the breathing, despite her mother stopping us mid-performance to ask if the boy's name in the story could be changed to the name of her son, which threw us a bit because we tried to stay in-role but it was difficult, so we said in-role, 'Oh this boy is called Timmy, remember he told you when he came in from the rain'. The mother was difficult. Then because we hadn't given her what she wanted she decided to talk to her sister about how the child was bored and tired.

(Journal, 26 July 2013)

Another report by an artist offers an example of parental interference with a negative impact on child participation during the performance.

The child was watching a video on a phone, playing with toys throughout, and the father was talking over the performance also. It made the performance the hardest yet as the child would smile at us if we said something that they liked. At one point, I was considering stopping the performance but felt it was worth it to carry on until the end. This child did require medical intervention during the performance so was also being spoken to by the nurses, again ad-lib was added in here to accommodate what was going on.

(Journal, 12 June 2013)

There is little that an artist can do when a parent has little respect for the artist and no understanding of intervention's effects. It is a case of performance that is attended by people who know nothing of what to expect from the performance or who do not know how to participate.

On ward 12 (cardiac) in the evening it was great to have the space for the opening before channelling all attention to the child. They had many family members watching which could have added to the tension of the child seeking permission from them every time we asked the child to breathe with the turtle.

(Journal, 12 June 2013)

The above quotes show that there can be some tension between the artist and the parent/ family who attend the performance with the child. Performances can be difficult when the parents participate in the performance. Those parents who want to participate actively in performance often show an authoritarian behaviour as if they seek to control the situation. Those children who do not know how to participate and ask permission from their parents to respond are sometimes children who are shy and non-confident, children who do not like to be the centre of attention, and children who feel uncomfortable in the presence of strangers and safe in the presence of family members, or children who are scared.

I witnessed the incident on ward 12 (cardiac). The child attended bedside theatre while some visitors were present. She shared reactions with them, asking her parents questions about the colours of the Rainbow, and where to go with her. Communication with family members and visitors during the performance could be an indication of enjoyment. However, on ward 12 the child–parent communication interrupted the child–artist relationship. The artists intended to establish communication with the child but that was difficult because the child was not focused on the artist. It became difficult for the artist to connect with the child because the child's attention was directed at the parent. It also became difficult for the child to engage with fiction and 'escape' through fiction because their attention was distracted by the adults' suggestions about what to say and what to do. The continuous communication with the parent kept the child with her feet on the ground, in reality. It constantly reminded the child of her role as a patient who is attending an event. What the parent did by interfering in the performance was to limit the possibility for transition from reality to a fictional situation. But theatre is intended to engage the child in fiction as much as possible. Thus, the artist aims to help the child make the most of the opportunity to engage with the dramatic. Therefore, they invite the child to share ownership of the play, and make a personal contribution to it, hoping that the child will respond to the play and not to their parents. This ambition sometimes fails and in itself it is frustrating. The artist learns from it that TCH requires focus, synergy of participation and effort to trust each other in the process of performance.

Through the years of witnessing parental pain caused by their children's illness, I have come to accept that the parent/carers deserve some level of involvement in TCH. They are welcome to be present during the show. They are encouraged to enjoy watching the bedside performance and sharing the experience with the child after the intervention. However, they should have minimum involvement during performance in order to let the child engage with the artist in a synergistic relationship in a fictional situation without guidance. The value of synergy in the process to those involved encourages the artist to explore new approaches to playing with sick children in one-to-one performance, to find methods to make the child more synergistic and confident in playing and more attentive to the performance. It also encourages the artist to negotiate personal meaning, to discover more about who they are in relation to others. The challenge for the artist is to respond to the child without ignoring the parents being present as an indirect audience. The challenge for the parent is to attend the performance as an indirect audience and free the child from their inspection during performance. Both the artist and the parent need to be aware of each other's roles in the moment and act with responsibility, respect and discretion. Is it too much to ask for awareness in the moment from parents who go through difficulties because of their child's condition needs some answers? I have always believed that the parents are subject to change for the better if they are educated. Ignorance and lack of information about children's health, education and progress can be the cause of many troubles, fears and anxieties in life. Therefore, it would be worth trying to inform the parents about their role in the performance, what is required from them to do and what is expected of them not to do. Such information could be included in the leaflets that the artists hand in to the nurses who, then, distributes them to all patients and their families prior to the performance. Ideally, the artists would have an opportunity to meet with the parents in a hospital room for a few minutes to talk to them about their intervention, answer any possible questions, gain the parents' trust and help their understanding of TCH. Investment in human relationships makes the formal informal, the general personal, the unknown familiar and the challenge less impossible. Practically, this is possible with the help of link nurses, members of the arts department and play specialists who will arrange for this informal training.

Another welcome finding from the study is that the artist learns to work for the community. This requires an expansion of the artist's skills through experience. The artist follows a process of personal learning about self through audiences through theatre.

> To be able to give a child a smile is priceless and should make more people want to volunteer. It was an experience and journey that I may never get again, to be able to entertain a child who may have never even visited a theatre and bring something to help them relax but at the same time entertain them was an amazing opportunity which I will never forget. Those children have been through so much, so young that it makes you grateful for what you have and encourages me to want to give more. I was thrilled to be given a badge with 'community artist' on it! I felt professional! However, it made me realize that being an artist within the community and hospital setting is important as you are providing an experience for others that no one else is!
>
> (Questionnaire, 30 July 2013)

> I love to get involved in community projects, it's a wonderful way to grow as a person and give to your community. My role as community artist is to do the best to educate, entertain and tell your community beneficial stories.
>
> (Questionnaire, 5 August 2013)

The balance between aiming at professional experience and giving something to the community was achieved for most artists. That the artist gave entertainment and relaxation to the children and their families is a clear indication of their ability to sense the interrelation of both roles: artist and citizen – perhaps above all being a human being. This is a sophisticated element of TCH work, and with less careful training for the artists on the concept of community the professional development could easily have resulted in some underestimation of the purpose of TCH as a community activity. The first-hand experience of performing in hospitals appeared to be in itself a great stimulus for the artist to continue their efforts in creating and promoting TCH.

> When I first volunteered I think that I was not as aware of the benefits for future development of this project and others like it but now I am really looking forward to being involved in similar projects in the future.
>
> (Questionnaire, 30 July 2013)

After my visit to the hospital I see that community artist is a very important role and one that I have great pride in having. I can contribute to the benefits the children may gain from bedside theatre.

(Questionnaire, 24 July 2013)

From the enthusiasm of the responses in the questionnaires it is obvious that the majority of the artists were clearly engaged with volunteering and enjoyed their participation in the project. The experience they gained was insightful to the way they were seeing their role as artists in healthcare before they participated in the project. There is evidence on camera that the artists treated children as the audience but there is also evidence from their journals that they referred to children as patients, an ill audience, and not as a theatre audience. The identity of the patient overpowered the role of spectator. Perhaps, in some cases, the messages of the clinical environment, including the images of children in bed, the sight of machines and equipment, were too 'medical', too dominant. As a result, the artist experiences the relationship with the child as one of artist–patient/spectator. Even so, the 'artist–patient/spectator' connection offers the artist the possibility of discovering a way of stepping out of traditional relationships with audiences and turning towards new experiences and skills including the ability to use theatre to improve child wellbeing. Practice proves that the artists felt positively motivated by those images to assist those in need by using theatre creatively. They were proud of being able to outreach to children's audiences in hospitals.

The artists' replies also provide us with a context for discussion about the development of volunteering artists in healthcare. Through volunteering, the artist tests artistic forms, strategies and techniques such as storytelling, short games and intimate performances with audiences. Through these and other strategies volunteer artists are led to do things in hospital wards that they would not have the opportunity to try in the studio, things that they would not have expected to work with audiences, things that surprise themselves. Verbal communications, trust-building dialogues, improvisation based on the moods and needs of the audience, are a few of the things that artists experience with audiences in hospital in ways that it would not have been possible to experience by reading texts. At the same time as the volunteer artist is learning skills, we should acknowledge that they need a continuing supported motivation before, during and after TCH performance. Preparation includes the ability to inspire them in rehearsals; to enable them to value the learning experience as important to their personal and professional development and employability; and to provide them with information to understand the process, such as a clear plan of rehearsals and performances. Supported motivation during and after performances involves emotional support, de-briefing, excellent organization of scheduled performances, and the provision of publicity opportunities (photo-calls, websites, local newspapers, etc.) and opportunities of networking.

One of the successful factors in supporting the artists' volunteering was the close collaboration with the arts department at the hospital. The arts manager will promote volunteering to the ward managers, the link nurses and the play specialists. Without the arts manager's support even volunteering can be difficult. Thus, in many hospitals the arts manager is the link between the volunteer artist and the audience. In the absence of arts managers in some hospitals, organizational problems in booking theatre companies arise, especially if the arts department is inactive or if the hospital has urged its closure due to managerial decisions related to small budgets and cuts of expenditure. From working with NHS hospitals, it is clear that the reduction of arts managers' posts reduces the number of art activities in the hospital. In some hospitals, there will be a play specialist or a lead nurse to operate as a point of contact. The artist can begin to link and associate with these people in advance to secure a volunteer place and enroll for an induction in the host organization.

The study reveals that where arts managers and experienced staff are involved in the coordination of the TCH project, the implementation of the project is improved. More parent/carers show interest in the performance and more children receive it. This does not come without effort. Those hospital staff taking part, especially if it is a new experience for them, have to be encouraged to stay present during performance and gain a personal opinion about the intervention. I did not take the hospital staff's understanding of the importance of TCH for granted. I had to invite arts managers, nurses and play specialists into the ward to watch children participating in the performance from a distance. At times, I had to gently persuade hospital staff into watching the show, and make up their own minds about the benefits of bedside theatre for the children. To establish a positive relationship with the hospital staff, to overcome their possible reservations and inhibitions about the effects of TCH on children, and to create an atmosphere of collaboration, I involved them in the event as indirect spectators. The following quotes show that hospital staff can become engaged with the work and that they develop an appreciation of TCH:

Breathing with Love worked well on the children's ward and was warmly welcomed by staff, patients and parents/visitors. It was suitable for children ages 2+. We found that the oldest child who wanted to take part was 11yrs. I watched every performance and was impressed with the way the artists were able to adapt their performance to each individual patient. In hospitals nothing is straightforward, which was apparent on a number of occasions with children who were upset, in pain, shy and agitated. On the last visit the performers saw a 2-year-old boy with learning difficulties and hearing and vision issues. He was also in traction, which meant he was lying down at an awkward angle. The performance took place in the playroom rather than the bedside. The boy was very excited during the performance and pointed a lot to the performers and made lots of happy noises. The performance confirmed how important it is to provide fun and enjoyable activities to patients in hospital to help distract and lower their anxiety. Often there is a lot of activity on the wards and patients are required to have different checks by nursing staff, generally the nursing staff leave any interruptions until after the performance as they understand how beneficial these activities are to patients. The show fits well into ward life. Before CADLab started at Heartlands Hospital, discussions were had between various members of staff including matrons and play specialists to decide what time of the day would be most appropriate for the performances to take place, between 3 and 5 p.m. was agreed most suitable. The benefits of the performance are that breathing techniques help the children to relax, which leads to a less stressful time in hospital for patients, parents and staff. Practically, sometimes there are other patients in the bays who may not want to take part and/or are maybe asleep, which may restrict the volume of the performance. If there are a lot of visitors by patients' beds sometimes there may not be enough performance space. The CADLab project has been received extremely well at Heartlands Hospital by all concerned. Children have benefited hugely by the relaxing, gentle and thoughtful way the students have performed. Each child is an individual and the students adjust every performance to each individual's need. All the staff have been impressed by the professionalism of the artists and the overall reaction by the patients and parents. One parent suggested that some songs might be 'a nice touch', [...] a nice idea; however, they would need to be of a slow, relaxing, almost lullaby style. The hospital is currently in discussions with CADLab over future projects.

(Arts Manager at Heartlands – Questionnaire, September 2014)

It was my first experience of the bedside theatre today, and as a staff member I thought that it was excellent. One patient in particular that a staff nurse and myself had identified reaped benefits as she was waiting all morning for the actors to arrive. She had got out of bed into a chair so she was comfortable and smiled throughout the performance. This was a patient that had been very sick and had had an operation the previous day. The performance was just the right length of time for herself and her mother to enjoy after a traumatic time for the family. Thanks for visiting us.

(Nursery Nurse – Questionnaire, April 2014)

Great session. It was good to see two very different children taking part in the performances. The students were able to adapt the drama to suit the child's needs which in my opinion was the loveliest thing to see. One child even moved closer to the actors because from her facial expressions she was really in the zone of the performance and really enjoyed the story. Well done all.

(Nursery Nurse, Arts and Health Monthly Report, Heartlands Hospital, Heart of England NHS Foundation Trust, June 2014)

The feedback expresses a growing appreciation of bedside methodology but it also recognizes that there are benefits for the nurses as their awareness grows about the role of the arts in healthcare. For example, while TCH, particularly bedside theatre, offers each child an opportunity to contribute to the performance that takes place, it also offers nurses an opportunity to discover more about the audience's abilities to be playful and creative while being ill. This also relates to how TCH artists challenge the healthcare culture for change, in ways such as breaking the hospital routine; symbolizing the space as a dramatic location; and encouraging participation and dialogue. The nurses who may be present during TCH projects observe how the child is participating in TCH and can use what they discover about the children's feelings and abilities to treat them accordingly and support them better, more compassionately, as patients. Practically, the nurse can learn about the child from watching the child responding to the play and use such discovery to consider how their patients feel and behave. For the nurse, one of the benefits of TCH could be to help develop awareness of the patients' personalities and needs for special care. My discussion of the study has narrowly focused on the partnership between the academic institution that employed the researchers and the healthcare system, but its implications can extend to patient participation in creative activities and their satisfaction during treatment and recovery.

> It has not only been fun and creative. We know that it [bedside theatre] is researched and that there is evidence and we know that no harm is coming to the child. We know that it has improved the overall experience of the child and family in hospital. The partnership between [hospital] and [university] was a new one for us and it has been great in improving that understanding between us of the importance of health and wellbeing of the child in hospital and the use of theatre in that context. There has been a sharing of knowledge between the two organizations and that has worked both ways, both from the academic institution to here, and just bringing theatre to the environment, and also the sharing and the learning of the project back into the classroom.
>
> (Lead for patient experience, Birmingham Children's Hospital, June 2013)

Using this feedback, I seek to extensively engage and connect university students, artists, audiences and health professionals with arts-participatory TCH projects in the future. Such connectedness aims to increase collaboration between organizations; increase the sharing of knowledge and expertise; and contribute to an awareness of theatre practice as a necessary component of child healthcare in hospitals in the United Kingdom and abroad. It is hoped that this will lead to the development of more 'bilingual' theatre and wellbeing projects that will not only represent the responses of the audience, the artists and the health professionals but will also act as a catalyst for creative individual and group projects that foster creative theatre practice in healthcare. This is something that needs further investigation in order to judge the effectiveness of partnership between theatre and health organizations.

When the artists were asked if the provision of TCH could become a constant provision for children in hospitals, the great majority of them replied positively to this prospect. They showed great enthusiasm to continue visiting children in hospitals and recommending TCH to other drama students who were undertaking the course. However, there was one participant who struck me with his answer. He wrote:

> I didn't want to believe in it [TCH] because it seemed unnatural to perform in hospitals, but I do now. [...] I was so pleased to discover that children, like myself, were interested in what we did. I feel I have experienced so much, I have learned so much about theatre

and human relationships [...] but I became convinced and still am that theatre in hospital is a luxury.

(Questionnaire, 3 August 2013)

This artist appears to be saying that TCH should not be considered a right for the children. How is the artist going to deal with the anxiety of their work being perceived as a luxury, a low priority in clinical settings? It is true that many artists have mentioned the practical challenges that they have experienced in attempting to perform on hospital wards. I have personally admitted the complexities that I have experienced in attempting to connect with the NHS. This does not mean that encountering difficulties in performing in hospitals is a reason to disregard the benefits of TCH for children and their families. It is also not a reason to halt efforts to prove that TCH should be integrated in hospital life on a constant basis. But this has of course to do with the right for healthcare and recovery and what is seen as 'luxury'. In health systems that choose to ignore or neglect the benefits of arts in healthcare, TCH is likely to be seen as a non-essential activity. Some of these considerations may bring smiles to the faces of nurses who recognize the truth in these words but also acknowledge the practical challenges of integrating arts projects in the busy hospital-ward timetables. We need to consider the challenges of bringing the arts on-site in health environments but we should not stop fighting for a sincere recognition of the arts as important bases towards progression in healthcare provision. It is in the nature of the arts to reflect, portray and, in some cases, interrogate society. Theatre is a mirror in which societies, communities and people observe their reflection: the beauty and the ugliness, the wealth and the poverty, the achievements and the shame, the pride and the wounds. In this sense, theatre is everyone's right. Every citizen should have the right to see and gain insight into life. Every child should have the right to become involved in theatre as an audience, either in the theatre or in the hospital. This process gives us an opportunity to watch things from a different angle and, hopefully, become more skilled in remaining calm and positive during the good and the bad times of life. TCH is a right for every child as it is for every artist.

Summarizing the main key learning points from the bedside theatre methodology,

- There are positive effects of using a participatory, child-centred bedside theatre approach, helping the child achieve a sense of normality of life in hospital, and resulting in an improved wellbeing.
- The strength of TCH is a special type of bedside one-to-one and moment-by-moment audience participation.
- Successful audience participation assists children to regain a sense of confidence and a sense of control over their experience while they are in hospital.
- Successful audience participation distracts children from clinical stress and diverts their minds to more enjoyable experiences through theatre.
- Successful audience participation exchanges the identity of the passive child-patient with an active and cheerful child-participant in theatre.

- Bedside theatre interventions are highly appreciated by the child and the family for their intimacy and effectiveness on the child's positive mood.
- Bedside theatre interventions, incorporating relaxation practices, are highly suitable for children with critical illness.
- Relaxation practices that are incorporated in bedside performance are beneficial to the child in preparing for an operation and taking their medication.
- The use of soft toys during performance increases the communication between the child and the artist and encourages the child to be active while they are in bed.
- Interaction between the child and the artist within the fictional is an investment for better communication between the child and their parents during their stay in hospital.
- A flexible structure of bedside performance enables the child and the artist to walk the journey of imagination together and creates opportunities for positive interaction between the two of them.
- TCH is effective in breaking the child's isolation and boredom and bringing joy to the child in hospital.
- TCH is effective in offering the child moments of calmness and maintained optimism.
- TCH makes children happy and by extension their parents, by seeing their children smiling and having fun.
- For TCH to continue growing, a certain commitment and a devotion to theatre practice in hospitals is necessary.
- For TCH to continue growing, governments and health systems need to invest more in patient wellbeing. They should realize the importance of the arts in healthcare and support the accommodation of art projects within their operation with better commitment in the future.

In this chapter, I presented and analysed my TCH bedside theatre practice as research methodology based on collected views from the children, their parent/carers and the artists who were involved in the study, as well as on personal observation and conversations with hospital staff. Extensive space was given to the description of incidents that took place in hospitals, including dialogues between the artist and the child, quotes from the responses that we collected from the children and their families pre- and post-performance, and quotes from the artists who evaluated practice from their perspective. I have examined bedside theatre itself and described it as a participatory theatrical synergistic process. From this proposition, I have asked what aspects of the practice that is involved in this study become opportunities for entertainment, distraction from the experience of illness, relaxation and opportunities to have fun and socialize with others in the hospital. I also asked myself how this happens in aesthetic terms; what involvement in the fictional may feel like for the child and the artist; how the ownership of the event is shared between the two; and how the role of the patient changes into the role of the audience. I asked the children as direct audiences, the parent/carers as indirect audiences and the artists as vital components of the TCH practice, to describe their experience and express their views about the benefits and challenges of taking theatre bedside.

There were no easy interpretations of the participants' responses to our practice, but the style of the bedside one-to-one intervention supported the children in re-winning a lost sense of enjoyment, confidence, trust and ways of 'being' present in their illness without despair. The evidence creates the possibility for the artist in healthcare and for the healthcare practitioner to envisage together the kind of art and the kind of healthcare system they want to be a part of in the future. I would like to believe that this evidence contributes to the better understanding of children's worlds when they are in hospital and the role of theatre in improving their hospital experience. The study reflects my view that ill children are fit to evaluate TCH practice because they are the audience for whom it is created and offered. Obviously, more research is needed about the benefits and complexities of children and actors interacting in performance within hospital contexts, but the bedside theatre study illustrates how TCH as a methodology can potentially support and comfort children in hospital.

The bedside theatre practice that I have critically discussed here offers something that the healthcare system appears to appreciate but has not the means to provide on its own. The artist faces a mission to offer children the benefits of emotional, physical and social wellbeing that doctors and nurses might find hard to provide as individuals from a completely different background, and with different roles and responsibilities to the artists. The bedside theatre study also made a unique contribution to the professional and personal development of the artist who experiments with different approaches, improvises with the unknown, and performs to children in particularly difficult conditions. This reactive response to the uncertainty that actors experience in hospitals suggests a new possibility for their work – it is possible that they will learn to embrace the unexpected and become better aware of the conditions in hospitals. Part of this learning can inform the development of new TCH projects and new ways of connecting and working with hospital staff. The artist might, then, want to incorporate this experience in their lives as a useful lesson of patience and flexibility.

Chapter Three

TCH as a choice: 'I want to make a difference!'

A philosophical approach to TCH

In this book so far I have examined some of the ways that an understanding of the nature and significance of bedside theatre for children in hospital can help the reader see the potential of TCH, and consequently do more to contribute to its growth. Chapter Two provided space to discuss the artists' perspective of developing TCH practice and what they think TCH means to them. This 'meaning' is easier to describe by using the artists' responses to performances. This third chapter returns to the theme of 'meaning'. It is about the personal choice of the artist to explore the meaning and importance of their role in the community in relation to the concepts of happiness, acceptance, empathy and compassion, and the use of theatre in that context. Finding personal meaning in TCH will help artists to give their art a significant purpose. This chapter offers the artists who may become involved in TCH another, more philosophical, psychological and spiritual dimension to their role, without which their mission in child healthcare cannot be fully appreciated.

When the artists in this study were asked what their role in healthcare is, they responded with great enthusiasm about their desire to make a positive difference in the lives of children in hospital. There was no, 'It will look good on my CV. Employers love community experience'. There was no, 'I don't know why I volunteer, and I don't have the answers to these children's problems'. There was no, 'Children in hospital are suffering and we come to heal them'. There was no, 'I come to solve children's problems with pre-decided solutions' or 'I am here to save them'. Instead, the artists know that they are coming as participants in theatre and outsiders to hospital life. They desire to give something back to the community but they do not necessarily aspire to change the world, although they start to understand that they can explore the child's world through the art form. In fact, they know that they are not drama therapists, or healers, or evangelists, and they know that they have no right to claim therapeutic powers. They are artists and as artists, they need to understand the complexities of the art that happens in clinical contexts. Complexities relate to illness that is threatening the wellbeing of children, illness that is putting the wellbeing of families at risk. It would be unwise to ignore the particular context of illness within which TCH develops. It would not be sensible to avoid the discussion about the artist's intentions, the journey they travel in healthcare and their personal growth in relation to their understanding of illness and wellness. Indeed, we should make an effort to understand the demands of the context on our artwork and the difficulties of interacting with audiences who are suffering with illness. It is part of the artist's journey to understand the meaning of theatrical experience and the core of the human experience in hospitals.

There is a series of questions for artists to use in thinking about their responsibilities when producing TCH. These are some of them:

Can illness be seen as part of the journey of life and the process of change? Does TCH practice require the artist to have a warm and compassionate heart, and if so can this warmth be put into caring during the performance? Does TCH create opportunities for the artist to experience happiness and fulfilment? How do artists view their responsibilities in interacting with children as audiences who are feeling unwell? Do we really know that artists develop empathy in being present with children in performance?

What it means to be happy as an artist and to aim at happiness through the artwork has not always been easy to state. However, I have learned to accept that exploring happiness and wellbeing together is a great opportunity to negotiate personal meaning in the arts – a process of using theatre to learn about self through others who suffer with illness. This learning I share here as a way of encouraging the reader to explore their relationship with audiences in hospital further, and to better position their work in relation to the context within which they perform. If one does accept that it is beneficial for artists in healthcare to know about happiness, should there be a canon of using certain theories?

Aristotle

There are several theories of happiness introduced worldwide, but I use Aristotle's theory of *eudaimonia* (Barnes 1984) to start the discussion. A modern translation of *eudaimonia* could be 'flourishing' or 'doing well' or 'being well' or 'being happy' or 'perfection' (Jackson, R. A. 2007). Aristotle argues that it is possible to experience an all-inclusive sense of happiness that relates to *eudaimonia*. He identifies happiness in the light of excellence both in terms of intellectual and human goodness.

If happiness is activity in accordance with excellence, it should be in accordance with the highest excellence; and this will be that of the best thing in us. Whether it be intellect or something else that is this element which is thought to be our natural ruler and guide and to take thought of things noble and divine, whether it be itself also divine or almost the most divine element in us, the activity of this in accordance with its proper excellence will be complete happiness.

(Aristotle 350 BCE: Book I, 7.11–18)

In Barnes's translation of *The Complete Works of Aristotle* (1984), it becomes clear that Aristotle's perception of happiness is not simply what is enjoyable, be it bodily pleasures or that which brings emotional joy and satisfaction. Happiness is more of a gift that one may experience through being guided by what is good inside him and also by acting for the good.

Aristotle distinguishes activities in respect of goodness and badness. Worthy activities are good and bring an element of excellence and unworthy activities are bad and do not enable and lead to the good (Barnes 1984: 1858). Speaking of good and bad activities, the same activity can be perceived as good or bad by different people; the same things please some people and discomfort others, but what matters is the good intention of a worthy activity. The good intention comes from within a person and can target others in both private and public life, although not all well-intended activities produce good results. However, my understanding is that Aristotle's happiness does not depend on the judgement of what is good and what is bad. Rather, he encourages excellence in activities and believes that excellence can only be claimed as a result when it is shared in society. We are happy when our actions are well chosen and when they are characterized by a certain 'rightness' or appropriateness, which for Aristotle is virtuous and ordered towards some interaction with others.

In Aristotle's work, I see a practical wisdom in developing one's personal growth in harmony with the community and not simply as an individual. Our understanding of how to become virtuous is not an individual but rather a collective, social process. Aristotle's *eudaimonia* embraces an element of discovery into how we can reach our own potential in private life but as we engage in this process, we find ourselves associated with others and we realise that the road towards *eudaimonia* cannot be walked alone. According to Gallagher, Lopez and Preacher (2009), the eudaimonic model of wellbeing has an intrapersonal focus (Ryff 1989), but from Aristotle's perspective, goodness is only understood as an action of generosity and kind sharing in the social world. *Eudaimonia* is, then, extended to whether, how and to what degree individuals overcome challenges of social integration, coherence and acceptance and how they function in interaction with others (Keyes 1998). Considering Aristotle's idea that *eudaimonia* is what makes for a worthwhile private life and is what one should aim for in social life, highlights the ways in which applied theatre practitioners may find meaning in working from a community perspective.

To put Aristotle's ideas into an applied theatre context, I would argue that applied theatre practice incorporates one of the main principles of *eudaimonia*; that is, the principle of interaction with others. As I have discussed earlier in this book, applied theatre is not a one-way process, but rather a synergetic and symbiotic practice that is open to the idea of gaining experience through interactions between people. Therefore, it is very hard to make a distinction between performance and the community for which it is created. Through many years of practising theatre in the community, I have come to realize that the *eudaimonic* approach to life can be relevant to the making of art. In fact, it requires us to accept others as participants in our lives in order to invite them to be participants in our art-making. This is not a weakness but a strength. What I mean by 'strength' is that the artist learns to accept the influence of others and involve them in their work, promoting discussion and exchange of common experience. 'Strength' requires a caring interest, an empathic understanding of other people's emotions and a capacity for warmth, according to Gilbert (2005). 'Strength' in this context is a word that presents a powerful competence in care-giving that includes the positive effect of acceptance: warmth. I think that what Gilbert means by 'warmth' is a warm heart, one that is not cognitively driven but emotionally engaged. But does this mean that happiness requires a warm and understanding heart? And, do relationships with others in applied theatre depend on the development of the artist's caring interest in others? In this case, the word 'interaction' helps applied theatre take on another meaning that reconnects the art form with the ability of caring and sharing good activities in the community. Caring and sharing refers to actions that take theatre practice away from egoism and towards to the 'collective' and to 'connecting'.

However, this is not easy. Not all people have the resources they need to put into caring. Not all people know how to become better versions of themselves, to grow intellectually and emotionally. Not all people have the support of their environments to reach their potential. Not all people know how to *be* with others. Not all people are able to reach out to another person. Not all people know how to be happy. And yet, *being* with others through theatre can be a great example of strength. Actually, it would be naive to argue the opposite, knowing that each person is a significant other to us even if their part in our lives has been a very small one. I believe, and I am sure that many of you will agree, that each person leaves footprints on our minds and marks in our hearts, both positive and negative. These experiences become our personal luggage, metaphorically speaking: belongings that we take with us wherever we go and inevitably put into not only our practice as artists, but into anything that we think, feel and do.

Thompson (2012: 29) expands on this idea by arguing that 'applied theatre can be an experience that develops links between people – above, around and through the existing shapes of the participants' lives'. He believes that interactive exchanges leave marks on our lives and create paths of knowledge, experience and behaviours that we use (perhaps unconsciously?) in making theatre a collective process that draws on past and present experiences of being. This argument not only introduces a fresh look at the system of applied theatre behaviours and the role of the artist but it also strengthens my argument that interaction creates opportunities for the artist to recognize the importance of others. It helps us to acknowledge that others (families, groups, communities and audiences) participate in our art through patterns of existing experiences and behaviours. This may be partly related with 'emotional socialization', which is a process of 'finding the truth in what we feel and think' (Leahy 2005: 195). Leahy argues that theatre and especially tragedies – 'and the human predicaments of suffering that they reflect – appeal to us because they validate our emotions, our own mistakes, misfortunes and suffering. They give nobility to our emotions, and make us feel we are not alone' (Leahy 2005: 195). This observation leads me to say that theatre creates opportunities for the artist and the audience to explore the range of feelings and emotional learning that we have gained from our interaction with others, because it reflects our lives onstage. The others and what we have experienced with them become significant to the process of making and watching theatre, because theatre gives nobility to our emotions and life experiences. What we see happening to the character onstage means something to us. We are witnesses, as Leahy (2005) continues, who see the truth in the dramatic and we are affected by the characters' struggling.

Leahy's (2005) emotional socialization theory appeals to me and I find it interesting to discuss it along with Thompson's (2012) view on previous marked histories and experienced emotions in applied theatre practice. In applied theatre we, the artists, first witness the emotional experiences of others (individuals and communities) almost in the same way an audience witnesses the lives of fictional characters onstage. Later, we 'zoom' in on their stories to see what is happening to them. If what we see means something to us, this meaning will become our personal pull, our motivation to work, for example, with a particular community of refugees, or patients, or prisoners, or children in schools. Something in our witnessing has done the trick for us. Some of our own emotions have been given greater value and meaning by witnessing others. Something in the truth of suffering in real life has given a purpose to our art, either to represent it and raise awareness about it or to comfort the wounds of those people and communities. Theatre gives greater meaning to how humans feel and think and applied theatre is no different. This is because the process of relating to communities through theatrical action is possible through validating the importance of people's emotions and feelings to theatre. Validation means that the artists process emotions through their own 'luggage'; we become involved in learning to empathize with others, inviting them to the centre of the making of theatre, such as sharing stories (or respecting their right to keep their stories to themselves). Interaction becomes a vehicle for learning and cultivating feelings through theatre. Applied theatre may become a significant enhancement to the acceptance of others as participants in our lives.

I am aware that Aristotle's *eudaimonia* has led me to a discussion about relationships, connections, emotions and empathy. These are all concepts that interrelate with each other and blending them together is not only inevitable but also fascinating. I will try to place TCH performance in the discussion as an example of creating opportunities for the artist to make meaning out of how children feel through a shared theatrical experience, and an empathetic connection with the child in hospital.

Each performance in a hospital ward is a journey of emotional validation through understanding behaviours of illness. In some cases, the artist has had previous knowledge of illness and suffering from first-hand experience as a patient or carer. In this case, empathetic understanding of how the child feels during illness can be easier because the artist draws on personal material from their own past. This means that the artist with previous experience of illness may respond more empathetically to the illness in accord with the child's behaviour in the moment, but it does not mean that an artist without knowledge of illness may respond less empathetically. The artist becomes witness of difficulties and pain through the empathic understanding that develops between the artist and the child-audience. Similar to *eudaimonia*, this journey is not walked alone. Whether this journey always leads to actions of excellence and whether happiness follows from performance is difficult to claim. It is not always possible to 'measure' the cause and effect in theatre because theatre is ephemeral (a short-lived experience), but I believe that no matter how short a hospital performance is, it works better for the child and the artist when they communicate their feelings in respectful, sensitive, calming, optimistic and reassuring ways within the protection of the dramatic frame. The artist, then, would be successful in showing empathy and compassion towards the child, and as a result lifting up the mood of a child on a difficult day in hospital would become easier.

Obviously, an achievement like this requires a good deal of empathy. The artist may develop empathy as a response to the situation of the child, feeling with the child and feeling their own emotions within the context of connection. Why is empathy an important component of the communication between the artist and the child in hospital performance? How does empathy relate to acting with care for the audience? Can the artist empathize with audiences in hospital?

Psychologists Zaki, Bolger and Ochsner (2009: 486) describe empathy as the social ability of understanding and responding to the emotional state of others, including 'a feeling of concern over the wellbeing of others'. Vreeke and Van de Mark (2003) further explain that 'empathy starts from affiliation or rather, the need for affiliation'. Such empathetic behaviour is motivated by the feelings of the other person who may be in need or in pain, and not by the information about the clinical condition of the person. We all know that artists do not have access to the medical record of the child or the details of their physical condition. Therefore, the artist cannot react to information regarding the history of the patient or the risks of the illness. But because empathy is based on understanding the emotions of the patient, the chances for the artist to develop an empathetic behaviour are affected by the artist's interpretation of the child's emotions, and the expectancy generated by the situation. If that is true, then the artist's efforts to empathize with the audience would depend on a very subjective understanding of the emotional state of the child, which may not necessarily be the truth. This is the 'blind man' metaphor I used in the discussion of altruistic artists in Chapter One. Perhaps the artist is even projecting their feelings and thoughts onto the audience. For example, an anxious artist might misperceive a child as an anxious patient. The reader might think that this view almost suggests that the artist in TCH is prone to making biased judgements about the emotions of their audience. This is a possibility I cannot deny. But in its best form, empathy in a TCH context is defined as the ways in which the artist reacts to the child's emotions and behaviour, mostly bodily and vocal expressions, and responds to them throughout the performance with discretion. The reader needs to remember that empathetic communication can rely on a range of social and environmental factors, such as type of personality and relationships, and cultural or language boundaries (Anderson and Keltner 2002). Therefore, any failures in empathizing with the child should not be seen as entirely the artist's responsibility, but they may affect the outcome of the communication. Empathy cannot be judged, measured or described in words easily. It is something that one cannot witness but only experience in performance.

In TCH, empathy requires the artist to position the child 'centre stage', so to speak. It requires effort to understand the child's emotions as these may not always be clearly communicated to the artist, but it is worth making the effort because the more the artist gets a sense of what the child needs the better they will respond to the children during performance. By doing so, the opportunities for communication with the child will be increased. The lack of empathetic communication reveals the artist's utter incapacity to transition from 'I' to 'You', and to communicate with individuals with a health condition.

I am thinking that if the artist sees the child as a sick person and not as an individual, they will fail to see the child as the audience who should be treated respectfully and without pity. Everything that is expressed or communicated by the child, even fear or emotional pain, is easily cast aside by the artist who develops a narcissistic attitude towards the performance. Lack of empathy, then, may lead the artist to fail in one of the most important aspects of TCH: to care for the audience. If the artist sees the world with themselves at the centre of the performance, they will fail to see the child as an important individual who should be placed at the centre of the artist's attention during the performance.

Jackson and Vine (2013) describe this as the 'self-expressive mode', where the emphasis during the performance is

> [...] on the 'I', the actor, that is, the actor as actor, where the performance itself becomes the primary focus of attention, with the audience more conscious of the skill, inventiveness and virtuosity of the performer than of the character she may be playing; this is 'See what I can do' [...] rather than 'Let me convince you that I am the character I play'.
>
> (Jackson and Vine 2013: 122)

The 'See what I can do...' attitude would be a disaster for the actor–child relationship in bedside performance. The attention should always be on 'You', the child, in a 'collaborative mode' where interaction between the artist and the audience is important to the interaction of the two in drama. For the artist in hospital, a lack of empathetic interaction can be considered professional poverty. Sometimes, professional poverty becomes personal poverty, which plunges the artist into loneliness. From the artist's perspective, if s/he cannot empathize with the child, s/he will find it difficult to create intimacy during the performance. The performance will, then, feel distant and 'empty'; but if the artist empathizes, he will start observing clues concerning what the child is seeking from the performance and the special circumstances within which the audience 'exists'. He will start judging the moment in order to respond to the child's emotional state and make decisions about his acting and his relationship with the audience on each occasion. The artist wonders:

'The child is pointing to my guitar with excitement but he/she does not want to speak. What is h/se trying to tell me? What should I do?'

'The child turned his/her back to me. Is he/she afraid of me? Is he/she in pain? Does he/she want to be left alone? Should I leave the room?'

'The child is ignoring me. He/she is playing a game on his/her phone device. Is he/she bored? Is he/she blocking me out of his world? Is he/she after my attention? Is he/she testing my patience? Should I wait and see?'

'The child has closed his/her eyes. Is he/she asleep? Is he/she pretending to be? Is he/she feeling sad or tired? Should I try to regain his/her interest? Should I sing him/her a lullaby? He/she is not responding. Should I worry?'

'The child becomes anxious at the sight of the puppet. Is he/she scared of the puppet? Should I put the puppet back into the basket? What else can I try with him/her?'

'The child is using his Lion (soft toy) to communicate with Mr Turtle. Is he/she protecting his/her private space by doing that? Is he/she setting him/her own boundaries in the dramatic? Or is this a sign of trust? Should I carry on responding to Lion through Mr Turtle?'

How the child feels and what they mean by doing or not doing certain things in performance is not easy to judge, but the artist who attends to the child and their reactions to the performance will begin to discover that the purpose of their journey in the hospital is to meet the child. Through empathy, the artist is connecting with the audience so that they can inter-play with the child and improve the child's experience of staying in hospital. Then, soon, the artist will come to the realization that in order to connect with the audience with some form of empathy, they will need to connect with something in themselves; to understand their own emotions better in order to know how the child is feeling. And although I do not know how to describe the artist's experience of knowing themselves better, I do know that what can make a TCH artist better in their profession is to find their own potential in compassionate performance.

Compassion has been linked to empathy and is associated with acceptance, kindness and love; it is similar to sympathy, a feeling of sorrow that is related to someone else's suffering, but it includes the desire to ease suffering and alleviate the burden of the other person (Ekman 2015). Compassion is a process of acknowledging that the other person is experiencing health difficulties and wanting to do something about it. Central to this process is the ability of the artist to *see* the child, to connect with them and care for them. This is relevant to the caring mentality that an artist develops in healthcare. 'Care and compassion require that we are in some way in tune with the feelings and needs of others' (Gilbert 2005: 41). My feeling is that if you want to know your audience in hospital then make sure that you really understand how they feel; try to feel how they feel and see what is in their minds. If you fail to connect with them properly there is a risk of failing to acknowledge their experience of being in hospital or to find meaning in performing in hospital. My experience of entering hospitals to perform to children helped me realize that theatre in hospital creates preconditions of working within illness, helping the artist to come to terms with the images of pain they see. Being in the moment helps, the artist and the audience see things as they are in the present freed from what they 'should' be. It helps them make a commitment to enjoy the play in the presence of illness.

From a 'Mindfulness' cognitive behavioural-therapy (MCBT) perspective, connecting with things becomes a necessity for acceptance of things as they are. Acceptance does not mean that we like everything that is going on in our lives or that we do not look at different avenues of change or that we do not look at ourselves from the perspective embracing change. It means that we accept and see things as they are, take each moment as it comes and are open to what we feel, think and see. Acceptance means attending to what is happening and being open to what will change in the next moment (Kabat-Zinn 2013). Since we all are imprisoned in our own likes and dislikes, it becomes common to find the non-judgemental approach to how things develop in life to be challenging. The problem is that judgements occupy our minds. They dominate our thinking and cause us to like and dislike throughout the day, to approve and disapprove. Mindfulness suggests that it is wise to observe and recognize judgemental thinking when it is happening, to watch it, be aware of it and avoid acting on it. The ideas that Mindfulness encourages: paying attention to the moment; being non-judging of the moment; and accepting of the moment, are positive because they protect us from developing bad habits of denying the world around us. This attitude sets the conditions for broadening our understanding of illness through theatre by accepting it as part of life (temporary or permanent). This concept needs attention from the artist if we are to experience theatre in hospital wisely.

If we as artists accept that we can find a passage through theatre to accepting illness in the lives of the children with whom we perform, then we can produce theatre of significance for these children. First, we need to accept illness as something that is here right now in the lives of the children in hospital. The artists are creating a practice of acceptance in response to the fact that the child is isolated from the world because of illness. They do not make efforts to judge the child's condition or demonstrate that illness needs change because it causes suffering. Acceptance of illness does not mean that we like it, nor that we take a passive attitude towards it, nor that we tolerate it without taking action towards cure and healing. Acceptance in this context means that the artist aims to take illness as it is, be with the children fully while they are suffering, and go with the flow of the performance, encountering the possibility that illness will or will not be here forever. Of course, one can only speculate on the effects of acceptance on the artist's performance. Within the artist–audience relationship, sometimes the artist carries the fear that something might go wrong in the performance and cause the child to reject the play. It is the responsibility of the artist to take measures to create dramatic safeness in their relationship with the child as the audience, by regulating their own fears about illness and creating an atmosphere of warmth. This, however, does not mean that those actors who are fearless in the face of illness turn out to be successful performers in hospitals, nor that those with a limited ability to accept things as they are do not make successful efforts to perform to children in hospital.

Heraclitus

It is speculation of course, but considering Heraclitus' (544–484 BCE) theory of change may be one way to help the artist come to terms with and accept the fact that we are all part of a changing universe and a component of that change could be illness. Interestingly, from this perspective, acceptance is not a static process but it embraces the possibility of change. Smith (2013) provides evidence on Heraclitus theory from Plato, Plutarch and Theaetetus:

Plato says that Heraclitus believes, 'All things flow and nothing stands' (401d); after this, Plato says, 'Heraclitus is supposed to say that all things are in motion and nothing at rest; he compares them to the flowing of a river, and says that you cannot step into the same water twice' (Fr. 12; Crat. 402a; see Plutarch, who adds 'for fresh waters are flowing on' [Qu. Nat. 912c]). Heraclitus uses the river as a metaphor to depict the nature of all things: superficially a river may appear to be a permanent and stable entity, but closer inspection reveals that it continually changes, not being the same river from one moment to the next. As Plato puts it, 'All things move like flowing streams' (Theaetetus, 161d).

(Smith 2013)

Wellbeing, to Heraclitus, involves understanding and accepting the necessity of change. Rayner (2008) also discusses Heraclitus' evolving theory evident in the epigram, 'We both step and do not step in the same rivers. We are and are not'. Heraclitus is saying that every time we step into the same river, we step into different waters and, thus, a different river. Moreover, we as people change too and every time we step into the river, we are different people. So, the river changes, and so do we. In fact, as we are all aware, change is associated with acceptance. Shunryu Suzuki Roshi ([1965] 2010), a Buddhist monk and teacher, writes, 'Without accepting the fact that everything changes, we cannot find perfect composure. Nevertheless, unfortunately, although it is true, it is difficult for us to accept it. Because we cannot accept the truth of transience, we suffer'. He talks about the eternal effort to accept things as they are and to change our way of thinking as a practice of realization that we possess selfish selves who find it difficult to accept the truth of things. I am not qualified to speculate on whether or not our sense of self is an admission of narcissism and weakness – except to say that it is natural to suppose that our resistance to accepting illness as an aspect of change may influence our wellbeing. We do not accept illness easily. It is hard to appreciate the borders of wellness and illness. When we feel well and healthy, we need some way to stretch ourselves further from what we know so that we may catch a glimpse of what illness is and how people who suffer with it really feel. All people need this, but the artist in healthcare needs it more than others do. Illness as an audience condition can transform the theatrical experience from entertainment to personal understanding, making it an extraordinary life incident for the child and the artist rather than a performance of events. The artist comes to performance with awareness of change. This means that what could be frightening to both the child and the artist in real life can become less terrifying in the dramatic. Ross's (2011) view of 'change with creativity' may help us improve our thinking about our attitude to illness in TCH performance.

Ross argues that we should accept that 'our destiny is to live with change, to negotiate personal meaning in the face of uncertainty, to remain active in a world that is forever urging us on, always threatening to unsettle us' (Ross 2011: 193). Ross argues for a consciousness that is open to possibility. Like Heraclitus and Shunryu Suzuki Roshi ([1965] 2010), Ross

(2011) does not seek to provide uncertainty but rather to raise awareness about change, a road that leads to possibility. To do otherwise would be to ignore the rules of the universe and our role as humans within it. Ross argues for the means that are supplied by the arts to adapt to change with creativity. Deep in his notion of the usage of the arts and creativity lies a conviction that change with creativity matters when 'it is for its own good and for the collective good' (Ross 2011: 193), which coincides with Aristotle's view of *eudaimonia*. Using the arts in understanding illness as a form of change and achieving evolution by using the arts seem inseparable. Illness can be seen as part of the journey of life and the process of change. Thus, illness can be seen as part of the journey of theatre in hospital and the process of creative change. The wise artist will accept their role as creators adaptable to change and become open to the possibility of change. Adaptability to change will allow the artist to approach the experience of performing to sick children as an opportunity to convert what is unknown about illness to what is, accepting it and working within it, but not explicitly with it in performance.

Of course, it would be unwise to deny that performing in hospital settings might cause moments of psychological distress. The artist might inappropriately become emotionally involved with the child. They might want to solve the child's or their own emotional challenges, as we can see happening in incidents that I presented in the previous chapter. The artist can either perform with acceptance of the child's condition, or attempt to remain disconnected from the experience and perform without emotional involvement. Ideally, the artist should be able to do both: be aware of the fact that the child is ill and be aware of their own emotions, while also remaining in-role as professionals. But thinking of ill children as 'victims', 'sufferers' and 'vulnerable human beings' can create an unfair, 'damaged' image of the child, a false pattern of experiencing TCH and a wrong approach to performing to children in hospital. Not everyone may agree that understanding illness as part of the changes that happen in our lives makes for a better artist, but the awareness of illness as a condition for change, even a condition for personal growth, offers a more profound and revealing account of children as human beings, and not just as patients. The acceptance of illness as change could even lead us to a more sincere appreciation of illness as a positive factor that affects our theatrical learning. Whether or not this happens, it is essential that the artist acknowledge illness more but fears less. I will share the following experience to illustrate the above.

The first time I visited children as theatre audiences in hospitals was in my birthplace city, Thessaloniki, in Greece in 2008. It was a performance scheduled for a group of children in oncology. It was not a bedside intervention. The night before, I observed myself thinking of the hospital visit in a particular way. I was terrified of the thought that I was going to see children with an uncertain future. I prepared emotionally to deal with the images of the children with cancer and the physical changes in their appearance during the course of their illness. The following morning, I walked into the oncology ward with my best smile on my face. That feeling I will never forget. The smile felt like a sticky mask. I had never thought before that smiling can make one feel breathless. Years later, an artist who performed in intensive care reported the same feeling. 'No air!' she said. The feeling of breathlessness was probably a physical reaction to the stress I experienced when I entered the ward, but I convinced myself that everything would be fine. I was there to support my actors during the play. I kept reminding us, 'It will all be fine'.

It is 10 a.m. I am waiting with three actors in the staff room. 'The children are waiting for you. They are all excited!' says a nurse. The nurse had briefed the children about the play before our arrival on the same day so that they would know what to expect from our visit. We soon find out from the nurse that she has given the corridor to perform. The corridor is long and narrow. It is crowded by chairs that have been placed there for the audience. We have ten minutes before we begin. While we are waiting for the children, I can hear them taking their seats in the corridor. I open the door slightly to see them coming in the corridor. In view of the limited space, I am beginning to worry. Not only would the three actors have to stand in a row as there was no space to manoeuvre, but they would also have to perform extremely close to the children. The children could literally smell the actors' breaths. 'Why use the corridor?' I ask the nurse. 'The corridor is easily accessed by children from all the rooms we have on this floor', is the answer. I ask, 'Is there surely not another room that we can use? Is it good for the children to have the artists so close to them?' She replies, 'Yes, there is a room on the fourth floor but we are hoping that you will agree to perform on this floor. You see, if you do, the children will not have to move to another floor. It is easier for everyone to keep it on this level'. I am thinking of the children who are supported by medical equipment and therefore cannot not move easily. 'What about the children who are in bed?' I ask. 'Will they be able to come to the play?' I can see that my questions are annoying the nurse but she is trying to be polite: 'Don't worry', she says, 'they will hear it from where they are'. I say nothing. There is no point. She would not understand. For her, we are just another scheduled activity in the ward from 10 a.m. to 11 a.m. Not a big deal. However, I am uneasy with the idea that there will be children hidden behind the doors, children who can hear but not participate in the performance. To hear but not be able to see; to hear but not be able to speak; to hear but not be able to enjoy. What a torture! I have no more time to think. It is time to begin. The actors are entering the 'stage' and I am following them. I stand next to the nurse watching from a distance. We have a small audience of not more than a dozen children, leaving many empty chairs to occupy the space unnecessarily. Then, I have the most revelatory experience. Some of the children are attached to breathing machines but that does not stop them from interacting with the artists. In fact, they are laughing extensively. Some of these children face uncertain futures but they are clapping with cheer. I have not seen such an enthusiastic audience before. I feel grateful to them. They give me hope that there is life in critical illness. They help me question my stereotypical assumption that children with serious health conditions have a limited capacity to do things. They help me observe the situation and decide what in my thinking about children in hospital needs changing.

McCormic (2012) argues in her book about change that

> unless we are able to look deeper, at the patterns of thinking, feeling and responding that we've got used to, external changes may be short-term solutions. Just being prepared to look at ourselves from a different perspective is already to be embracing change.
>
> (McCormic 2012: 9)

So I did. I observed the experience and looked deeper at the patterns of my thinking about illness as a negative condition of living. Thinking of illness as a 'bad thing' was an old pattern that had become a habit. I realized that the stereotypical thinking of the ill person, the suffering child and those who care for them, was powerful but it was also subject to change. Sometimes this is a hard task because when we do begin to see a need to change our thinking, we wreak the unconscious fear that we are not entitled to reject a stereotype and that we will make the wrong change, and then we will lose our confidence. However, this is an attitude that can be re-viewed, re-examined and revised.

In the years that followed, I had many opportunities to re-view and re-examine the impact of theatre on children in hospitals, to renegotiate my perception of hospitalized children and my role as an artist in healthcare. I removed the 'smiley mask' from my face and replaced it with the real me, trying to understand children's and parents' emotions, positioning myself with the child at the same level of experience in the moment of the performance. Through acceptance and intimacy, I could refine my view, shifting away from the stereotypical perceptions of a child with a serious illness. If TCH is a process of trying to understand and support the child through the aesthetic with intimate access to healthcare environments, a shift in the perception of illness is necessary. This is because performing in a clinical setting where illness is a fact necessarily leaves the artist with a decision to make: 'Illness exists. What do I do with it?'

Religious elders, psychologists and therapists of our times suggest praying and meditation. They also suggest thinking with love and compassion and developing a kind and loving response to the 'injustice' of life – and illness is often seen as an aspect of this injustice – in order to replace negative feelings with compassion and empathy, particularly in healthcare environments and especially in palliative care (Blacker and Deveau 2010; Ross 2011). They point towards empathy, love and compassion as ways of having hope in adversity. The artist neither can change nor get rid of the illness because illness is a fact. Nevertheless, they can create moments of joy, happiness and relaxation for the child. This is because compassion has nothing to do with facts. Compassion is, amongst other things, about developing a capacity to empathize with vulnerability without making judgements. As I understand it, love in this context means to feel compassion for the child's condition and position. Love means to see the world through their eyes, as well as to act positively towards others, accept the injustice of children suffering, recognize fragility and accept working in an environment of illness, despite the fact that illness may have caused the children, and their families, pain and harm. To be able to do this, the artist needs to develop more than artistic skills: they need to develop a kind-hearted and compassionate self. Becoming a compassionate artist can also be something that may happen if the artists learn to engage with the audience in ways associated with caring *for* the audience through the heart. This potential grows out of a loving approach to audiences who suffer from illness.

Two examples from literature are appropriate in this discussion. One is from *Le Petit Prince/The Little Prince* (1943), a story by Antoine de Saint-Exupéry about a strange and wonderful boy who tells wise and enchanting stories about his planet where there are three volcanos and one rose. A fox presents the Little Prince with a gift, a secret. 'It is only with the heart that one can see rightly; what is essential is invisible to the eye' (Saint-Exupéry 1943: 68). Perhaps I am too young to know how to love, the Little Prince says, I sometimes do not know how to understand things as life is so complicated. I think that I ought to judge by heart more often, not by words. Artists, like most people, may often judge by words. We need explanations to understand things. Explanations serve our rational thinking, but not everything can be answered with assumptions or facts. Seeing through a warm heart (*kardía*) helps us to accept that, for example, there are children in hospitals who suffer with terminal illness and are facing death, without judging or getting depressed about it. TCH is an opportunity for the artist to develop a sense of kindness towards all that happens to children in hospital; and an opportunity to accept that the performance that took place in hospital was the best it could be, considering what was going on in the child's life and with what the artist had at that time.

The other example is *The Manual of the Warrior of Light* (2011) by Paulo Coelho, a Spanish poet who offers his views on love and kindness, saying that underneath the masks that people tend to wear there is a burning heart. That is why the Warrior of Light takes more risks than others. He is always in search of someone's love because he knows that without love, he is nothing. Coelho symbolically uses the title of the Warrior of Light to address the power of love that is hidden within each one of us. He talks about love as a medium of learning about ourselves and about others, a way of appreciating the gift of life, a way to reach one's potential. Rooted and supported by love, compassion satisfies the search for meaning in what an artist does and justifies the choice of making theatre in some of the oddest conditions for performance outside the theatre. The heart can explain what the mind sometimes cannot. This is a useful skill for the artist in healthcare. Being a good artist requires knowledge of the art form but this alone may not be enough to respond deeply to the needs of TCH practice. TCH requires commitment and determination to face all the pressures and problems of delivery of theatre in hospital. I know from experience that TCH can be a great challenge for the artist, as working in a hospital differs significantly from working in a theatre, but if the artist arrives at the hospital with an open mind and an open heart, then the possibilities increase for creating spontaneous moments of successful interaction and communication with the audience. Compassion is the medium for a loving relationship between the artist and the child in hospital, a relationship of creative artistic play, respect and care. No one can deny that children in hospital, as any other audience, deserve to be approached sincerely and treated with respectful consideration of their feelings and aspirations (Korogodsky 1978: 16–17). The TCH artist's capacity for compassion and respect is a healthy response to the suffering they witness in children's hospital wards, a way to become motivated to excite a child facing difficulties in their life through art. Compassion does not offer the artist an understanding of health risks and the kinds of medical treatments used in hospitals. But the attitude of compassion may support new meanings of theatre and new ways of using the art form in hospitals.

After all these years, I am certain that to take just one aspect of the artist's work and one aspect of the child's life as a basis for judging the success of the artwork betrays a lack of understanding of art and the world of children. What meaning the artist gives to their performance and what benefits the children take from it are only part of the experience of being an artist and part of the experience of being an audience in healthcare. However, exploring the relationship between art and the concepts of happiness, acceptance, empathy and compassion informs both the work of the artist and their identity. This does not imply that every artist will use this knowledge well, for either themselves or their audiences but I hope that the emotional depths and insights, which may come from this exploration of meaning, will reveal the rewards and complexities of TCH projects in artists' individual worlds. Different meanings, each in different ways, will provide better understanding of artists' own talents and expectations of performing in hospitals. Consequently, the artists will create TCH more consciously, and can look forward to meeting children with a feeling of competence, fulfilling their potential as artists in healthcare.

My philosophy

My philosophy is that each artist in hospital theatre should be an expert in being with their audience in the best way that they can, by understanding what is involved in the TCH performance. The artist who is willing to share soon discovers that giving something to the community brings changes to their personal and professional growth. This often happens in conjunction with social growth, developing the artist's self while contributing to interpersonal relationships, such as giving something to the child in illness. The experienced artist comes to a realization that working with children in hospital is a rewarding experience, a sustainable joy, and *eudaimonia*. There is a sense of fulfilment in this experience, a sense of 'rightness' and goodness. The charismatic artist knows how to be in agreement with the child in the fictional, not simply to be physically present in hospital. There is an extraordinary feeling of living life differently when performing theatre in participation with a sick child. There is a sense of harmony contained in this experience, in which the dramatic is lived in a new way, in the light of what the child agrees to happen. The intuitive artist develops a notion that the wellbeing of the child is bound to the wellbeing of the artist as they share the theatrical experience in the moment that it is executed.

To you, the artist, I have a confession to make. TCH will never be easy but it is full of rewards, gifts of wisdom for you and for others. As you embark on your own journey of applying theatre in hospital and of discovering your own inner resources, all you need to remember is to commit yourself to the child and to the moment, observing for yourself what is happening to the child and to you as the performance unfolds. You will be learning from within, from your experience and what you are capable of thinking, feeling and doing as an artist. The journey of TCH is full of adventure, including successes and failures in interacting with children who suffer, connecting with professionally, and caring for them through theatre. Do not be disheartened by the challenges but rather use the experience to find out how to interact with your audience. Although we may know little about the experiences of children in hospital, we can learn more through our relationships with the children as audiences. By accepting things that we see in hospital as they are; believing in the possibility of change; and looking deep into ourselves in order to better understand how the children feel, and what they expect of us. You will, then, feel blessed with the sense of achievement that is gained through the applied theatre profession. You will realize that the secret of good community art lies in the ability to be part of a network of relationships and human interactions with others. Making the child feel special and well cared for facilitates such a network. Effectively, being a practising TCH artist will reveal the purpose of theatre in hospital: to participate with children in the real live moment of theatre wherever they may be.

Chapter Four

Concluding thoughts

Summary

When Jonathan Seagull joined the Flock on the beach, it was full night. He was dizzy and terribly tired. Yet in delight he flew a loop to landing, with a snap roll just before touchdown. When they hear of it, he thought, of the Breakthrough, they'll be wild with joy. How much more there is now to living! Instead of our drab slogging forth and back to the fishing boats, there's a reason to life! We can lift ourselves out of ignorance, we can find ourselves as creatures of excellence and intelligence and skill. We can be free! *We can learn to fly!*

(Bach [1970] 2014: 17)

As I have maintained throughout this book, this is my personal account of exploring and understanding Theatre for Children in Hospital as a growing phenomenon of interest and recognition. I have made a promise to offer the reader who might want to bring theatre to children in hospitals a definition of TCH, an example of practice followed by research evaluation, and a 'guide' to finding a personal meaning in their own artistic journey in hospital wards. I believe that I have met my promise within the slim spine of this book. I have acknowledged the circumstances of children in hospital and the conditions of the location. I have offered an extensive account of examples to illustrate bedside theatre practice. And I have critically discussed my data together with observations and conversations with those who were involved in the study. I have argued for the potential of theatre practices to bring entertainment, relaxation and normality to children's lives in hospital, therefore positively affecting their wellbeing. In this chapter, I conclude my thoughts by summarizing the key concepts of the book. The reader will find in this last part of the book a discussion about the future of TCH in the United Kingdom and in other countries, considering environmental factors such as the status of the arts in health provision, the quest for compassionate care and the role of finances in TCH's growth.

The book begins with an introduction to the work and the acknowledgement that TCH is situated within the larger arts and health framework in the United Kingdom and internationally. The core of the book is divided into four main chapters. In Chapter One, I offer a definition of TCH as a form of applied theatre practice with focus on the participatory purpose and nature of the work. My aim has been to reflect upon the role of theatre as an integral part of child entertainment and wellbeing in clinical settings. At the same time, I have discussed the wealth of opportunities inherent in TCH for the artist to learn new skills, observe their emotions and to find themselves, in Bach's ([1970] 2014) words, as 'creatures of excellence and intelligence and skill'. I have looked into the challenges that the artist faces in hospital but I have not doubted, not for a minute, that these can be overcome. I have looked at the culture of inviting children to participate in a synergistic performance: a process of communication between the artist and the child. I have discussed the benefits and complexities of connecting with the audience within the distinctive context of hospital, the restrictions of that context and its demands on the work. I have argued that audience participation in TCH carries ethical considerations in the collecting of stories from children in hospital and the devising plays on illness. In terms of its content, TCH raises a plethora of other ethical considerations, including the individual truths expressed by the artist; the possible stigmatization of the sick child; the representation of illness in the dramas and the consideration of the audience's health condition; the artist's perception of their role in healthcare; the risk of believing that the artist is the therapist or the healer; and the risk of facilitating the wrong forms of narrative and performance. The clinical stressors that affect child wellbeing in clinical settings compounded these key ethical concerns.

With attention paid to the specific purpose of TCH and the particular nature of the audience, I have introduced devising as a process in relation to applying theoretical frameworks of creativity, imagination and community collaboration. My definition of TCH also combines a discussion about the site-specific nature of TCH. Here, the role of audience participation in the hospital aesthetic experience, and the transformation of the hospital into a theatrical environment through dramatic symbolization, are discussed. The need to challenge the dominant message of 'vulnerability' in healthcare through TCH and offer the children opportunities to engage in the fiction as an audience and not as a victim of illness was explicit. I recognize that TCH is a rather new area that cannot be easily defined and described. Meeting this, we need to understand that TCH is still evolving from practice and that it is the artist's and the researcher's responsibility to be alert to improvements and discoveries that are not easily measured or assessed.

Chapter Two contributes to this need. I assembled resources for new understandings of TCH from a bedside theatre study, as an example of using mixed research methods to evaluate TCH practice. The study reported on a specific type of interactive performance for children in pathology, cardiac and cancer NHS Trust hospital wards in the United Kingdom. It provides evidence for the positive impact of theatre. Evidence is based on the personal responses of children, parent/carers and the artists who participated in the performance. Transcribed dialogues between the child and the artist during performance; incidents of communication and participation; examples of success and failure in engagement with the child; discussions with parents and hospital staff; and moments of personal participation in the events through observation, brought practice to life. These examples have been chosen for description because they are not representative of the typical dramas in which most artists find themselves in schools, youth clubs and recreation centres. These examples are unique illustrations of significant events that take place during TCH performance. I believe that practice has been illustrated, providing food for thought for the planning of new TCH projects in the future.

The main concern of Chapter Two is the explanation of the aims and the methodology of the study as important to understanding the rationale and the purpose of the work described. Because TCH is such an unexplored area, the evaluation of the project from three different perspectives – the child, the family and the artist – aimed to offer some indications about what is out there and some suggestions about the development of arts strategies for the benefit of the child in hospital. I have explained my choice to use a mixed method of traditional qualitative and ethnographic research tools, combined with elements from applied theatre *as* a research methodological model. In this chapter, I considered the child's experience united with the experience of the artist as important in enabling the researcher to collect valuable data about the intervention and reflect back on it through practice. This was intended to contribute to the limited knowledge we have about the level of child engagement and participation in arts projects in clinical settings. While the literature in this field is growing, the evaluation of TCH continues to be affected by anxieties around the politics of appropriate research methodologies. Admitting this, it nevertheless remains the case that TCH evaluation can be an exciting space for discovery and experimentation with a variety of research methods, for the process of developing TCH as well as for the effect of theatre on the wellbeing of children, families and artists. Chapter Two offers the reader inspiring but also realistic illustrations of what the artist faces in hospital, and how they use their skills to deal with these unique situations through drama.

Chapter Three is semi-autobiographical. I relate TCH to the artist's notion, interrogation and exploration of illness as a condition in TCH performance; as an opportunity for the artist to discover new meanings of happiness in the art form; as a form of life change; and as an opportunity for improved empathy, love and compassion. Of all the work in this book, the discussion of illness was probably the most revealing to me – not to say that exploring theatre as an art form and the research findings were not. I have learned that the liberation from prejudices about making art for the unwell, and the connection of theatre with practising kindness and responding to suffering with respect and sensitivity, are great gifts for the artist. I came to realize that the artists have to know themselves better in order to empathize and to understand the child's situation, in order to emotionally resonate with the child but also to shift into the child's perspective in order to create TCH. This requires a level of self-knowledge and an attitude of compassion in the artist. I do understand the challenges that an artist may face during the project, including the hospital space, routines and regulations; the health conditions of the children; ethical issues; the interference of other adults; and other factors that cannot be predicted in such an unpredictable environment. This understanding brought up the question, 'Why, despite all the challenges, are there artists who want to perform in hospital?' The discussion of concepts including happiness, empathy and compassion in relation to the role of the artist in healthcare that took place in Chapter Three, provided us with possible answers.

The future of TCH

To conclude my work, I have chosen to give space to some considerations about the future of TCH in this final chapter. It is challenging to make predictions about how exactly TCH will develop in healthcare systems where it already exists in some form. It is also hard to predict whether it will emerge in other countries where it does not exist, because TCH practice, as any other theatre, depends on so many social factors. It will be useful to examine briefly some of these factors – also known as demographic analysis (PESTLE framework). These include, amongst others, current trends in the field of arts and health; financial factors that may influence people's involvement in TCH; and how society might react to it (Lynch 2006). I have spent a lot of time thinking about what conditions need to be in place to increase the possibilities for children to experience theatre in hospitals. The majority of the factors that are included in the next paragraph are common sense, but I think that recording them, though in no particular order, will bring to the reader's attention a 'screening' of the needs of TCH for their consideration.

For TCH to grow further where it exists and emerge where it does not, some of the factors that need be considered are the following:

- the artists' perceptions about theatre in healthcare;
- the artists' understanding of their role in the community and the benefits of their work on children's experiences in hospital;
- the artist-in-healthcare training provision in higher education;
- the development of trained actors in healthcare who can carry out research on the role and impact of the arts in healthcare (Moss and O'Neill 2009)
- the progress of accreditation of the artist-in-healthcare profession;
- the existent realities in theatre companies (finances, staff employment and development);
- the existent realities in healthcare systems (finances, staff employment and development);
- the value systems, priorities, responsibilities and attitudes of healthcare systems;
- the nurses' understanding of what theatre can do in hospitals;
- the kinds of patient participation encouraged in child healthcare;
- the hospital governors and ward managers' attitudes towards providing TCH for their patients;
- the awareness of the public in order to support TCH through fundraising activities; and,
- the effects of the global financial crisis, which affects the operation of both the arts industry and the quality of healthcare provision.

We need:

- brave, enthusiastic and inspiring theatre practitioners to commit to TCH;
- arts departments in hospitals to host TCH performances;

- more trained researchers to evaluate TCH;
- the governments to improve their arts and healthcare policies;
- the public health sector to invest more money in arts for care;
- local councils, trusts and charities to support TCH financially;
- arts organizations to become strategic about marketing and networking issues and establish partnerships with healthcare institutions;

Being passionate about TCH is one thing and being practical and realistic is another. According to a World Health Organization (2012) report, which was about the financial crisis in Europe, the crisis caused a shock on healthcare:

> Health systems require predictable sources of revenue. Sudden interruptions to public revenue streams can make it difficult to maintain necessary levels of health care. Cuts to public spending on health made in response to an economic shock typically come at a time when health systems may require more [...]. Arbitrary cuts to essential services may further destabilize the health system if they erode financial protection, equitable access to care and the quality of care provided.
>
> (World Health Organization 2012)

The report reflects an ongoing climate of general insecurity, frustration and financial constraints in healthcare systems around the world. The picture of national health funding in the United Kingdom is also, rather disappointingly, not ideal. NHS announced a £200 million cut in June 2015 as an additional measure to bring down debt (Thompson 2015). Massive redundancies of medical and administrative staff seem to be the easy way (or an easy excuse) for making savings in the healthcare system. Arts departments located in public hospitals are sometimes easy targets when the NHS budget is slashed. The art team of the Birmingham Children's Hospital was redundant in 2012, and at the operation of the arts department at Heartlands Hospital in Birmingham was terminated in April 2016 after a long consultation period, which tortured the staff and kept them in agony about their jobs for months. It is devastating to witness the abandonment of the arts. It is upsetting. It makes one wonder what healthcare provision we want for our patients and if the improvement of healthcare that the politicians promise to their people is possible by talking steps backwards. It makes one feel furious about the discriminating treatment of the arts on some occasions. However, there are arts departments in NHS hospitals who survive the reduced budgets and continue offering patients a range of arts-based projects and activities. This is thanks to the hard work of their fundraising teams and the generous donations of money that come through charitable trusts and foundations. A number of trusts and foundations in the United Kingdom are known to have grant programmes that cover arts-based projects in healthcare or at least some aspects of the work. These include the Anchor Foundation, Arts Council of England, the Baring Foundation, BBC Children in Need, the Big Lottery Fund, the Charles Hayward Foundation, Comic Relief, Concertina Charitable Trust, the Clothworker's Foundation, the Franda Foundation, the Esmee Fairbrain

Foundation, the Frognal Trust, the Garfield Weston Foundation, the James Tudor Foundation, the John Ellerman Foundation, the Lankelly Chase Foundation, the Leverhulme Trust, Lloyds TSB Foundations, Man Group plc Charitable Trust, the People's Postcode Trust, the Rayne Foundation, the Welcome Trust, Youth Music, and others that are not included here (NAAHW 2012). The extended support of trusts and foundations also save individual artists and small theatre companies whose operation is threatened by the severe cuts in the arts in the United Kingdom. Despite governmental decisions, communities find their ways to support one another, rely on their criteria about the necessary priorities in society and make their own decisions for the further improvement of public services.

It takes courage to fight for what is important to the many. The artist needs to be proactive, flexible with arrangements and open to changes of plans when these are necessary in order to survive financially. I have seen hospital artists, managers and play specialists fighting together for the provision of the arts during periods of insecurity. I have been in situations where I had to face delays and frustrations caused by the closure of the arts departments in public hospitals. I have learned to be flexible with my projects timelines, and make serious decisions about the viability of the projects. It has never been easy to make a selection of hospitals and wards but the guide to make choices about the venue has always been the children and the number of audiences. The larger the audience and more diverse, the better. The more children we outreach with bedside performances, the more children will benefit from the arts. Even with a healthcare system that faces financial problems, the effort, creativity, passion and determination that have been invested in the arts in health and wellbeing by trusts, foundations, arts organizations, practitioners and researchers in the last twenty years give me hope for the future.

I believe that the brave and inspired artist who wants to make a positive difference to the lives of children in need will be guided by the increased recognition of the impact of the arts on patient experience and satisfaction in healthcare in the United Kingdom. The TCH artist is not alone in their efforts to promote the arts in healthcare. It is true that we do not really know if governments will fund TCH projects in the future and what cost-effective criteria will guide their decisions. We also do not know if arts departments in public hospitals will survive for much longer and if there will be new vacancies for permanent artists-in-residence in the future. We cannot be sure how many artists will be able to afford to fully commit to TCH, and how many will practise TCH sporadically. Some artists might choose to work freelance in the healthcare sector on a project-by-project contract basis. We do not know how many of them will develop their dramatic work further when or if funding stops. Funding insecurity is a difficult reality that thousands of employees face every day in the world. How could the arts be an exception? However, TCH artists should know that they will learn valuable skills, gain life-changing experiences and sense of fulfilment that not many jobs can offer. It is encouraging that there are artists who will continue to make TCH led by their enthusiasm and passion, their appreciation of theatre's effectiveness on the child's experience in hospital, and their willingness to reach their own potential as community artists. There are young artists, such as the ones who participated in the study, who believe in the power of applied theatre and of reconnecting communities with theatre. These are artists who believe in making the arts accessible to all in healthcare, and thus they use theatre as a tool to enhance wellbeing, creativity and relaxation in the most difficult conditions. These are artists who have been inspired by TCH and aim to inspire the community as a whole and instigate positive reactions to theatre in the service of child wellbeing.

It is only informed speculation, of course, that there will be an increase in actors who want to expand their work in healthcare, but I have faith in young actors for their fresh outlook on the world. These will be actors, like my students, some of whom have already committed to TCH as an alternative path for their career development. I hope that there will be drama graduates from universities who have had training in applied theatre and who may look for new and less obvious theatre jobs in the community. For the most courageous and passionate drama graduates, TCH could be their opportunity to make something new and identify their names with a great innovation in theatre in healthcare. It is important to recognize that TCH requires the artist's commitment to make every performance a powerful, innovative and necessary practice that benefits children and their families in hospital. I encourage theatre companies to see TCH as a way towards audience development and experimentation with dramatic forms, and also as an opportunity to attract the attention of their local communities and gain publicity for their well-intentioned work. Funding is always an issue for the arts but after many years of researching theatre groups and communities, I am convinced that funding does not necessarily make the artist feel passion for theatre and compassion for the child, but passion for theatre and compassion for the child can create some unforgettable moments in hospital performance that may attract funding.

TCH needs to be considered as one of the answers to the demand for a compassionate healthcare and a society of equal opportunities for all patients to receive quality care and support in illness. According to Ballatt and Campling (2011) over 9,000 nurses, midwifes, care staff and patients attended the Chief Nursing Officer for England (CNO) conference in December 2012 in London, where a three-year vision and strategy was launched with the title 'Compassion in Practice'. The strategy proclaimed high-quality care based on empathy, respect and dignity – described as intelligent kindness, a way of reforming the culture of healthcare. The strategy acknowledges that the quality of care is as important as the quality of treatment. In a way, it proposes an ideal relationship between the nursing staff and the patient who is treated kindly, with respect and dignity. The recognition of compassion in healthcare as it was defined by the British government, identifies that those who work in healthcare and are compassionate are considered as good health professionals. They offer a better quality of care to the patients compared to those who are considered to act without compassion. The discussions about compassionate health and quality care for all practices continue within the NHS today and there are hopes that the development of a scheme for compassionate and caring staff will be further supported in the future. However, modern healthcare is often criticized for lacking compassionate care.

[M]any modern-day healthcare practices are driven by a production-line, procedure-centred, target-obsessed mentality. [...] the fundamental idea of finding time to think, to talk, and to feel and to share often appears in danger of being entirely lost.

(International Health Humanities Network 2012)

This statement challenges the notion that healthcare prioritizes compassionate care. In fact, it advances new challenges to explore more inclusive creative practices in clinical settings and their benefits for those who are often marginalized from medical research studies, including, for example, patients, carers, nurses and health professionals (Crawford, Brown, Tischler and Baker 2010). This seems to be a good opportunity for hospitals and artists to work together towards addressing the request for compassionate care through arts-based applications in NHS healthcare provision.

Partnerships between hospitals and theatre companies can stimulate debates and cause anxiety about the collaboration between two very different organizations. In particular, persuading hospitals to host theatre performances and commit to working with artists can be a demanding task. Brodzinski (2010) argues that it can be particularly difficult for theatre companies to find venues (hospital sites) to accommodate them: 'For those hospitals that are willing to explore the possibilities of performance it seems that a commitment to dialogue from both sides is very important' (Brodzinski 2010: 54). It is important to take this into account during communications with hospitals. I suggest considering alternative, multiple options for 'staging' the performance in more than one hospital in case the dialogue between one hospital and the theatre company fails. This will not solve the lack of established, mutual appreciation of the arts in healthcare but it may ease the search for hospital audiences and minimize the risks of denying theatre for children who need it but are unable to receive it in hospital. It may also benefit larger number of children under treatment in more than one hospital sites.

The commitment to connect with hospitals is significant, but efforts that are more systematic are necessary to inform hospitals of the benefits they can gain from partnerships with theatre companies. A significant aspect of these efforts is to put the proposal of partnership in the right context. By this, I mean that theatre companies are required to invest time in making proposals for partnerships with healthcare organizations for two reasons. First, theatre companies need to acknowledge the problematic, labyrinthine bureaucratic administrations of hospitals and give the hospitals enough time to study the proposal and explore the practical implications of visiting artists on-site. From experience, I can say that hospitals need more time to process, consider, digest, approve or disapprove, and reply to the artists than do other organizations. Second, theatre companies need to be as precise as possible in writing well-thought out, detailed and clear descriptions of the project's aims, stages of implementation, activities and estimated costs. In Appendices Three and Four the reader will find a step-by-step guide for writing a proposal and a letter of application. In their preparation, the companies should examine the particular dynamics of hospitals; consider their priorities and finances; estimate the potential practical problems of working in hospitals (routines, times, visitors' zones etc.) and make realistic propositions of workable frames of collaboration and promotion of the artwork, and demonstrate clearly and carefully the benefits for both the host and the visitors. Theatre companies have no other choice but to invest time in this. The return on this investment is that hospitals can make decisions based on sufficient information about well-designed projects with clear benefits for the audience; clear stages of implementation; clear methods of evaluating the effects TCH will have on audience's lives; and clear financial expectations from the funder. The hospitals will know that they can get entertainment for their patients with benefits for their wellbeing. They will know that they can improve patient satisfaction and participation by helping children feel better, experience lower anxiety levels, and be happier and more relaxed through their participation in theatre. They will see the potential of interacting with a network of local and regional charities and trusts who support the arts, health and wellbeing.

Thousands of people fundraise to make a difference in children's lives. We are grateful to them. For example, according to BBC Children in Need (2015), since their first major appeal in 1980, Pudsey has raised over £790 million, all of which has gone to help disadvantaged children and young people around the United Kingdom. Some hospitals are aware of the benefits of arts provision but some are not. Therefore, there is scope for the possibilities for a broad and creative healthcare system that provides equal opportunities for effective, compassionate care to be increased, but there is no guarantee. Being optimistic, I hope to see more opportunities for improved patient satisfaction of children and families from all cultural, social and economic backgrounds, and for children of all abilities, skills and needs who undertake treatment in hospitals. Equal opportunities to experience the benefits of theatre in healthcare can be proposed as an ideological basis to justify the purpose of partnerships. This is something that TCH artists need to consider in their decision to open up a dialogue with community and healthcare systems. This is something that hospitals need to consider in their decision to host the arts. The purpose embodies principles of showing respect to children. If governments, healthcare professionals and artists wish to lay claim to supporting children in hospital, a deeper appreciation of the need for new, alternative forms of caring for children in hospitals through theatre should begin.

The artist should also be prepared to answer some new, yet familiar, questions:

- How can TCH meet its artistic objectives under the demands and pressures of the clinical context?
- Can it respond to theatrical priorities and aesthetic values without causing conflict with the healthcare system of values and priorities?
- How can TCH artists increase their opportunities to start and maintain partnerships with health organizations?
- Can TCH artists be financially independent?
- Will they be able to protect their artistic autonomy?

- Will they survive in a financial climate of global insecurity?
- What does TCH want to develop, and how will it change to adapt to the future without compromising its artistic and humanistic mission and its values?
- How will TCH emerge in countries with unstable healthcare infrastructure and provision?
- How can TCH be accessible to all children of all cultural, financial, social and educational backgrounds?
- What is it that we, the artists and researchers, can do to expand our efforts and improve public appreciation that theatre is beneficial to the child and to the overall delivery of care to children in hospital?

At the moment, there is evidence from children, parent/carers, artists, arts managers, nurses and play specialists in hospitals about the beneficial role of Theatre for Children in Hospital, but we cannot deny that more efforts are needed to create a sustainable TCH future. Arguably, there may not be any predetermined answers to control the future of TCH, but I believe that we need to envisage the future in the long-term. We need to keep people engaged in the arts and audiences fascinated in the most challenging and continually changing social, political and financial situations. We need to keep actors open to the experience of theatre, concentrated on their audiences and willing to experience the joy of connection with others in some of the most difficult contexts of applied theatre practice. We should welcome the difficult nature of TCH, working in contexts of illness and pain, and we should welcome the challenge to better understand the world of children and the kingdom of illness through theatre. We should remember that TCH has its own values and the TCH artist faces their own missions.

Sophrony Sakharof of Essex, an Orthodox Christian Elder, in his stirring book (2004) 'We shall see Him as He is' uses a metaphor to describe the mission of the person who connects with God through prayer as similar to the mission of the one who connects with the universe. Inspired by the metaphor, and based on my experience of TCH, I make my own associations between travelling in prayer, travelling in a spaceship and travelling in hospitals. There is no intention to imply that the artist is or should be a person of prayer or a cosmonaut obviously. Rather I use the metaphor to illustrate some of the key highlights of my personal artistic experience in bedside performance that are also common, as I find it, when I pray. These are concentration, openness to experience, and joy.

Out in space, an astronaut is free from gravity, free in the universe away from the Earth, away from worries about everyday little things. The astronaut's whole focus and attention is on their mission. Their personal life is left behind them. Although they are caught up in a small spaceship, they are still able to channel their energy into their journey and observe the new. Something similar happens to the artists of TCH: they visit a child in a hospital ward and they perform in a small space. Although the artists are often restricted by the conditions in hospitals, they are still able to perform and enjoy their role as an artist. The artist will not seek any conditions similar to the experience of rehearsals in the main theatre. The artist will not be too upset or disappointed if the children fall asleep during the performance. The artist does not forget the mission of their visit in hospital but does not worry about their publicity, which is so very important to the actor profession. In the same way, though I am not sure if the astronaut is concerned about publicity at all, I want to believe that being in space and far from the Earth opens the mind to new experiences. The astronaut is open to making new meanings and gaining a new appreciation of things such as reputation and wealth, which have no value outside the Earth. The new experience is that of the astronaut being present in the unknown and the unexpected. The new experience is that of the astronaut being concentrated on their journey but flexible to resolve any possible turbulence in their spaceship. Similarly, to the artist in hospital performing with the child bedside is almost like performing in a spaceship – a confined space. Confined spaces help the artist being concentrated on their performance, being present with the child. The worries of the artist's personal life are left behind for as long as they are in the hospital ward, just as the astronaut leaves their worries on Earth and gives themselves to the experience of the universe. Every performance in a hospital is a journey into the unknown and the unexpected, because it depends so much on the child. Every journey into space is an adventure. Every moment of praying is a window that opens to the universe in the name of God. Every artist, cosmonaut and person in prayer is a courageous traveller, an adventurer who is ready to respond to the unexpected. Every performance also depends on the artist's ability to respond to the unexpected during the performance. In addition, if we judge the quality of the TCH performance, not by the expensive set, costumes and props, but by the artist's awareness of the audience, we shall understand what is included in the artist's experience and what it means to be present for the child. Therefore, if we know what is lying within the purpose of theatrical interventions in hospitals – the sustaining joy of being present with the patient within drama – then, all our concerns about the challenges that we as artists face in clinical environments can be overcome. We continue in the knowledge of the main principle of TCH: to make contact with the child through the art form rather than just performing to them. And this can be one of the most rewarding adventures on Earth.

I hope that I have shown that Theatre for Children in Hospital is capable of broadening our perspectives on the concepts of theatre, art, wellbeing and illness. I have learnt more about applied theatre in healthcare myself, but sometimes I wonder why I chose to initiate TCH projects, why I want to evaluate them and write about children who experience poor health. There is no simple answer, obviously, but for me what matters in life is what can give sustained joy within one's heart and a purpose for living. I am not denying that writing about theatre with children who experience pain and stress related to their illness is a complex moral issue for me. There is no doubt that there are positives to discussing illness – something that can sometimes be uncomfortable for the reader – as it can help to encourage a discussion of the effect of theatrical performance on children who suffer and on those who care for them – families, guardians and friends. But there is a dilemma when talking openly about theatre and child illness. For some people, pain and suffering are easier to keep in silence.

Keeping illness private provides a feeling of protection from the eyes of others, some dignity. While writing this book, I could not foresee how the reader might feel, or what they might think, or how they might relate to the words of children in oncology and cardiac hospital units, or how they might respond to the children's emotions as well as to their own emotions. Perhaps some of these quotes triggered the reader's personal private feelings and memories associated with the experience of illness. The task of researching and disseminating the results of Theatre for Children in Hospital was a difficult one, but I did not run away from it. I kept on reminding myself that what is unexamined stays in the dark and thus offers no help for improving the lives of children or the growth of the arts in healthcare.

Reminding ourselves of the importance of sharing examples of our applied theatre practice and research findings will help us to be better artists and better researchers. The communication of experience and knowledge may be brief and inadequate at times, but it can help us all to do the following:

- understand how children with a health condition experience theatre;
- understand the worlds of the audiences we work with;
- experiment with acting, improvisation, storytelling and puppetry;
- challenge our views about illness and reflect on how families and staff view illness;
- pay attention to the child as someone special but not as a sick person;
- use our creativity and imagination to deal with emergencies and unexpected interruptions during the performance;
- become better in reporting and documenting our experience in performing 'with' rather than 'to' audiences in hospital;
- improve our compassion, sensitivity and generosity through the arts;
- improve our flexibility in engaging children in the fictional world when they experience a difficult reality;
- understand our research participants and treat them as individuals rather than 'objects';
- develop awareness of research ethics in theatre in healthcare;
- meet the requirements of sensitivity in our approaches to children's narratives;
- avoid reproducing stereotypical images of illness and ill people in the performance;
- strengthen our confidence and patience when hospital rules delay the progress of our work;
- interact with hospital staff and reflect on the design of the project; encourage interdisciplinary research across the arts and healthcare;
- develop respect for the artists who are motivated to perform in some of the most discouraging places;
- create new opportunities to reassess previous theatre practice in healthcare and make sense of how theatre projects for children in hospital could be further improved;

- set high standards of artistic quality in what the artists achieve given the constrains of the environment in which they perform;
- become determined to continue investigations into TCH as a way of life.

It is my hope that this book may prove to raise awareness of the importance of applied theatrical practices that currently exist in hospitals and propose new ways of creating and evaluating theatre in hospitals. It may prove to be a valuable tool for reasoned advocacy when artists, clinicians, researchers from the arts and healthcare, public arts and health policy-makers, and commissioners speak about the efficacy of theatre interventions in the context of child healthcare. Above all, it is my hope that my experience of working with talented artists, passionate researchers and the most wonderful children, parent/carers and supportive hospital staff, may inspire and encourage more people to explore, produce and disseminate Theatre for Children in Hospitals as a gift of compassion to the world.

Appendices

Appendix One: *Breathing with Love*, the script

The play was devised around the story *A Boy and a Turtle* written by Lori Lite (2001) and adapted for hospitals by Newman University (UK) CADLab students and the author of this book.

TIMMY: Oh no, it's raining again! Typical weather for a summer! British summer in Birmingham. Where is my beautiful sun? I got off the bus and a big splash covered me and I got all wet. Look! Hello. Can I take a seat to dry off. Thank you. *(He starts playing his guitar)* What's your name? [Reply]

That's a beautiful name. Do you want to know mine? Mine is Timmy. I guess you're wondering why I'm here… Why am I here? I just want to relax with you. Is it okay if I just relax here with you? *(Pause, plays guitar)*

I am a traveller, an adventurer. Sometimes I get lost but I always find my way back. I have travelled a lot and heard many stories. I have seen some magical things. I have seen Grass that was silver, a sky that was red and sparkling water that calmly flowed. *(Music plays)*

But do you want to know what the best thing about today is? I met a very special friend. Do you want to meet her? Well, first we have to make up a song to call her so that she knows that we are here. What about this. *(Tries a few notes…) (Music plays)* Tell me when you see her. [Reply] Oh, there she is coming!

(The Rainbow enters the room or the ward with gentle movement/dance. The Rainbow approaches the child's bed)

RAINBOW: Hello, Timmy.

TIMMY: Hello, Rainbow. *(Voice-over music plays)*

RAINBOW: Hello.

TIMMY: Where have you been hiding?

RAINBOW: I have been waiting behind a bush for the rain to stop and come out.

TIMMY: You are beautiful, Rainbow. You should come out more often.

RAINBOW: Thank you. *(Pause)* Who is s/he?

TIMMY: This is … [child's name].

RAINBOW: That's a beautiful name. Hello … [child's name]. I am Rainbow! Do you like my colours? I am made of red, orange, yellow, green, blue and purple. All the other rainbows are jealous of me cause I am the most beautiful rainbow ever.

	But you know what my favourite thing is of all? *(Waits for response)* I love the rain!
TIMMY:	I don't like the rain. I love the sun! I want to relax in a field with the warm sun playing my guitar. *(He stops playing his guitar)*
RAINBOW:	I like the sun and the rain. Do you want to know why?
TIMMY:	Why Rainbow?
RAINBOW:	Because when the sun comes out after it rains, my colours are the brightest and everyone is pointing at me cause I am so special. Rain allows me to be.
TIMMY:	Oh Rainbow. Shall we tell our new friend a story?
RAINBOW:	Can I be part of the story? I want to be part of the story. (Yes, a story! Can I be part of the story?!)
TIMMY:	I want to be part of the story too. Do you [child's name] want to be part of the story? [Reply]
RAINBOW:	Great! Let's begin. Let's use our imagination to travel to a special place.
TIMMY:	What should our story be about, Rainbow?
RAINBOW:	Can it be about me?
TIMMY:	She thinks everything is about her.
RAINBOW:	About the adventure we had today in the park?
TIMMY:	Shall we tell her about the water?
	(Music plays)
RAINBOW:	Yes, the water. *(Pause)* Let's imagine that there is a pond, a calm blue pond with little yellow and white flowers around the edge of the water, purple butterflies that flutter in the air; and swimming across the pond is a duck followed by all her baby ducklings, while the birds above are tweeting, then underneath the calm blue water is a little golden goldfish swimming across the waters. And above it all is a clear blue sky.
TIMMY:	And silver grass… !
RAINBOW:	Hmm, I can smell the grass. Can you smell the grass?
TIMMY:	I can smell the grass. Can you smell the grass too? *(To the child. Waits for a reply)*
RAINBOW:	And I can feel the warm sunshine against my colours. Can you feel the sunshine, Timmy?
TIMMY:	Yes, I can also feel the sunshine warming up my hair… I feel dried off now. It's lovely! Can you also feel the sunshine coming into the room? *(And the music starts…)*
	(Music)
RAINBOW:	I'm ready to tell our story. Are you [child's name] ready to hear the story? A boy is sat watching the quiet pond…
TIMMY:	A rainbow danced at the water's edge. *(R dances)*
RAINBOW:	A turtle on the other side of the pond also noticed the Rainbow. *(The music comes on)* The boy removed his shoes, shut his eyes and put his feet into the

water and imagined that the colours of the Rainbow that filled the pond could also fill his body. *(The R lifts Mr Turtle from the prop box and animates it)* The turtle, curious about what the boy was doing, also put his feet into the warm water and shut his eyes. The boy drew a breath of warm air in through his nose and felt all the stress of the day slip away.

(T stops playing his guitar and R passes Mr Turtle [puppet] on to him)

TIMMY: Hello, Mr Turtle. Say hello to [child's name]. *(T animates the turtle. He improvises a short dialogue with the child as 'Mr Turtle')* The turtle also drew the warm air in through his nose and gave a gentle sigh as he let the air out through his mouth.

(From now on R will demonstrate her colours [each one at a time] by using the fabrics that are stitched on her hat with gentle movements and a soft voice. T will animate the turtle and change his voice to differentiate his character from 'Mr Turtle')

RAINBOW: The boy imagined that the colour red was flowing up from the pond into his feet, making them float like petals on the water.

TIMMY: The turtle also felt the red flow into his feet and he started to drift towards the boy. Shall we do the breathing together now [child's name]? Do you want to try it with the turtle? *(Demonstrations follow with the child repeating the practice)*

RAINBOW: The boy felt the red turn into orange as it travelled up his legs. The orange allowed his legs to relax and let go of all their tightness.

TIMMY: The turtle also felt the orange travel up his legs as he drifted closer to the boy. *(Brings the turtle to the colour)*

MR TURTLE: Oh, I liked that. I feel quite orangey now!

TIMMY: Me too. I feel good. Are you [child's name] feeling good too? [Reply] Shall we do the breathing together again [child's name]? *(Demonstrations follow with the child repeating)* Very good. That was a good try. What do you think, Mr Turtle?

MR TURTLE: I think [s/he] is great. I want to do it again myself.

RAINBOW: The boy felt the orange turn into yellow as it warmed his stomach and chest. The yellow filled his body with an inner glow.

TIMMY: The turtle also felt the yellow warm his body as he drifted even closer to the boy.

RAINBOW: The boy felt the yellow turn into green as it touched his heart and poured into his arms and hands. The gentle green filled his heart with love and made his arms feel like blades of grass swaying in the breeze.

TIMMY: The turtle also felt the green touch his heart and pour into his arms and hands as he drifted still closer to the boy. Shall we do the breathing together again [child's name]? *(Demonstrations with the child repeating)* Well done! You are becoming an expert now!

MR TURTLE: I am becoming an expert too! Green is lovely. I feel so relaxed now. *(Dreamy voice)*

RAINBOW: The boy felt the green turn into blue as it explored his neck and jaw. The blue felt peaceful, like the ocean rising with the tide.

TIMMY: The turtle felt the blue explore his neck and jaw as he drifted even closer to the boy. Shall we do the breathing [child's name]? Are you ready? What about you, Mr Turtle? [Reply] *(Demonstrations with the child repeating)* Well done [child's name]. You look very relaxed to me now.

RAINBOW: The boy felt the blue turn into purple as it swirled around his head. The purple washed all the thoughts from his head, leaving his mind completely still.

TIMMY: The turtle also felt the purple swirl around his head as he drifted so close that his head touched the boy's hand. Hey there, Mr Turtle. You are so cute. Shall we do the breathing together once more with [child's name]? *(Demonstrations with the child repeating)* Excellent! Well done!

RAINBOW: The boy smiled, and together the boy and the turtle felt the Rainbow's colours embrace them in a soothing white glow.

TIMMY AND RAINBOW: In their newfound oneness, they knew that they had experienced the wonder of colours!

[The ending was devised with CADlab students and improvised mostly on the day based on the child's condition]

TIMMY: Oh, I feel completely relaxed now.

MR TURTLE: Me too. That is magical! Breathing through the nose and out through the mouth really works.

TOGETHER: [Improvised] Remember us when you do your breathing exercises. Remember the turtle. *(Rainbow gives the child a memo card showing Mr Turtle and the basic breathing instructions)*

RAINBOW: The sun's out now, I've got to go.

TIMMY: I'm all dried off now. It's time for me to go too. Thank you for letting me relax with you [child's name]. I enjoyed relaxing with you. Did you enjoy it too? *(Small talk with the child about the performance; the favourite characters and colours)*

(Timmy says goodbye to the Rainbow and Mr Turtle, who leave first. He then improvises a dialogue with the child before he departs playing his guitar.)

Appendix Two: The shape of our bedside theatre rehearsals

The following text consists of notes taken from an artist's journal, reflecting the creativity of the work-in-progress.

- Scripts are given and read through.
- An imaginary world is created for characters to be developed and an understanding of the benefits of relaxation is gained.
- The story is acted out a few times.
- We write on the script what words should be enforced and motives and reasons for the words are created.
- A beginning is improvised over a couple of rehearsals.
- The beginning is practised alongside the main story.
- Publicity in production and drafts of posters are shown.
- An opportunity for taking the *Breathing with Love* project to West Africa is discussed and explored.
- So is an opportunity to perform in a hospital in Dudley, after being watched in rehearsal.
- The introduction and main story become polished with music being implemented.
- With the music learnt, the story flows better and the whole performance comes together.
- The only thing that we need now is an ending for the performance.
- The ending is improvised with both groups, just like the introduction was.
- Full prop and costume runs begin.
- Feedback is gained from lectures and staff within Newman.
- All the while CVs are processed, completed and a tour of the hospital is conducted.
- Final rehearsals are done and the performances start. (Stefan, Journal, 5 August 2013)

In more detail

Week One
Relaxation exercises – breathing.

Reading the story. Discussion of the story, analysis of the text, picking out which words appeared most relaxing to the cast.

Improvisation of scenes using the characters of the story as a starting point.

Week Two
Adapting the story to hospital settings.

Discussing the audience's age, needs, abilities, health conditions.

Discussing the suitability of the story to the particular features of the audience.

The relationships between the characters of the story.

The Rainbow as a phenomenon. She's not in a hospital, which helps the children imagine they are somewhere else. Pauses between descriptions of colours, giving the children a chance to absorb these colours and think about what the colours might mean to them. Symbolic use of the rain. The Rainbow loves the rain, as she needs it to be – perhaps making the children critical of things we may not necessarily like but are needed (e.g. the rain, being in hospital).

Rain as hospital procedures (symbolism).

Week Three
Going through the script.

Improvisation of scenes relating to the story's plot.

Writing up of improvisation and creation of draft script (1).

Rehearsal:

Body work.

Voice work.

Where to put the gaps. When to talk and when to wait – finding the pauses to allow the child to absorb what is happening and respond.

How the actor changes his/her mood, and how music is incorporated with the words.

Work with Rainbow, creating more depth to the character, working on their story.

Writing up of draft script (2).

Week Four
Improvisation. Travelling from a rainy place (by train/car/going for a jog, etc.).

Discussion regarding Timmy's attitude during his entrance. How does s/he feel before s/he enters?

Breaking the ice. Pre-pubescent boy. Grumpy about everything. Timmy enters complaining. Not angry, but upset.

Rehearsal:

Engagement through imagination.

Projecting the images into the room and engaging the child in the dramatic context.

Timmy – imagine that you are a child in a hospital, give time to take in the signs you are receiving from the child. Wait for a reply. Pause. Making the child feel important.

Homework – imagine what it would be like on these adventures, imagine what you are describing in the dialogue. Recalling experience, not just communicating information.

Timmy's reaction to Rainbow enjoying the rain… Surprise, confusion, defiance?

What is usually by the pond on a lovely quiet day by the pond. Birds?

Rainbow's attitude toward the boy. What air are you bringing into the room? Happy, happy beings. Happy goddesses. Graceful? Think highly of yourself? But not posh, approachable. Indulging voice.

How did the Rainbow get there? You came through the atmosphere. Pause, because you're looking around you and taking in your surroundings. Non-stigmatization of the child. Because they're not a patient to the Rainbow as the Rainbow doesn't know why people are in hospitals… Doesn't know about treatments, etc. Naive and innocent. Helps to take the child out of their situation.

Rainbow is like a beautiful woman walking into a darkened room.

Using hands and fingers to illustrate the descriptions of the pond. As if you are hypnotizing, and engaging. Providing a distraction. Novel and imaginative.

Just listening to the sound of the characters' voices, not focusing on movements.

Rainbow is something ethereal and the boy is solid and real life.

Can I sit next to you? Etc… Treating the child equally in the performance. Not as a patient or spectator, but as a participant on equal terms.

Rain allows me to be – very important. Symbolic rain.

Think of each colour of the rainbow and something which represents each colour.

Red = love. It's as if you say love instead of red.

Using the blue cloth as the pond, but then let it drop. Hopefully it will stick in their imagination. Combination of both hands and cloths.

Describing the smells and sense of touch too.

Week Five
Musical improvisations.

Discussing the suitability of musical pieces to the performance alongside the purpose to relax the child.

Selection of music for guitar.

Rehearsing music with words.

Voice work.

Week Six
Rehearsal:

Further analysis of the text.

Symbolizing the space that is next to the child's bed. Rainbow is defining the space between the chair and the space. Changing the semiotics of the space.

Symbolic use of characters. Juxtaposition – Timmy is like the child in the hospital – creates empathy and therefore connection with the piece.

Week Seven
Rehearsal:

Additional voice work – making your voice relaxing. Not too high-pitched. Not too eccentric, inviting.

Child following the Rainbow's hands when she describes the pond: 'Let's imagine there's a big pond'. Making them focus and creating an 'image' for them. Added in more to the script in the description of the pond.

Added improvisation of pond scene into script. Finalizing the script.

Week Eight
Ensuring actors are aware that the set-up is not set in stone.

Using the props basket.

Final decisions on costumes.

Actors prepare on characters. 'Who are you? What has just happened to you? What is your mood? Your energy? How are you feeling now? As a boy, as a rainbow... Remember that you are here to bring a smile to the child's face. Bring some magic into this unit. Relax the child. They are a friend that you don't know but is waiting for you'.

Animating the turtle puppet.

Cue to pick up the turtle after you've turned around and done your movement [Rainbow] is 'A rainbow danced at the water's edge'. Bring up the turtle in a ceremonious way. Bring the turtle to life. Give it life. Use the guitar as a fishhook.

Guitar hook thing needs more rehearsal... It causes the action to slow down. Doesn't work after the child has just been drawn into the story. Disengaging.

The turtle's voice needs to be calming.

Rainbow rehearses with her props (coloured organza fabrics).

Week Nine
Practising the breathing.

Practising the Rainbow's movement-dance with music. Airy fairy movements from the rainbow. Need to practice with the change of the colours and the turtle being with the colours.

Working on different challenges: projecting your voice and moving the turtle and working with the Rainbow. Being aware of the space you may be in. Each performance will be in a different space.

Rainbow: practising with the turtle and the coloured organza fabrics, almost like shadow puppet theatre. As if you're putting filters on a camera lens.

Every time the turtle shows one of the colours, it needs to cover her completely and then cover the turtle.

Timmy: rehearsing the movement of the colours and the accent of the turtle. Different projections.

Week Ten
Run through.

Developing Rainbow entrance – Rainbow dancing when she enters with the basket.

Hold the turtle away from Timmy and bring him closer as the story progresses? Have hand on your lap when the turtle comes closer and touches you with his head.

Avoid overdoing the parental engagement. Focus should be on the child. Only address the parent/carer at the end.

Suggest to the parent know that they remember the breathing exercises and help the child with them.

Dress rehearsals.

Appendix Three: Writing a TCH proposal plan (bid)

According to *Abilis Foundation's Manual 1* for project proposal writing (Fricke 2003), all funders ask the same questions: Who are you and who will benefit from the project? Why are you planning a project? What do you hope to achieve? Where and when will the project take place? How will you proceed? These questions appeal to professionals and trainees in the field of drama and theatre studies and include a series of sections that the company or the individual artist needs to fill in with as much detailed and accurate information as possible. A TCH proposal should provide information about the following areas: a brief history of your company and projects; aims and objectives of the project; a brief description of the characteristics of the beneficiaries (children in hospital); a detailed description of the difference the project will make in the lives of children; an outline of the content of the project; the stages of work including how the proposed project will be researched, rehearsed, managed and evaluated; awareness of ethical issues and the ways of coping with the ethics of participation and representation of personal experience (i.e. children's stories); benefits for the wider community; cost estimations; suggestions for partnerships; and associations with institutions and bodies in the performing arts in health and wellbeing.

Name(s) of the artist(s) or theatre company

A brief history of your company and projects: Background of your theatre company, starting date, previous experience of projects, events and activities, company members, skills and expertise, awards and support from partners and associate organizations.

Title of the proposed TCH project (25 words): A title needs to be short, easy to remember, 'catchy', up-to-date, and use key words that apply to the content, context and aims of the project.

Drama theme (approx. 150 words): This paragraph will include a short description of a TCH project and the reason for its selection.

Summary of the project (approx. 200 words): In this paragraph, you will summarize the context, content and aims of the proposal. You might find it easier to write it after you finish the proposal.

Research into the context in which the drama intervention will take place (approx. 200 words): Organization/social group or individual. The aim of this paragraph is to demonstrate knowledge and understanding of the particular circumstances and the needs of your TCH 'audience'. This paragraph will include a description of the characteristics of the children in the hospital, clinic or rehabilitation centre.

An understanding of the humans who inhabit it (approx. 200 words): You will need to define the age group of the children, the health condition (i.e. paediatrics, cardiac, orthopaedics, chronic illness, recovery stage, etc.), and the condition of the 'audience'. For the needs of this paragraph, you will need to do research about your potential 'audience' and the culture of the hospital where you will meet them.

Aims and objectives (approx. 250 words): In this paragraph, you will provide the reader with clear, understandable, justified and to-the-point information about your aims and objectives, the whys and how you aim to do things.

The construction and delivery of the dramatic experience (approx. 350 words): This paragraph will include a description of your TCH project. In the description, you will write about the set of performances and activities chosen by yourself and will justify how the proposed project will flow (order of doing things).

Evaluation of the outcomes to judge the effectiveness of the intervention (approx. 200 words): Are you evaluating the TCH project? Most theatre companies tend to evaluate their practical projects and keep records of the results to use in future proposals and applications.

Ethics (approx. 200 words): In this paragraph, you will write about any possible ethical issues that might arise from your TCH project and your strategies of coping with these effectively.

The benefits (approx. 100 words): In this paragraph, you will write about the benefits of delivering the proposed TCH project to the children, their families, the hospital community and the wider community.

Management plan (approx. 250 words): In this paragraph, you will give an outline of your management plan, including duration, time management and justifications for actions. It is important to be as realistic about this as possible.

Bid and cost estimations (approx. 100 words): In this paragraph, you will include careful and detailed cost estimations and careful justifications for all your costs.

Potential partnerships (approx. 100 words): In this paragraph, you will provide information about any potential associations, arts organizations, health organizations, societies, networks, institutions or trusts that you feel may support your TCH project financially or in any other ways.

Author(s) or theatre company's biography: If you have a biographical press release, CV, production activity, funding records, etc., please attach.

Appendix Four: Example of application letter

Project title: _____

Dear Trustees

I am writing in support of my application for £_____ for the further development and implementation of the _____ project for children at _____ hospital(s). I hope that the information that this letter provides you is sufficient to cover the main areas of interest in the operation of the charity, the description, the outcomes and the benefits of the project and its finances.

About my organization

The [name of my institution/organization/theatre company] vision is _____ The proposed [title of the project] will be implemented under the auspices of [name of company].

[Information about the theatre company] _____ For more information about [name of the company], please visit the link: _____

About myself

I am [title, position, affiliation, expertise]. For more information about my work, you may read my CV attached to this application or visit the links: _____

Academic profile: _____

Description of the project

[Title of TCH project] consists of a _____ minutes theatre performance presented to children in hospital settings aiming at _____ We aim at children from [age group] in [specific wards?] at _____ Hospital.

Description of the performance: _____

History of the company: _____

History of the TCH project: _____

Targeted audience characteristics: _____

What are the estimated Outcomes?

1. Create a theatre performance that suits the needs of hospitalized children.
2. Outreach to [number] members of hospital audiences.
3. Evaluate the theatre experience _____
4. Disseminate the 2013 experience to the public _____

What are the estimated Benefits?

1. This project will outreach approximately a mixed population of _____ children and their families at [name of hospital] during [time-scale of the project]
2. Evidence of previous similar project conducted by the company: _____
3. Statement promoting health and wellbeing through the arts: _____

Grant sector

This is a note to clarify that I have selected the _____ [grant sector] as a programme sector for the project because _____

Previous support

[Title of the project] has received funding from [previous grants] _____

Current support

The theatre company currently operates with funding from: _____

Financial information

Company's total income: £_____

Total expenditure: £_____

Budget expenditure of this project: £_____

Amount requested: £_____

Secured amount: £_____

Where will your money go?

The grant will cover the following areas of expenditure: _____

I kindly ask you to support _____ with up to £_____. [Give reasons for the funding body to trust their money to your project securing delivery and sustainability] _____

If you need any further information or clarification regarding this application, please do not hesitate to contact me directly.

Yours sincerely
Name of applicant/company

The letter of application for funding provides a useful set of sections to help the artist(s) in the writing of a suitable and coherent proposal. It also provides a practical framework within which to approach the project to be assessed by the funding body. The letter above is a combination of personal experience, and various applications that have been shared with me by theatre companies and freelance artists, who I thank for their generosity. To present an attractive TCH proposal would mean that the company must have worked out the theoretical and practical aims, the strategy, the outcomes and the benefits of the project clearly. In some cases of small trusts, a letter of application may be all that is required to submit but with major funding it may serve as a good exercise before completing the main application online.

Appendix Five: Guidance for applying for NHS Research Ethics Committee approval (for researchers only)

Awareness of ethics is exceptionally important to the TCH proposal because it involves questions about safeguarding and confidentiality. Those courageous artist-researchers who might choose to undertake a TCH research study should go through the national health system's bureaucracy in their countries. For UK practitioners, the process of applying to the NHS REC (National Health Service Research Ethics Committee) is described in the following steps.

- Step One: Fill in the NHS REC form on the application system for NHS online by first creating an electronic account and getting a reference number.
- Step Two: Provide the system with detailed and accurate information about the nature of the research, its rationale, the aims, the schedule of the activities and their structure, the research methods that will be employed to evaluate the impact of the project's efficacy, the degree of the child involvement, data protection information, the activities that will be used for the dissemination of findings, ethical concerns and ways of dealing with those, the researcher(s)' CVs and contacts, and affiliation with their institution or organization.
- Step Three: Arrange and attend meetings with site-specific (SS) NHS organizations (hospitals). There, they will work closely with the arts department.
- Step Four: Speak about the project to the Research and Human Resources managers at SS organizations.
- Step Five: Produce leaflets and consent forms for the research participants and submit them with your application.
- Step Six: Make arrangements to complete NHS criminal-record checks for the artists who will be in one-to-one interaction with children. This process is straightforward and it is usually conducted through the arts department, who they also pay for the expense of the checks.
- Step Seven: Get a formal endorsement letter from an expert about the research project and provide evidence for the funding of the project.
- Step Eight: It is important to book a date for attending an NHS REC in good advance to the beginning of the project. Sometimes, the committees return the application with amendment suggestions.
- Step Nine: Submit NHS REC form online followed by a checklist and post it by Royal Mail. It is important to receive it within 3 days of the booking, otherwise the application is withdrawn.
- Step Ten: Attend the NHS Research Ethics Committee.

Note on the author

Dr Persephone Sextou is Reader in Applied Theatre at Newman University Birmingham (UK), and the Research Director of the Community & Applied Drama Laboratory (CADLab), leading theatre interventions in health and wellbeing. She has secured a grant from BBC Children in Need (2016–2019) to continue her research on the impact of specially developed participatory dramas for children's wellbeing while they are in hospital undergoing treatment. She develops projects in partnership with the NHS Trust in the United Kingdom, and educational organizations in Europe and West Africa. She is the author of peer-reviewed articles in international journals, commissioned chapters and three monographs in Greek. She acts as a member of the editorial boards for *Arts & Health: An International Journal of Research, Policy and Practice* in the United Kingdom; the *Applied Theatre Reader* in Australia; and the *Arts in Communities Journal* in the United States.

Bibliography

Works Cited

Aldiss, S., Horstman, M., O'Leary, C., Richardson, A. and Gibson, F. (2008), 'What is important to young children who have cancer while in hospital?', *Children & Society*, 23: 2, pp. 85–98.

Allain, P. and Harvie, J. (2006), *Theatre and Performance*, London: Routledge.

Anderson, C. and Keltner, D. (2002), 'Open peer commentary: The role of empathy in the formation and maintenance of social bonds', *Behavioral and Brain Sciences*, 25: 1, pp. 21–22.

Angus, J. (2002), *A Review of Evaluation in Community-Based Arts for Health Activity in the UK*, London: Health Development Agency.

Aristotle (*c*.350 BCE), Ἠθικὰ Νικομάχεια/*Nicomachean Ethics* (trans. W. D. Ross), http://classics.mit.edu/Aristotle/nicomachaen.1.i.html. Accessed 21 March 2016.

Armstrong, T. S. H. and Aitken, H. L. (2000), 'The developing role of play preparation in paediatric anaesthesia', *Pediatric Anesthesia*, 10: 1, pp. 1–4.

Arts and Health South West (AHSW) (2013), *International Culture Health and Wellbeing Conference*, personal notes, South West Regional Body of the National Alliance for Arts Health and Wellbeing, Bristol, 24–26 June.

Arts Council England (2004), *Arts in Health: A Review of the Medical Literature*, London: Arts Council of England.

—— (2006), *Arts, Health and Well-Being: A Strategy for Partnership*, London: Arts Council England.

—— (2007), *A Prospectus for Arts and Health*, London: Arts Council of England.

—— (2014), *The Value of Arts and Culture to People and Society: An Evidence Review*, London: Arts Council of England.

Athanassiadou, E., Tsiantis, J., Christogiorgos, S. and Kolaitis, G. (2009), 'An evaluation of the effectiveness of psychological preparation of children for minor surgery by puppet play and brief mother counselling', *Journal of Psychotherapy and Psychosomatics*, 78, pp. 62–63.

Atkinson, S. and Rubidge, T. (2013), 'Managing the spatialities of arts-based practices with school children: An interdisciplinary exploration of engagement, movement and well-being', *Arts & Health: An International Journal of Research, Policy and Practice*, 5: 1, pp. 39–50.

Bach, R. ([1970] 2014), *Jonathan Livingston Seagull: The Complete Edition*, New York: Scribner.

Balfour, M. (2009), 'The politics of intention: Looking for a theatre of little changes', *Research in Drama Education: Journal of Applied Theatre and Performance*, 14: 3, pp. 347–59, http://www98.griffith.edu.au/dspace/handle/10072/30346. Accessed 27 March 2014.

Balfour, M., Bundy, P., Burton, B., Dunn, J. and Woodrow, N. (2015), *Applied Theatre: Resettlement: Drama, Refugee and Resilience*, London and New York: Bloomsbury Methuen Drama.

Ballatt, J. and Campling, P. (2011), *Intelligent Kindness: Reforming the Culture of Healthcare*, London: RCPsych Publications.

Barnes, J. (trans.) (1984), *The Complete Works of Aristotle: Revised Oxford Translation,* vol. 2, Bollingen Series LXXI, Princeton: Princeton University Press.

BBC Children in Need (2015), 'Be a hero', http://www.bbc.co.uk/programmes/articles/5ShlK3D H4J6XyLMXXTw355h/frequently-asked-questions-faq. Accessed 26 November 2015.

Bergen, D. (2002), 'The role of pretend play in children's cognitive development', *Early Childhood Research and Practice*, 4: 1, http://ecrp.uiuc.edu/v4n1/bergen.html. Accessed 2 October 2014.

Birch, A. and Tompkins, J. (2012), *Performing Site-Specific Theatre: Politics, Place, Practice*, London: Palgrave Macmillan.

Blacker, S. and Deveau, C. (2010) 'Social work and interprofessional collaboration in palliative care', *Progress in Palliative Care*, 18: 4, pp. 237–43.

Boal, A. (1979), *Theatre of the Oppressed*, London: Pluto.

Brodzinski, E. (2010), *Theatre in Health and Care*, London: Palgrave Macmillan.

Bryman, A. (2008), *Social Research Methods*, 3rd ed., Oxford: Oxford University Press.

Burnard, P. and Campling, J. (1994), *Counselling Skills for Health Professionals*, 2nd ed., Hong Kong: Springer.

Calvert, D. (2015), 'Heroism and heroic action in applied and social theatre: A selection of provocations from TAPRA's Applied and Social Theatre working group', *Research in Drama in Education: Journal of Applied Theatre and Performance*, 20: 2, pp. 173–76.

'cardia' (2014), *Merriam-Webster Dictionary Online*, http://www.merriamwebster.com/dictionary/cardia. Accessed 6 January 2016.

Carel, H. (2012), 'Phenomenology as a resource for patients', *Journal of Medicine and Philosophy*, 37: 2, pp. 96–113.

—— (2013), *Illness: The Cry of the Flesh*, London: Routledge.

Christopoulou-Aletra, H., Togia, A. and Varlami, C. (2010), 'The "smart" Asclepieion: A total healing environment', *Archive of Hellenic Medicine*, 27: 2, pp. 259–63.

Clavering, E. K. and McLaughlin, J. (2010), 'Children's participation in health research: From objects to agents?', *Child: Care, Health and Development Journal*, 36: 5, pp. 603–11.

Clift, S., Camic, P., Chapman, B., Clayton, G., Daykin, N., Eades, G., Parkinson, C., Secker, J., Stickley, T. and White, M. (2009), 'The state of arts and health in England: Policy, practice and research', *Arts & Health: An International Journal of Research, Policy and Practice*, 1: 1, pp. 6–35.

Clore, G. L. and Huntsinger, J. R. (2007), 'How emotions inform judgment and regulate thought', *Trends in Cognitive Science*, 11: 9, pp. 393–99.

Coelho, P. (2011), *The Manual of the Warrior of Light*, London: HarperCollins.

Compas, B., Jaser, S., Dunn, M. and Rodriguez, E. M. (2012), 'Coping with chronic illness in childhood and adolescence', *Annual Review of Clinical Psychology*, 27: 8, pp. 455–80.

Cowell, E., Herron, C. and Hockenberry, M. (2011), 'The impact of an arts program in a children's cancer and hematology center', *Arts & Health: An International Journal of Research, Policy and Practice*, 3: 2, pp. 173–81.

Coyne, I. (2006), 'Children's experiences of hospitalization', *Journal of Child Health*, 10: 4, pp. 326–36.

Crane, R. (2009), *Mindfulness-Based Cognitive Therapy*, London: Routledge.

Crawford, P., Brown, B., Tischler, V. and Baker, C. (2010), 'Health humanities: The future of medical humanities?', *Mental Health Review Journal*, 15: 3, pp. 4–10.

Cultural Value Project (2014), Arts and Humanities Research Council, http://www.ahrc.ac.uk/research/fundedthemesandprogrammes/culturalvalueproject/. Accessed 21 March 2014.

Daykin, N., Orme, J., Evans, D., Salmon, D., McEachran, M. and Brain, S. (2008), 'The impact of participation in performing arts on adolescent health and behaviour: A systematic review of the literature', *Journal of Health Psychology*, 13: 2, pp. 251–64.

De Lima, R. A. G, Azevedo, E. F., Nascimento, L. C. and Rocha, S. M. M. (2009), 'The art of clown theatre in care for hospitalized children', *Revista da Escola de Enfermagemda USP*, 43: 1, pp. 178–85.

Economic and Social Research Council (ESRC) (2007), *Space to Care: Children's Perceptions of Spatial Aspects of Hospitals*, Swindon: ESRC, http://www.esrc.ac.uk/my-esrc/grants/RES-000-23-0765/read. Accessed 2 March 2013.

Eisner, E. W. (2005), *Reimagining Schools: The Selected Works of Elliot W. Eisner*, London: Routledge.

Ekman, P. (2015), 'All about empathy: Definitions of empathy', Centre for Building a Culture of Empathy, http://cultureofempathy.com/references/definitions.htm. Accessed 28 January 2015.

Emunah, R. (1994), *Acting for Real*, London: Psychology Press.

Eyre, R. (2009), *Talking Theatre: Interviews with Theatre People*, London: Nick Hern Books.

Fawcett, M. (1996), *Learning Through Child Observation*, London: J. Kingsley Publishers.

Fisher, R. and Williams, M. (eds.) (2004), *Unlocking Creativity Teaching across the Curriculum*, London: David Fulton.

Fricke, Y. (2003), *Abilis Manual 1 Project Proposal Writing*, Helsinki: Abilis Foundation.

Gallagher, M., Lopez, S. J. and Preacher, K. J. (2009), 'The hierarchical structure of well-being', *Journal of Personality*, 77: 4, pp. 1025–50.

General Council of the Bar (2012), *Fair Recruitment Guide 2012: A Best Practice Guide for the Bar*, http://www.barcouncil.org.uk/media/165213/recruitment_guidev22_18sept_merged_readonly.pdf. Accessed 7 January 2016.

Gilbert, P. (2009), 'Introducing compassion-focused therapy', *Advances in Psychiatric Treatments*, 15, pp. 199–208.

——— (2010), *Compassion Focused Therapy: Distinctive Features (CBT Distinctive Features)*, London: Routledge.

——— (ed.) (2005), *Compassion: Conceptualisations, Research and Use in Psychotherapy*, London and New York: Routledge.

Grainger, R. (1995), *Drama and Healing: The Roots of Drama Therapy*, London: Jessica Kingsley Publishers.

Green, D., Schertz, M., Gordon, A. M., Moore, A., Schejter Margalit, T., Farquharson, Y., Ben Bashat, D., Weinstein, M., Lin, J. P. and Fattal-Valevski, A. (2013), 'A multi-site study of functional outcomes following a themed approach to hand–arm bimanual intensive therapy for children with hemiplegia', *Developmental Medicine & Child Neurology*, 55: 6, pp. 527–33.

Greetham, B. (2009), *How to Write Your Undergraduate Dissertation*, London: Palgrave Macmillan.

Hall, C. and Reet, M. (2000), 'Enhancing the state of play in children's nursing', *Journal of Child Health Care: For Professionals Working with Children in the Hospital and Community*, 4: 2, pp. 49–54.

Heddon, D. and Milling, J. (2006), *Devising Performance: A Critical History*, New York: Palgrave Macmillan.

Hemingway, A. and Crossen-White, H. (2014), *Arts in Health: A Review of the Literature*, Bournemouth: Bournemouth University, http://www.artsandhealthsouthwest.org.uk/userfiles/Other_Resources/Reports/Arts%20and%20Health%20Literature%20Review.pdf. Accessed 1 March 2015.

Hoban, R. (2001), *Jim's Lion*, Cambridge: Candlewick.

Holderness, G. (1992), *The Politics of Theatre and Drama*, London: Macmillan Press.

Hughes, R. K. (2006), *2 Corinthians, Power in Weakness*, Illinois: Crossway Books.

International Health Humanities Network (2012), 'Innovation, involvement and impact research summary', Nottingham: Nottingham University, http://www.healthhumanities.org. Accessed 22 November 2012.

Jackson, A. (ed.) (1993), *Learning Through Theatre: New Perspectives on Theatre in Education*, 2nd ed., London: Routledge.

—— (2007), *Theatre, Education and the Making of Meanings*, Manchester: Manchester University Press.

Jackson, A. and Vine, C. (eds) (2013), *Learning Through Theatre: The Changing Face of Theatre in Education*, 3rd ed., London: Routledge.

Jackson, R. A. (2007), 'Aristotle on what it means to be happy', *Richmond Journal of Philosophy*, 16, http://www.richmondphilosophy.net/rjp/back_issues/rjp16_jackson.pdf. Accessed 22 May 2015.

Jarrett, L. (ed.) (2007), *Creative Engagement in Palliative Care*, Oxford: Radcliffe Publishing.

Jarvis, P. (1992), 'Reflective practice and nursing', *Nurse Education Today*, 12, pp. 174–81.

Jellicoe, A. (1987), *Community Plays: How to Put Them On*, London: Methuen.

Jennings, S. (2009), *Dramatherapy and Social Change: Necessary Dialogues*, London: Routledge.

Jones, P. (2007), *Drama as Therapy, Volume One: Theory, Practice and Research*, 2nd ed., London: Routledge.

Jun-Tai, N. (2008), 'Play in hospital', *Paediatrics and Child Healthcare*, 18: 5, pp. 233–37.

Kabat-Zinn, J. (2013), *Full Catastrophe Living: Using the Wisdom of Your Body and Mind to Face Stress, Pain and Illness*, 2nd ed., New York: Bantam Books.

Keyes, C. L. M. (1998), 'Social well-being', *Social Psychology Quarterly*, 61, pp. 121–40.

Korogodsky, Z. (1978), 'Respecting the child spectator' (trans. M. Morton), in N. McCaslin (ed.), *Theatre for Young Audiences*, New York: Longman, pp. 13–17.

Kostenius, C. and Öhrling, K. (2009), 'Being relaxed and powerful: Children's lived experiences of coping with stress', *Children & Society*, 23: 3, pp. 203–13.

Leahy, R. L. (2005), 'A social-cognitive model of validation', in P. Gilbert (ed.), *Compassion: Conceptualisations, Research and Use in Psychotherapy*, New York: Routledge, pp. 195–217.

Lite, L. (2001), *A Boy and a Turtle*, New York: Litebooks. Net, LLC.

London Arts in Health Forum (LAHF) (2012a), 'A charter for arts, health and wellbeing', http://www.artshealthandwellbeing.org.uk/what-is-arts-in-health/charter-arts-health-wellbeing. Accessed 15 March 2016.

——— (2012b), 'London hospital-based arts programmes', http://www.lahf.org.uk/resources/links/london-hospital-based-arts-programmes. Accessed 12 June 2012.

——— (2012c), 'What is arts in health?', http://www.artshealthandwellbeing.org.uk/what-is-arts-in-health. Accessed 15 march 2016.

——— (2014), 'Creativity week', www.lahf.org.uk/news/newsletter. Accessed 20 October 2014.

——— (2015), 'Creativity and wellbeing week this year', http://www.lahf.org.uk/news/newsletter/lahf-newsletter-%E2%80%93-24-june-2015. Accessed 17 November 2015.

Lynch, R. (2006), *Corporate Strategy*, 4th ed., Bloomington, IN: Indiana University, *Financial Times* and Prentice Hall.

Maguire, T. and Schuitema, K. (2012), *Theatre for Young Audiences: A Critical Handbook*, London: Trentham Institute of Education Press.

Mayall, B. (2008), 'Conversations with children', in P. Christensen and A. James (eds), *Research with Children: Perspectives and Practices*, Abingdon: Routledge, pp. 109–24.

McConachie, B. (2013), *Theatre Mind*, London and New York: Palgrave Macmillan.

McCormic, E. W. (2012), *Change for the Better*, Washington: Sage.

Miller, V. and Harris, D. (2012), 'Measuring children's decision-making involvement regarding chronic illness management', *Journal of Pediatric Psychology*, 37: 3, pp. 292–306.

Mitchell, D. T. and Snyder, S. L. (2015), 'Global in(ter)dependent disability cinema: Targeting ephemeral domains of belief and cultivating aficionados of the body', *Negotiating Space for (Dis)ability in Drama, Theatre, Film and Media Conference*, University of Łódź, Poland, 25–27 September.

Moss, H. and O'Neill, D. (2009), 'What training do artists need to work in healthcare settings?', *Medical Humanities*, 1, pp. 1–5.

National Alliance for Arts Health and Wellbeing (NAAHW) (2012), 'A charter for the National Alliance for Arts, Health and Wellbeing', http://www.artshealthandwellbeing.org.uk/sites/default/files/A%20Charter%20for%20Arts,%20Health%20and%20Wellbeing.pdf. Accessed 28 February 2014.

Negus, K. and Pickering, M. J. (2004), *Creativity, Communication and Cultural Value*, London: Sage.

NHS England (2014), 'Compassion in practice: Our culture of compassionate care', National Health Department, http://www.england.nhs.uk/nursingvision/. Accessed 20 July 2014.

Nicholson, H. (2005), *Applied Drama: The Gift of Theatre (Theatre and Performance Practices)*, London: Palgrave Macmillan.

——— (2014), *Applied Drama: The Gift of Theatre (Theatre and Performance Practices)*, 2nd ed., London: Palgrave Macmillan.

O'Connor, P. and Anderson, M. (2015), *Applied Theatre: Research: Radical Departures*, London and New York: Bloomsbury Methuen Drama.

Oddey, A. (1994), *Devising Theater: A Practical and Theoretical Handbook*, London: Routledge.

Osborn, D. (2015), 'Hellenic medicine', Greek Medicine.Net, http://www.greekmedicine.net/whos_who/Hippocrates.html. Accessed 27 January 2016.

Oyebody, F. (2012), *Madness at the Theatre*, London: RCPsych Publications.

Pederson, C. (1995), 'Effect of imagery on children's pain and anxiety during cardiac catheterization', *Journal of Pediatric Nursing*, 10: 6, pp. 265–375.

Peerhoy, D. and Bourke, C. (2007), 'Icebreaker: The evaluation', *Health Education Journal*, 66: 3, pp. 262–76.

Peterson, L. and Shigetomi, C. (2006), 'The use of coping techniques to minimize anxiety in hospitalized children', *Behaviour Therapy*, 12: 1, pp. 1–14.

Philipp, R. (2010), 'Making sense of wellbeing', *Perspectives in Public Health*, 130: 2, p. 58.

Pölkki, T., Pietilä, A.-M., Vehviläinen-Julkunen, K., Laukkala, H. and Kiviluoma, K. (2008), 'Imagery-induced relaxation in children's postoperative pain relief: A randomized pilot study', *Journal of Pediatric Nursing*, 23: 3, pp. 217–24.

Prádier, A. (2011), 'Theatre and compassion: The aesthetic criteria in the theatrical staging', *Proceedings of the 5th Mediterranean Congress of Aesthetics: Art, Emotion and Value*, Cartagena, Spain, 4–8 July, pp. 421–47, https://www.um.es/vmca/proceedings/docs/38.Adrian-Pradier.pdf. Accessed 20 January 2015.

Prendergast, M. and Saxton, J. (2013), *Applied Theatre: International Case Studies and Challenges for Practice*, Chicago: University of Chicago.

Prentki, T. and Preston, S. (2009), *The Applied Theatre Reader*, London: Routledge.

Prkachin, K. M. (2009), 'Assessing pain by facial expression: Facial expression as nexus', *Pain Research and Management*, 14: 1, pp. 53–58.

Putland, C. (2012), *Arts and Health – A Guide to the Evidence: Background Document Prepared for the Arts and Health Foundation Australia*, Sydney: The Institute for Creative Health, http://instituteforcreativehealth.org.au/wp-content/uploads/2013/03/A-Guide-to-the-Evidence.pdf. Accessed 4 April 2014.

Rayner, T. (2008), 'Heraclitus on change', Philosophy for Change, http://philosophyforchange.wordpress.com/2008/04/07/heraclitus-on-change/. Accessed 6 January 2016.

Readman, G. (1993), 'New partnerships in new contexts: A consumer's viewpoint', in A. Jackson (ed.), *Learning Through Theatre: New Perspectives on Theatre in Education*, 2nd ed., London: Routledge, pp. 267–84.

Reason, M. (2010), *The Young Audience: Exploring and Enhancing Children's Experiences of Theatre*, Stoke-on-Trent: Trentham Books.

Reed, K., Kennedy, H. and Wamboldt, M. Z. (2014), 'Art for life: A community arts mentorship program for chronically ill children', *Arts & Health: An International Journal of Research, Policy and Practice*, 7: 1, pp. 14–26, http://www.tandfonline.com/doi/abs/10.1080/17533015.2014.926279. Accessed 2 December 2014.

Regents of the University of Michigan (2013), *Child Care and Early Education Research Connections*, http://www.researchconnections.org/childcare/datamethods/fieldresearch.jsp#direct. Accessed 15 June 2015.

Rokach, A. and Matalon, R. (2007), '"Tails" – A fairy tale on furry tails: A 15-year theatre experience for hospitalized children created by health professionals', *Paediatrics & Child Health*, 12: 4, pp. 301–04, http://www.ncbi.nlm.nih.gov/pmc/articles/PMC2528678. Accessed 10 February 2013.

Ross, M. (2011), *Cultivating the Arts in Education and Therapy*, London: Routledge.

Royal Society for Public Health (RSPH) (2013), *Arts, Health and Wellbeing beyond the Millennium: How Far Have We Come and Where Do We Want to Go?*, London: RSPH Working Group on Arts, Health and Wellbeing.

Ryff, C. D. (1989), 'Happiness is everything, or is it? Explorations on the meaning of eudaimonic well-being', *Journal of Personality and Social Psychology*, 57, pp. 1069–81.

Saint-Exupéry, A. (1943), *The Little Prince*, New York: Reynal Hitchcock.

Sakharov, S. ([2004] 2006), *We Shall See Him as He Is* (trans. R. Edmonds), Essex: Stavropegic Monastery of St John the Baptist.

Scarry, E. (1988), *The Body in Pain: The Making and Unmaking of the World*, Oxford: Oxford University Press.

Scott, K. W. (2004), 'Relating categories in grounded theory analysis: Using a conditional relationship guide and reflective coding matrix', *The Qualitative Report*, 9: 1, pp. 113–26, http://www.nova.edu/ssss/QR/QR9-1/wilsonscott.pdf. Accessed 15 February 2012.

Seymour, A. (2009), 'Dramatherapy and social theatre: A question of boundaries', in S. Jennings (ed.), *Dramatherapy and Social Theatre: Necessary Dialogues*, London: Routledge, pp. 27–36.

Sextou, P. (2004), 'A proposal for the establishment of Hellenic theatre-in-education: Possibilities and problems in developing aspects of the British TiE experience in Greece towards the provision of professional theatre with an educational purpose in pre-school and primary education', Ph.D. thesis, London: Goldsmiths College, University of London.

——— (2011), 'Theatre for children in hospitals', in S. Schonmann (ed.), *Key Concepts in Theatre/ Drama Education*, Rotterdam: Sense Publishers, pp. 313–18.

Sextou, P. and Hall, S. (2015), 'Hospital theatre promoting child wellbeing in cardiac and cancer wards', *Applied Theatre Research*, 3: 1, pp. 67–84.

Sextou, P. and Monk, C. (2013), 'Bedside theatre performance and its effects on hospitalised children's well-being', *Arts & Health: An International Journal of Research, Policy and Practice*, 5: 1, pp. 81–88.

Sextou, P. and Trotman, D. (2013), 'Devised drama, Shakespeare and creativity; Practical work on Othello's pathos', *International Journal of the Arts in Education*, 7: 1, pp. 47–56.

Shunryu Suzuki Roshi ([1965] 2010), 'Thursday morning lectures, "Change"', http://suzukiroshi. sfzc.org/dharma-talks/?p=373. Accessed 30 July 2013.

Smith, B. D. (2013), 'Ancient Greek philosophy: Heraclitus', http://www.mycrandall.ca/courses/ grphil/heraclitus.htm. Accessed 16 March 2016.

Somers, J. (2003), 'Jukebox of the mind: An exploration of the relationship between the real and the world of drama fiction', *International Conference of Drama Education*, North Taiwan Arts Education Centre, Taipei, pp. 53–74, http://ed.arte.gov.tw/uploadfile/Book/470_53-74.pdf. Accessed 18 November 2015.

Somers, J. (2009), 'Drama and well-being: Narrative theory and the use of interactive theatre in raising mental health awareness', in S. Jennings (ed.), *Dramatherapy and Social Theatre: Necessary Dialogues*, London: Routledge, pp. 193–202.

Sontag, S. (1978), *Illness as Metaphor*, New York: Farrar, Straus and Giroux.

Strauss, A. and Corbin, J. (1998), *Basics of Qualitative Research: Techniques and Procedures for Developing Grounded Theory*, New York: Sage.

Thayer, J. (1995), *Thayer's Greek-English Lexicon of the New Testament: Coded with Strong's Concordance Numbers*, Massachusetts: Hendrickson Publishers.

Theatre and Performance Research Association (TAPRA) (2014), *Tenth Anniversary Annual Conference*, 3–5 September, http://tapra.org/archive/conference-2014/tapra-2014-schedule. Accessed 30 October 2014.

Theatre-Rites (2005), 'Hospitalworks', http://www.theatre-rites.co.uk/index.php/archive/site-specific-shows/hospitalworks. Accessed 20 June 2013.

Thomas, N. and O'Kane, C. (2000), 'Discovering what children think: Connections between research and practice', *British Journal of Social Work*, 30: 6, pp. 819–35.

Thompson, J. (2005), *Digging up Stories: Applied Theatre, Performance and War*, Manchester: Manchester University Press.

—— (2009) 'Ah Pava! Nathiye: Respecting silence and the performances of not-telling', in S. Jennings (ed.), *Dramatherapy and Social Theatre: Necessary Dialogues*, New York: Routledge, pp. 48–62.

—— (2012), *Applied Theatre: Bewilderment and Beyond*, 4th ed., Oxford: Peter Lang.

Thompson, R. (2015), 'Public health blow is just an NHS funding cut under another name', *RCN Nursing Standard*, 29: 52, pp. 32–33, http://dx.doi.org/10.7748/ns.29.52.32.s41. Accessed 5 January 2016.

Trotman, D. (2010), 'Deliberate impression: Critical directions in researching imaginative education', in T. W. Nielsen, R. Fitzgerald and M. Fettes (eds), *Imagination in Educational Theory and Practice: A Many-Sided Vision*, Cambridge: Cambridge Scholars Publishing, pp. 129–51.

Van de Water, M. (2012), *Theatre, Youth, and Culture: A Critical and Historical Exploration*, New York and London: Palgrave Macmillan.

Vreeke, G. J. and Van de Mark, I. L. (2003), 'Empathy, an integrative model', *New Ideas in Psychology*, 21: 3, pp. 177–207, http://dx.doi.org/10.1016/j.newideapsych.2003.09.003. Accessed 8 March 2013.

Way, B. (1981), *Audience Participation*, Boston: Walter H. Baker Co.

White, G. (2013), *Audience Participation in Theatre: Aesthetics of the Invitation*, London: Palgrave Macmillan.

Wilson, M. (2006), *Storytelling and Theatre: Contemporary Storytellers and Their Art*, New York: Palgrave Macmillan.

Wisker, G. (2009), *The Undergraduate Research Handbook*, London: Palgrave Macmillan.

World Health Organization (WHO) (2012), *Policy Summary: 5 Health Policy Responses to the Financial Crisis in Europe*, http://www.euro.who.int/__data/assets/pdf_file/0009/170865/e96643.pdf?ua=1. Accessed 28 January 2015.

Zaki, J., Bolger, N. and Ochsner, K. (2009), 'Unpacking the informational bases of empathic accuracy', *American Psychological Association*, 9: 4, pp. 478–87.

Useful Reading

Adams Jr, C. N. (2013), 'TiE and critical pedagogy', in A. Jackson and C. Vine (eds), *Learning Through Theatre*, 3rd ed., London: Routledge, pp. 287–304.

Aked, J., Marks, N., Cordon, C. and Thompson, S. (2008), *Five Ways to Wellbeing*, London: New Economics Foundation, Centre for Wellbeing, http://www.artsforhealth.org/resources/Five_Ways_to_Well-being_Evidence_1.pdf. Accessed 12 June 2014.

Allen, D. (2005), 'The children', in D. Davis (ed.), *Edward Bond and the Dramatic Child*, London: Trentham Books, pp. 145–62.

Aristotle (*c.*335 BCE), Περὶ ποιητικῆς/*Poetics* (trans. S. H. Butcher), http://classics.mit.edu/Aristotle/poetics.html. Accessed 6 April 2016.

Battrick, C., Glasper, E. A., Prudhoe, G. and Weaver, K. (2007), 'Clown humor: The perceptions of doctors, nurses, parents and children', *Journal of Children's and Young People's Nursing*, 1: 4, pp. 174–79.

Bennet, S. (1990), *Theatre Audiences: A Theory of Production and Perception*, London: Routledge.

Bishop, K. (2010), *The Experience of Waiting in an Emergency Department: What's it Like for Children and their Families?*, Gladesville: Association for the Wellbeing of Children in Healthcare (AWCH).

Bharucha, R. (1993), *Theatre and the World: Performance and the Politics of Culture*, London: Routledge.

Blatner, A. with Wiener, D. J. (2007), *Interactive and Improvisational Drama: Varieties of Applied Theatre and Performance*, New York: iUniverse, Inc.

Bleeker, M. (2011), *Visuality in the Theatre: The Locus of Looking*, London: Palgrave Macmillan.

Boal, A. (2005), *Games for Actors and Non-Actors*, 3rd ed., London: Routledge.

Bond, E. (2000), *The Hidden Plot*, London: Methuen.

British Medical Association (2011), *Psychological and Social Needs of Patients*, London: British Association of Medicine.

Brook, P. (1968), *The Empty Space*, London: Penguin.

Brown, B. (2013), 'The power of empathy', Royal Society for the Encouragement of the Arts (RSA), http://blazenfluff.com/the-power-of-empathy-animated-short-explains-the-difference-between-empathy-and-sympathy/#. Accessed 29 December 2013.

Bueno, J. (2011), 'Promoting wellbeing through compassion', Therapytoday.net, 22: 5, http://www. therapytoday.net/article/show/2515/. Accessed 19 August 2014.

Cain, F. (2014), 'What is the cosmic microwave background radiation?', Universe Today, http://www.universetoday.com/110221/what-is-the-cosmic-microwave-background-radiation/. Accessed 19 August 2014.

Centre Forum Commission (2014), *The Pursuit of Happiness: A New Ambition for Our Mental Health Report*, London: Centre Forum Commission.

Churton, M. and Brown, A. (2010), *Theory and Method*, 2nd ed., Hampshire: Palgrave Macmillan.

Clift, S. (2012), 'Creative arts as a public health resource: Moving from practice-based research to evidence-based practice', *Perspectives in Public Health*, 132: 3, pp. 120–27.

Collard, P. (2014), *Mindfulness for Compassionate Living*, London: Gaia Books.

Cooper, C. (2013), 'The imagination in action: TiE and its relationship with drama in education today', in A. Jackson and C. Vine (eds), *Learning Through Theatre*, 3rd ed., London: Routledge, pp. 41–59.

Cooper, M. (2013), 'The playwright in TiE', in A. Jackson and C. Vine (eds), *Learning Through Theatre*, 3rd ed., London: Routledge, pp. 103–19.

Creative Health CIC (2014), 'Collaborating in quality arts in public health in the future', personal communication with Kate Gant, 10 July.

Currier, H. and Garbin, P. (2014), *Artist in Healthcare Certification*, Washington, DC: Society for the Arts in Healthcare, http://thesah.org/doc/Artist%20in%20Healthcare%20Final%20%282%29.pdf. Accessed 19 June 2014.

Curtis, P. (2007), 'Space to care: Children's perceptions of spatial aspects of hospitals: Full Research Report', *ESRC End of Award Report*, RES-000-23-0765, Swindon: ESRC.

Dolan, J. (2005), *Utopia in Performance: Finding Hope at the Theatre*, Michigan: University Michigan Press.

Done, A. (2001), 'The therapeutic use of story-telling', *Paediatric Nursing*, 13: 3, pp. 17–20.

Fenech, A. (2010), 'Inspiring transformations through participation in drama for individuals with neuropalliative conditions', *Journal of Applied Arts & Health*, 1: 1, pp. 63–80.

Freeman, J. (2010), *Gifted Lives: What Happens When Gifted Children Grow Up*, London: Routledge.

Glaser, B. G. (1978), *Theoretical Sensitivity*, Mill Valley, CA: Sociology Press.

Goldberg, M. (1974), *Children's Theatre: A Philosophy and a Method*, Upper Saddle River, NJ: Prentice Hall.

Goldfinger, E. (2011), 'Theatre for babies: A new kind of theatre?', in S. Schonmann (ed.), *Key Concepts in Theatre/Drama Education*, Rotterdam: Sense Publishers, pp. 295–300.

Gretton, A. (2013), 'Video: Touring theatre group spread panto cheer at Norfolk children's hospital', *Eastern Daily Press*, 12 January, http://www.edp24.co.uk/news/health/video_touring_theatre_group_spread_panto_cheer_at_norfolk_children_s_hospital_1_1790273. Accessed 28 July 2013.

Harvey, M. (2010), 'Staging the story', seminar material, 27 January, Cardiff: University of South Wales, George Ewart Evans Centre for Storytelling, http://storytelling.research.glam.ac.uk/media/files/documents/2010-03-01/Staging_the_Story_Final_version.pdf. Accessed 12 June 2015.

Hetherington, E. M. and Park, R. D. (1986), *Child Psychology: A Contemporary Viewpoint*, 3rd ed., Singapore: McGraw-Hill.

Iyer, A. (2009), 'Portrayal of intellectual disability in fiction', in F. Oyebody (ed.), *Mindreadings*, London: The Royal College of Psychiatrists, pp. 115–26.

Jones, P. (1996), *Drama as Therapy: Theatre as Living*, London: Routledge.

——— (2007), *Drama as Therapy: Theory, Practice and Research*, 2nd ed., London: Routledge.

Johnstone, K. (1999), *Impro for Storytellers*, London: Faber & Faber.

Kemp, M. (2003), 'Acting out: A qualitative evaluation of a mental health promotion project for young people', *Journal of Mental Health Promotion*, 2: 3, pp. 20–31.

KidsHealth (2013), 'Relaxation techniques for children with serious illness', The Nermours Foundation, http://kidshealth.org/parent/_cancer_center/feelings/relaxation.html. Accessed 1 May 2013.

Kingsnorth, S., Blain, S. and McKeever, P. (2011), 'Physiological and emotional responses of disabled children to therapeutic clowns: A pilot study', *Evidence-Based Complementary and Alternative Medicine*, 4, http://www.hindawi.com/journals/ecam/2011/732394/. Accessed 10 December 2012.

Krietemeyer, B. C. and Heiney, S. P. (1992), 'Storytelling as a therapeutic technique in a group for school-aged oncology patients', *Children's Health Care*, 21, pp. 14–19.

Landy, R. (2010), 'Drama as a means of preventing post-traumatic stress following trauma within a community', *Journal of Applied Arts & Health*, 1: 1, pp. 7–18.

Low, K. (2010), 'Creating a space for the individual: Different theatre and performance-based approaches to sexual health communication in South Africa', *Journal of Applied Arts & Health*, 1: 1, pp. 111–26.

Margalit, T., Farquharson, Y., Bashat, D. B., Weinstein, M., Lin, J. P. and Fattal-Valevski, A. (2013), 'A multi-site study of functional outcomes following a themed approach to hand–arm bimanual intensive therapy for children with hemiplegia', *Developmental Medicine & Child Neurology*, http://www.dailyherald.com/assets/pdf/DA12800691.pdf. Accessed 3 September 2013.

McCarthy, J. and Light, J. (2001), 'Instructional effectiveness of an integrated theater arts program for children using augmentative and alternative communication and their nondisabled peers: Preliminary study', *AAC Augmentative and Alternative Communication*, 17, pp. 88–98.

Meeting of Cultural Ministers (CMC) (2014), *Australian National Arts and Health Framework*, http://mcm.arts.gov.au/sites/default/files/National%20Arts%20and%20Health%20 Framework%20May%202014.pdf. Accessed 22 May 2015.

Moore, J. (2006), 'Theatre of attachment: Using drama to facilitate attachment in adoption', *Adoption and Fostering*, 30: 2, pp. 64–73.

NHS Dudley Public Health Report (2011), *A Strategy for Marketing Mental Health and Wellbeing in Dudley 2011–13*, http://www.nhsdudley.nhs.uk/sites/documents/cms/979-2012-4-13-2860584.pdf. Accessed 23 June 2013.

Niscer, J., Martin, D. K., Bluhnm, R. and Daar, A. S. (2006), 'Theatre as a public engagement tool for health policy development', *Health Policy*, 78, pp. 258–71.

O'Neill, P. (2013), 'How do we measure healthcare and compassion: Why should we bother?', NHS Leadership Academy, 27 September, http://www.leadershipacademy.nhs.uk/blog/about/blog/how-do-we-measure-healthcare-and-compassion-why-should-we-bother. Accessed 2 October 2015.

O'Toole, J. (1992), *The Process of Drama*, London: Routledge.

Patte, M. (2010), 'The therapeutic benefits of play for hospitalized children', in E. E. Nwoknh (ed.), *Play as Engagement and Communication: Play & Culture Studies*, pp. 3–23.

Peaceful Lion Productions (2014), 'Theatre for Hospitals initiative', http://peacefullion.com/hospitals.php. Accessed 16 July 2014.

Prentki, T. (2015), *Applied Theatre: Development*, London: Bloomsbury Methuen Drama.

Rae, W., Worchel, F., Upchurch, J., Sanner, J. and Daniel, C. (1989), 'The psychosocial impact of play on hospitalized children', *Journal of Pediatric Psychology*, 14: 4, pp. 617–27.

Raw, A., Lewis, S., Russell, A. and Mcnaughton, J. (2012), 'A hole in the heart: Confronting the drive for evidence-based impact research in arts and health', *Arts & Health: An International Journal of Research, Policy and Practice*, 4: 2, pp. 97–108.

Ritchie, J., Spencer, L. and O'Connor, W. (2003), 'Carrying out qualitative analysis', in J. Ritchie and J. Lewis (eds), *Qualitative Research Practice: A Guide for Social Science Students and Researchers*, London: Sage.

Schonmann, S. (2006), *Theatre as a Medium for Children and Young People: Images and Observations*, Dordrecht: Springer.

Schuitema, K. (2012), 'Intercultural performances for young audiences in the UK: Engaging with the child in a globalised society', in T. Maguire and K. Schuitema (eds), *Theatre for Young Audiences*, London: Trentham Books, pp. 69–79.

Schweitzer, P. and Bruce, E. (2008), *Remembering Yesterday, Caring Today*, London: Jessica Kingsley Publishers.

Sedgman, K. (2012), 'Review', *Participations Journal of Audience and Reception Studies*, 9: 1, pp. 122–25.

Sextou, P. (2012), 'Devising monologues on domestic violence for the development of inter-professional training and community support services', *Drama Research: International Journal of Drama in Education*, http://www.newman.ac.uk/files/w3/applied-drama-lab/pdf/Sextou%20Drama%20Research%20International%20Journal.pdf?q=415. Accessed 7 January 2016.

Staricoff, R. L. (2004), *Arts in Health: A Review of the Medical Literature*, London: Arts Council of England.

—— (2006), 'Arts in health: The value of evaluation', *Perspectives in Public Health*, 126: 33, pp. 116–20.

Staricoff, R. L., Duncan, J., Wright, M., Loppert, S. and Scott, J. (2001), 'A study of the effects of the visual and performing arts in healthcare', *Hospital Development*, 32, pp. 25–28.

Stickley, T. (2011), 'A philosophy for community-based, participatory arts practice: A narrative inquiry', *Journal of Applied Arts & Health*, 2: 1, pp. 73–83.

Stuttaford, M., Bryanston, C., Hundt, G. L., Connor, M., Thorogood, M. and Tollman, S. (2006), 'Use of applied theatre in health research dissemination and data validation: A pilot study from South Africa', *Health*, 10: 1, pp. 31–45.

Theatre Modo (2010), *Sick*, http://www.modo.org.uk/projects/2010/sick. Accessed 14 May 2013.

Weaver, K., Prudhoe, G., Battrick, C. and Glasper, E. A. (2007), 'Sick children's perceptions of clown doctor humour', *Journal of Children's and Young People's Nursing*, 1: 8, pp. 359–65.

White, G. (2015), *Applied Theatre: Aesthetics*, London and New York: Bloomsbury Methuen Drama.

Willard, C. (2010), *Child's Mind: Mindfulness Practices to Help Our Children Be More Focused, Calm, and Relaxed*, Berkeley: Parallax Press.

Index

Index